ON THIN ICE

ISBN: 978-1-7334176-7-9
LCCN: 2020912100

Most TechnologyPress titles are available at special quantity discounts for bulk purchases for sales promotions, premiums, fundraising, and educational use. Special versions or book excerpts can also be created to fit specific needs.

For more information, please write:

TechnologyPress
520 N. Orlando Ave, #2
Winter Park, FL 32789
or call 1.877.261.4930

TechnologyPress
Winter Park, Florida

CONTENTS

CHAPTER 1

HISTORY OF CYBERSECURITY

BY TONY OLSON

Over the history of mankind, whenever something new has been developed for good, there have been people that have twisted that new functionality and redeployed it for evil.

Computers have not been immune to this twisting of good for evil intention. In fact, by their very design, they serve as the perfect vehicle to distribute evil-concocted payloads. Today, computer devices have been universally deployed. Some estimate that there are 24 billion computer devices in the world today. These devices are all connected on a worldwide scale. This tremendous and ever-expanding computing and communication power, has turned out to make the perfect tool to enable, amplify, and spread anyone's evil intentions rapidly and globally.

In the short history of computers, the number, cost, and scope of cybercrimes committed have taken off like a rocket. And these evil efforts continue to escalate exponentially. Over the last forty years, we have already gone through what I categorize as the 4-movements of cyberdisruption:

1) Cyber Curiosity
2) Cyber Criminality (Theft)
3) Cyber Espionage, Terrorism & Warfare
4) Cyber Organized & Commercialized Crime

CYBER CURIOSITY

The initial opportunity for someone to disrupt other people's lives using a remote computer came about when the first computer network link was established on October 29th, 1969. The network was called the ARPANET, and it was funded by the United States Department of Defense. Even though this early computer network was on a closed-circuit system consisting of three computers that were being used only by scientists, it still served as the earliest laboratory project for cybersecurity.

During an ARPANET research project in 1971, Bob Thomas conceived of the possibility of a computer program moving across the network from one computer to another. This idea had great practical potential, for example, deploying useful programs remotely across the network to numerous systems. He created a small program to test his idea. His test program made that journey, and as it traveled, it left proof that it had been there, by printing a message on the local TENEX terminals. The printout said, "I'M THE CREEPER: CATCH ME IF YOU CAN." This program, now referred to simply as "The Creeper," was the first computer virus.

Another computer scientist, Ray Tomlinson, saw the Creeper program in action. He further advanced the idea by making the Creeper self-replicating. With this extension, he created the first computer worm. Then, Tomlinson wrote another program that was designed to chase the Creeper around the ARPANET and delete it, wherever it found it. He called this program the Reaper. It was the first antivirus program.

These three basic programs were created by two curious scientists with good intentions. They were simply working to advance the state of the art of network capability and communication. Even with humble beginnings, these three programs still today, serve as the model for most antivirus software.

That model, at its core, consists of four parts:
- First, identify a new threat.
- Second, write an antidote program to find it.
- Third, root it out and eliminate it.
- Fourth and finally, blacklist it so others will benefit from the knowledge gained by the operation.

While this method is effective, and it has worked well for many years, there is an inherent flaw in this model. That is, in this method of malware combat, the software must wait to develop an antidote until after a new threat has emerged. In other words, there cannot be a cure until after the disease has struck and is understood. Therefore, this method guarantees that some computers will always be infected by new forms of malware before it can be stopped.

One other fact of history that must be noted here is that the same Ray Tomlinson that created the Reaper program also conceived the idea of communicating from one person on one host computer, across the ARPANET to another person on a different host computer. This idea was the invention of email. Tomlinson had to design a new format for addressing the emails. He created the idea of using the format user@host – a setup that is still in use today.

Why did I mention the invention of email at the close of this Cyber Curiosity segment? Because it is another perfect example of a development with good intentions being twisted for evil purposes. The invention of email was for good. It has gone on to positively impact the way the entire world communicates. Yet, at the same time, it has been twisted to serve an evil purpose. It has turned out to serve as a perfect vehicle for the delivery of malware payloads to the masses around the world.

CYBER CRIMINALITY

Cyber Curiosity formally turned to Cyber Criminality in November of 1988. Robert Morris, then a graduate student at Cornell University, was curious. He wondered, "How big is the ARPANET?" The way that he thought he could tell was to count how many devices were connected to the ARPANET. So, he wrote a program that traveled from computer to computer and asked each device to send back a notice (sound familiar?) to his server, where he planned to tabulate the results.

His problem occurred because the message he sent traveled faster than he expected. On top of that, it went to more devices than he expected. When all those devices started generating internet traffic by sending back their notices, along with the traffic that his original replicating messages generated, the whole mess started to clog up huge sections of the internet. When Morris realized what was happening, he tried to send out warning emails to network administrators. But he was too late. His warning emails got caught in the massive traffic congestion that he created. His warning emails didn't make it out.

The trail of devastation was dramatic. Today, historians estimate that the Morris worm affected 10% of the total ARPANET. (As a percentage of scope, no other single piece of malware has had near that effect.) By 1988, the ARPANET had grown to have over 60,000 computers. Berkeley, Stanford, and Purdue universities, as well as MIT, NASA, and the Pentagon, were just some of the organizations that had systems infected. It took research scientists at Purdue and Berkeley, as well as other institutions, over 72 hours to debug and stop Morris' worm. It took much longer to clean up the mess.

Even though his efforts had no malice, and were based only on intellectual curiosity, Robert Morris was prosecuted under the then recently-passed Federal Computer Fraud and Abuse Act. Trying to make an example of Morris, in an effort to deter copy-cat computer crimes, the Justice Department charged Morris with a felony. He was convicted by a jury and sentenced to serve three years of probation, to perform 400 hours of community service, and to pay a $10,000 fine. Many in the computer industry at the time thought his punishment was excessive. But it is now a matter of history. Robert Morris was the first person ever prosecuted for a cybercrime.

In 1988, the ARPANET was a place akin to small-town Americana. All the "neighbors" pretty much knew and trusted each other. The internet neighborhood of that day was innocent. There was no need for security. It was the equivalent of the neighbors leaving their front doors unlocked and keeping their keys in the ignition of their cars sitting in the driveway.

The Morris worm changed all that. Although it originated as innocent curiosity, the Morris worm served as the spark that ignited cybercrime. In retrospect, it is now obvious that criminals began to realize the potential scope of access at their fingertips. The Justice Department's desire to shut down cybercrime before it started didn't even serve as a speed bump to criminals. It's quite possible that the publicity given the Morris worm served to act as an accelerant to cybercrime.

Since Morris, acceleration and proliferation of cybercrimes have occurred. Individuals are targets for identity theft and ransomware, which can occur through hacking, virus dissemination, phishing, and malvertising (targeted, compelling-but-fake Ads, ever wonder why those ads follow you around your browsing?) Other rising forms of insidious cybercrimes against individuals include cyberbullying, cyberstalking, child pornography, and sex trafficking.

Businesses are increasingly targeted by BEC (Business Email Compromise) attacks. These sophisticated scams first compromise, then steal legitimate email accounts to gain access to people, information, and funds across the entire business. The FBI's 2019 Internet Crime Report states the BEC attack has risen to become the costliest cybercrime-type against businesses. Another major business attack vector is DDoS (Distributed Denial of Service) attacks, where their websites are flooded with bogus requests to the point that the webserver crashes, and the business caves into the attacker's extortive demands.

CYBER ESPIONAGE, TERRORISM & WARFARE

Cyber Espionage is the act of gaining access to secrets without the permission or even knowledge of the owner. Once information is obtained, how it is used determines if it is an act of crime, terror, or warfare.

Individuals, businesses, political parties, military units, and increasingly, national-level governments can be targets of these attacks. At the global level, the two cyber entities making the most headlines these days are the USA and China.

One example of massive cyber-espionage at the global level is the operation that has been coined Titan Rain. These coordinated series of attacks are believed to have persisted for three years in the early 2000s. They originated in Guangdong, China, and targeted U.S. defense contractors. One U.S. official postulated that the attacks were so sophisticated and were carried out with such discipline that they had to be military in origin.

In addition to military contractors, Titan Rain also attacked the FBI and

NASA. Information that was stolen allegedly disclosed U.S. strengths and weaknesses. Information leaked from this operation has served to cause distrust between other countries as well. The full extent of the damage is unclear.

The Stuxnet virus, uncovered in 2010, was targeted specifically at Iranian nuclear facilities. It is the first cyberweapon that is known to have crossed the digital/physical barrier. The virus wreaked havoc in the digital world by infecting over 200,000 computers. More importantly, it physically destroyed a significant portion of Iran's nuclear centrifuges. Stuxnet was able to do this by first using Cyber Espionage to gather information on how the machines were being controlled. Then, using that information to reprogram the devices, Stuxnet was able to cause the centrifuges to spin at such a high speed that they tore themselves apart. It is widely believed that this cyberweapon was jointly developed by the USA and Israel. To date, no country has openly admitted responsibility.

CYBER ORGANIZED & COMMERCIALIZED CRIME

It is predicted by I.T. security experts that the global economic impact of cybercrime will hit $6 trillion annually by 2021. To put that in perspective, that means cybercrime will be more profitable than the total global illegal drug trade.

Why is Cyber Organized crime growing so fast? Because that is where the opportunity is. Over the last five years, we have had the perfect trifecta of growth.

I. First, the growth of internet-connected devices is estimated to be approaching four devices for every single person on the planet.

II. Second, the growth of the total amount of data and the percentage of it that is internet accessible. Microsoft estimates that the data volume online this year alone will be 50 times greater than it was in 2016.

III. Third, the growth of cyberspending continues to increase at a rate of 15% per year. (And that was before the coronavirus accelerated online spending this year.)

More targets, more data, more money, and it is easy pickings.

At the same time, security defenses are sagging. According to a Cisco survey, 40 percent of manufacturing security professionals do not even have a security strategy. Palo Alto Research Center estimates over 3 million cybersecurity positions remain unfilled. Each year, cybercrime volume rises, and the resources needed to combat it falls further behind.

Ransomware is rising! In 2019, two-thirds of the ransomware efforts in the USA attacked state and local governments. In addition, over 500 schools were affected. Organized crime has moved to social phishing attacks. These attacks are well organized and sophisticated. One group will conduct research on companies and people, searching for a vulnerable entry point, and targeting a specific person or position within an organization. The next group will craft an email specifically designed to entice that person to click a link or open an attachment. Another group will have written the malware that infects the network, encrypts the data, and sends the ransom message. Finally, there will be an accounts payable group that will work with the affected company to receive payment, usually in a cybercurrency. The entire transaction is conducted in a business-like fashion.

Riviera Beach, Florida, has the dubious distinction of having made the largest known ransomware payment in the USA in 2019. The city paid out $600,000 in 65 bitcoins. Riviera Beach was a vulnerable target. On May 29th, a person in the police department opened a ransomware-infected email, and nearly all the city's system crashed. The ransomware-impacted systems included phones, email, Police, City Attorney's office, Public Work's office, and the library. Riviera Beach was a ripe target because their computer systems were drastically outdated. In addition, they had an interim I.T. manager in place as well as a city government filled with interim department heads. Apparently, decisions and actions were hard to come by. What makes this story even worse, the city had already bought a new computer system costing nearly $800,000. It had not been deployed.

While data remains the main target, a ransom is not always the main goal. The new breed of organized cybercriminals increasingly looks to destroy data, or even change it in an attempt to create confusion or breed mistrust. The most sophisticated criminals enter a network and remain undetected, simply watching and learning everything they can about an organization.

In the early days of computing, an in-depth working knowledge of the computer system was required in order to exploit network nuances. Today, many of these attack vectors are available for sale on the dark web as prepackaged utilities that give even novices the ability to hack systems.

It is sad to look back from where we are now, realizing that the earliest cyber-problems were about as harmful as litter on the street. Now, in an era of ransomware, social phishing attacks, 'fileless' malware, and nation-state attacks, the cyber-problems we face are capable of stealing money, stealing identities, and even damaging property.

After reading about the rapid increase and sophistication of cybercrime, you should realize that we are on thin ice, and it is starting to crack! But there is hope. If you rely on I.T. security professionals, like my company D2, and many of my colleagues and co-authors of this book, you will get back to operating your organizations on solid ground.

About Tony

Tony Olson is a leader in the computer industry where he has worked for nearly 40 years. An entrepreneur, Tony founded D2 Worldwide in 2004, and as president, continues to lead the effort to provide great solutions for D2's clients. An innovator, Tony is an inventor with over two dozen U.S. Patents. His education includes a Bachelor's degree in Electrical Engineering from Illinois Institute of Technology and a Master's degree in Computer Design from the University of Massachusetts. And most importantly, as a family man, Tony and his wife Cindy of 36 years have four beautiful children.

Tony founded D2 on the principle of servant-leadership. Servant, because Tony drives D2 to always understand I.T. clients' business goals and needs. Tony directs D2 to ultimately serve clients by taking work off their plates and worry off their minds. Tony drives D2 to leadership by researching emerging trends in technology, culture, and behavioral changes in society. This, in turn, helps clients understand and serve their customers better. In addition, D2 leads clients by designing systems to fit perfectly into their business ecosystem. These efforts combined, promote D2's clients to work safely, efficiently, and with a competitive advantage in their industry.

Through Tony's leadership, D2 is an active participant in the cybersecurity industry. Most recently, he provided significant commentary content to the draft of the federal government specification on "Detecting and Responding to Ransomware and Other Destructive Events."

Tony's servant-leader culture extends a helping hand into the community by providing books to elementary school kids that need them. The D2 "Books for Budding Brains" program has been in service for over ten years and has provided tens of thousands of kids with free books.

Prior to D2, Tony worked as the Vice President of Engineering and Product Development at Gateway Computer Company. Tony led the effort to design, test, configure, and deliver literally millions of award-winning desktop, notebook, server, and network-based products. One of the first P.C. companies to employ Human Factor Engineers, Tony helped Gateway pioneer the design of delightful customer experiences. They were so wonderful that customers were excited to see the cow-spotted box arrive on their doorstep.

Tony started his career at Zenith Data Systems as a designer of computer systems. Later, as Director of Engineering, Tony lead efforts that required government security clearance to design highly secure computer systems for branches of our U.S. military.

You can connect with Tony at:
- tony.olson@d2worldwide.com
- www.linkedin.com/in/tony-olson
- Work Phone (605)422-1322
- www.d2worldwide.com

CHAPTER 2

WHY SMALL BUSINESSES ARE A CYBERCRIMINAL'S #1 TARGET

BY PEDRO NUNEZ-BAUTISTA

When I began my career as an IT Professional over 20 years ago, I was finishing up an eight-year tour in the Army Reserves. For those of you who don't know, military training is built around drills, lots of drills. Drills are procedures that you do so often you no longer have to think, just respond. In my world of cybersecurity, I use what I learned as a methodical way to train my team to be prepared for every situation; we want to be prepared to face the "enemy" with minimal errors and response time. Can you see the connection? Cybercriminals, the enemy, prey on the unsuspecting and the unprepared, and our clients, small businesses, have become their number one target.

Don't let the label mislead you. Small businesses are a big target. They make up 90% of the United States' economy. To my company, small business has fewer than 50 employees with less than $10 million annual revenue. Most of those businesses assume they are too small to be a target of cyber-criminals. Media reinforces this idea because only reports about data breaches at large corporations make the news. What they fail to report are the instances of small businesses that lose $10,000 or $20,000 at a time because of ransomware, hackers that steal bank account information, and the like. Globally, the cost of cyberattacks has reached several trillion dollars a year. A small business that gets hit and isn't prepared could lose everything.

23

If you are a criminal and you want to target companies, who are you going to target?

Small businesses! Small businesses are the low-hanging fruit for cyber-criminals because they aren't protected properly for three main reasons: lack of resources, lack of understanding, and lack of ability.

First, most small businesses don't have the money in the budget to staff an IT department or hire a Chief Security Officer to implement what's needed in order to prevent cyberattacks. Well, that is short of the office manager or the most technically savvy person on the staff who wears multiple hats already. They struggle to include IT staff on the budget to reduce overhead, but they often times pay more in the end.

Second, they lack knowledge of cybersecurity risks, or worse; they think they know enough to protect themselves. They're very good at what they do, but they're not good at technology or cybersecurity, and because of that, they have a blind spot and don't perceive they are the target – no thanks to Equifax or Sony and other large corporations taking up the cybersecurity headlines. They assume that since they're not a billion-dollar company, they aren't worthwhile for the criminal.

It's estimated that by 2021, the cost of cybercrime will be about $6 trillion. The cybercrime market has become commoditized. Anybody can rent software to be able to orchestrate a cyberattack and hold a small business hostage that has no clue how to defend itself.

Despite that information, business owners often say, "That's never going to happen to me." Technology progresses, though. There's been a 30% increase year-over-year in cybercrimes. Cyberthreats are becoming more sophisticated and more vicious. The in-house IT guru that fixes everything might not be the best person for the job. There's an old saying that in the land of the blind, the one-eyed man is king. Companies come to rely so heavily on the expertise of their long-time IT specialist that they blindly follow that person's lead when it comes to cybersecurity without ever vetting his or her knowledge in that realm. This is a case where bad advice can be just as bad as no advice at all.

I sometimes wonder if the larger concern is the lack of knowledge and action, or the belief that as long as you have paid your anti-virus subscription through Norton or Trend Micro, you are good to go. Today, it's not that simple. Today, cybersecurity must be looked at as a strategy, and this strategy is composed of multiple layers. It's not a matter of install this one piece of software and you're done. Three out of four businesses asked about their cybersecurity will say, "Oh yeah, we're all set." Upon further review, I explain, "You're missing this layer. You're missing that layer. You mentioned this, and this is what's going to happen." Just because you have fifty employees and an IT staff and haven't been a victim of a cyberattack doesn't mean you've got the right strategy. That's sheer luck.

It's not a matter of if a business will be attacked, it's a matter of when. The business of cybersecurity is basically like insurance. It's about prevention. You're trying to prevent an attack and be prepared for when it happens. Nothing is impenetrable. It's a matter that if you have the layers set up in a particular manner, then you will not be caught off guard. One thing we know is that the enemy changes. Cybercriminals are evolving along with technology very quickly. Consider this, a lowercase password can be cracked within 11 seconds. A password with one capital letter, eight characters, and numbers can be cracked in about 30 minutes. It's not a human being doing this, it is a computer robot, an algorithm, just hitting the system repeatedly to break it.

The cost of a data breach extends far beyond the retrieval of records. If a company houses medical records with personal information, for example, and suspects they have been compromised, even if they don't have the forensics to prove it, they must alert the FBI that they have been compromised. Then, they must contact their insurance company.

The insurance company will assign attorneys to them to dictate how to handle the breach. How will they communicate all the information about this breach to the public? Next, they will have to contact the companies that are going to be responsible for providing identity theft monitoring. When a company has 25,000 records and is required to pay $20 to $30 a month for monitoring, the math is mind-boggling. Does your company have reserves to cover $750,000 a month, not for just one month but for at least a year or two?

Although insurance is available to cover cybersecurity losses, many businesses are underinsured in this area. A dentist with 10,000 records might think that his $1 million cybersecurity policy for which he pays $500 a year will cover him should a breach occur. As previously mentioned, if a business is mandated to cover monitoring for those clients affected by the breach, that million dollars won't go far. On top of that, the business will still have to pay for a forensics company to determine which records were compromised and then pay to rebuild their system. Don't assume that the $1 million policy recommended by the insurance agent is enough protection.

Some small businesses mistakenly think that they are only liable for the records that they have active in their system. For instance, a medical facility might have 50,000 total records because they have been in business 20 years, but only be concerned about the 7,000 patients they have seen this year. The reality is that they would still be responsible for the 43,000 archived records because they are required by law to keep patient records for ten years. Consequently, those archived records should also be protected.

Common cyber-attacks on small business' computers include ransomware, data breaches, and brute force attacks. Ransomware works its way into a network and encrypts the data so the business cannot access its own files. How does it get there? The data breach usually begins with a phishing attack when somebody sends an email or pop-up or something that says, "click here." When an employee clicks on it, it automatically opens the door to their credentials and access to the system to install ransomware.

Data Breaches often start with phishing scams that could be avoided if employees use common sense. If the employee has never purchased something from eBay, why would he click a link to change his eBay password? Hackers also use email attachments to get into a system. Let's say an employee receives a resumé via email. If that employee isn't a member of human resources, they shouldn't be receiving resumés via email and have no business clicking on that email attachment.

Data breaches also occur through third-party activity. Let's say an employee received a prompt to update Adobe. An untrained employee might think they are being helpful by updating Adobe so IT doesn't have to, however, if it is not their job to update systems and applications, they shouldn't do it. Leave IT tasks to the IT department. IT will know what a legitimate update request is and what is a potential hack. If that employee types his credentials in there, he will give the hacker a back-door access to the company system.

A brute force attack occurs when a cybercriminal repeatedly tries to crack usernames, passwords, and PIN codes to access the system. They often utilize a third-party whose software leads back to the company's database.

When the internet evolved into the internet of things, connecting previously independent elements of our lives, vulnerability and liability increased. That cable box providing entertainment to a business' clients in the waiting area connects to the network. Right? The DVR is connected to that same network. Guess what? All those devices are entry points to the business' network. Attacks have happened through the internet service provider during which hackers made it past the internet service provider's cybersecurity protections and onto the individual IP addresses stored within that provider's system. Remember, the hackers look for the weakest link, so you must defend every entry point to the network.

Out-of-date systems pose a significant threat to a business. Hacking isn't done by a single human sitting at a computer anymore. Sophisticated hackers actively look for older systems with known vulnerabilities using automated attacks. These vulnerabilities can be exploited in nanoseconds, so all systems that are connected on the network need to be patched and up to date.

Small businesses aren't powerless, but they must strategically implement a plan to protect their business' data. There are nine key things small businesses should know to protect themselves:

- **#1.** A single layer approach to cybersecurity is not a strategy. Utilize a multi-layer solution.

- **#2.** Perform risk assessments quarterly. What is measured is known. Don't rely on what was effective against yesterday's enemy.

- **#3.** Out of those assessments, you need to identify critical systems and vulnerabilities that can directly impact the business.

- **#4.** Address all the loopholes that were found during the assessments.

- **#5.** Perform end-user training and phishing simulation weekly. A fire door isn't effective if the employee doesn't know to keep it closed.
- **#6.** The right toolset for the job includes next-generation endpoint

protection, managed detection and response, dark web monitoring, gateway security and encryption, security policies, firewalls, and back-ups.

- **#7.** Business continuity depends on back-up, recovery, and continuity of records. Essentially, does the business have a back-up of its data housed in an offsite location? Continuity, then, is the ability to get the business back up and running within a matter of hours, not days. If the server just crashed and everything is lost, can I restore that server within the next two to three hours, or do I have to go in and reformat everything? Do I have to wait 1 or 2 weeks before I can restore the whole thing? Most small businesses cannot afford to lose two or three days waiting for their systems to function again.

- **#8.** Penetration testing should be performed annually. Basically, a third party forces an attack from the outside and from within – to make sure that there are no loopholes in the system.

- **#9.** Purchase Cyber Liability insurance. At the end of the day, if everything fails, a business can fall back on its insurance policy. Make sure that insurance policy covers 300% of everything for which you are liable. Liability varies by industry.

Eighty percent of small businesses are concerned about cybersecurity and understand that it's a threat. They see it. They perceive it. Only one-third of them do something about it, and of that one-third, many take the wrong measures or not enough to secure their business' data. They end up doing a mediocre job because they were advised by somebody that doesn't know how to devise and execute a strategy.

Effective cybersecurity is something a small business can accomplish. It's a matter of being aware as a small business owner that you need help, and knowing you can get that from an IT professional with a track record of delivering on what they're promising. If it isn't being measured or reported on, it probably isn't being done. Whatever is measured, improves dramatically. Whatever is measured and reported upon, improves exponentially.

About Pedro

Pedro Nunez-Bautista is CEO of IT Management Solutions, an organization that helps make life simple for successful businesses by providing Managed IT support and consultation. After spending 20 years focused on IT and technology, Pedro fully understands the importance of having reliable systems in place, and has trained his staff to share the same passion for helping businesses leverage their IT securely to become more efficient, and in turn, more successful.

Pedro believes strongly in continued education to stay abreast of ever-changing technologies as well as personal growth and development. Each year, he attends more than six educational courses throughout the US with the goal of being better able to provide the best service for his clients and improved mentorship for his employees and colleagues. His staff is provided with training and additional resources to meet quarterly professional and personal goals.

Mr. Nunez-Bautista served in the US ARMY Reserves for eight years, where he served as a 91B Combat Medic, 91D Operating Room Tech, and 74B Systems Analyst. While enlisted, Pedro completed his education at Northern Essex Community College, earning a degree in Computers and Information Science focused on Applications and Operations. After graduating, he furthered his education and technical skills by training on Network+, Security+, MCP, MCSA, MCSE, VMWare, HyperV, and obtained a CCNA Cisco Certification.

Pedro has been involved with accountability groups from Petra Coach, Darren Hardy HPF Business Mastery, and Robin Robins, where he serves as a captain sharing and helping his peers.

In 2019, he was a guest on *Cyber Security Today*, which aired on ABC, NBC, CBS, and Fox Affiliates, and was a guest speaker at The Cyber Security Forum at the United Nations Headquarters.

He was grateful to be featured in *MSP Success Magazine*, and at other times has appeared in *The Wall Street Journal* and *USA Today*.

Having won several awards through his career, he was most recently honored with a Speaker EXPY® Award as well as a Media and Communications EXPY® for his work.

Pedro is fiercely focused on helping his clients, but still makes time for what's most important to him. He enjoys spending time with his family and keeping up with his triplets, fishing, motorcycle riding, and of course, cooking.

To contact Pedro:
- 855-551-TECH (8324)
- pnunez@itmsolutions.us
- https://www.itsupportboston.us

CHAPTER 3

THE #1 WAY CYBERCRIMINALS HACK YOUR NETWORK

BY WIL MANGUAL

With all the reports in the media today about hackers stealing valuable data from major corporations, it would be hard to avoid the knowledge that there are people who would do harm to your business to make a buck. Between media reports and television shows, many people conjure visions of cyberthieves from elaborate hacking groups that mysteriously hack into a company. The reality is far less glamorous. Phishing emails are the primary way that cyberthieves attack. Essentially, the criminal knocks on the office door and an employee ushers him in.

A few years ago, networks were hacked mostly through downloading an image, visiting a website the user was not supposed to go to, or by watching a video that introduced malicious code onto the person's computer. Those attacks did not involve fake emails from well-known vendors, the company's attorney, or their CPA firm.

Viruses and malware also come in via email. Spam filters, while somewhat effective at sorting through the virus and malware rubble, are not 100% effective in catching phishing emails. The trouble with spam filters is by the time your IT department sets the parameters tight enough to filter out most of the fake emails, a handful of legitimate emails will end up in the spam folder, too. IT does not control what your clients send to your firm either. If they're sending something that sounds particularly 'sale-sy' in nature, a good spam filter might block that email as spam.

In addition to sales-sounding emails, that strong spam filter is going to block some legitimate business communications, potential sales, and orders. As an example, if your business makes more B2C sales, it will likely be receiving emails from personal home computers. Most personal computers lack security; their kids play video games, watch YouTube videos, and access Social Media all day. Who knows what's running on that machine that they then use to email orders to your business. If your IT department sets the filters high enough to deny delivery of potentially harmful phishing emails, it could block legitimates sales as well. So, automated filtering is kind of a double edge sword; it might save man-hours by filtering emails for the staff, but it could lead to a loss of revenue in the form of missed opportunities.

Since phishing emails have become the number one hacking method to break into a company's network, it is more important than ever before to be able to identify phishing emails before they unleash a monster into the network.

HOW CAN YOU IDENTIFY A PHISHING EMAIL?

Look carefully at the email address. An email from the CEO should not be coming from CEO@Hotmail.com. If a suspect email does arrive in the inbox, set ego aside, and call the person from whom you think the email has been sent. Better to verify that the email is legitimate than to open it and unleash a beast into your network. Check the file extension type. If the company from whom your business usually purchases paper from is OfficeSupplies.com, you should be critical of an email received from OfficeSupply.net. Cybercriminals rely on the fact that staff members are busy and will quickly open their email to dispense with it without inspecting it too closely.

If the emails you normally receive come from Tom Smith with the email address: tom@widgets.com, and the one you just received says: tom@mywidgets.com, then it is likely you are being phished. Second, look at the subject line. If there are misspelled words in the subject line, or if there are special characters in the subject line, those are red flags that it's a phishing email.

In this area, a smaller company might have an easier time identifying phishing emails for the simple reason that they could easily yell across the office or walk to the next cube to inquire if a coworker did, in fact, send the suspect email. In a larger organization, determining if a suspect email is legitimate or not might take a bit more effort. Either way, ascertaining the validity of an unusual email is still the second-best way to stop a phishing scheme in its tracks.

I've had plenty of clients that received suspicious emails. They always resemble an email coming in from the CEO of the company, a vendor that they work with, a client, or their CPA. Often those emails are disguised to make the recipient believe it is legitimate; that is called social engineering. The hackers will do their due diligence. They make their phishing emails fit an organization that has, for example, several hundred employees in several locations. They send an email that appears to be from within the organization or from a typical contact. However, there are always clues that an email is fake. Usually, someone at the bottom of the totem pole isn't talking directly to the CEO of the company and would not be receiving an email from him or her.

It's not like in a small organization in which there are a handful of users, and the CEO of the company works two cubicles down from you. In a small organization, you could say, "Hey, Bob (the CEO), this is Dave in accounting. Did you send me an email just a few minutes ago about resetting my password for our payroll system?" In larger organizations where you do not have access to higher-ups in the food chain, it's kind of hard to pick up the phone or yell over the cubicle.

Most people, until trained otherwise, would just say, "Oh, this came from Bob," then go ahead and do whatever the email directed. The CEO's name looks legitimate. Let me click on the link, take some redirects into another website where they are told to put in their login credentials for whatever system. For IT professionals, not a day goes by that we don't receive an email, a service ticket, or a phone call from a client that says, "Hey, I clicked on this link." or "Does this look suspicious?"

Spam emails, or phishing emails, are designed in different ways. The ones that we've seen recently don't immediately deploy a virus or malware. Instead, they are socially engineered to convince the user to willingly participate in the hacker's scheme. Some of the old school viruses still make their way through with malicious code embedded in the email, but those aren't as prevalent. Using the preview pane to view emails is generally safe and might even help a person to verify the authenticity of an email. It won't increase your chances of getting phished.

Curiosity killed the cat. Realistically, people—even if they have an internal IT organization—will click on the link in an email just to get that email off their plate for the day. They think if they must create an IT help ticket, it's going to take an hour or so to receive a response to that ticket. If it's almost lunchtime on a Friday, they want to finish and go home early, not wait for what feels like forever for IT to call back. They begin to rationalize, "I know Bob, the CEO, or I know Tom, the sales manager at this company that I buy my material from. I'll just go ahead and click on this link. I'm sure it's harmless because it came from him." Frankly, no one wants to put in the extra effort to call the person from whom the email is addressed to inquire if they really sent it, even if that is a commonsense approach. They don't want to stop what they are doing to call the IT professionals and ask, "Can you look at this email? Is it legitimate?" Better still, call the sender and ask. "Hey, I just received an email from you that says in the subject line that it includes a quote. I don't believe I asked for a quote from you recently. What is it for?"

A REAL-LIFE PHISHING EXAMPLE

I'll share an excellent example that happened to a client of ours. It is a ten-person company whose owner works remotely. The owner was in the process of building a new home in another state. During his absence, his office manager, whom he trusted, oversaw payroll and paying bills, had access to the checking account, and was able to write checks on the owner's behalf. The office manager received an email that looked like it came from the owner.

The email asked her to wire $50,000 to the owner. The email provided her instructions on where to wire the money and to use a specific money wiring service. The office manager went to the bank, gave them the wiring instructions and said, "I need you to wire $50,000 to the owner, and here is where I need you to wire it." Thankfully, the bank called the owner to verify because even though the office manager should have known better and called the owner herself, she did not. The owner was shocked, of course, but told them that he never asked her to send him $50,000. Thankfully, the bank intervened at that point or who knows where that $50,000 would have gone.

Why didn't she call the owner? They trusted each other. It was a small organization, and it was the middle of her day. She was doing so many other things that she just did not call. She failed to do that. This phishing email came at a time when the client had only recently begun implementing cybersecurity measures. It highlights the importance of training end-users because you can have the most sophisticated antivirus and antispam filters and a strong firewall, but if your users aren't educated, they become victims.

Ironically, we had just put those employees through a simulated phishing email campaign. All ten users in the organization passed, even the office manager. This phishing email was so convincing that she didn't spend the 30 seconds to verify.

This story demonstrates the importance of training end-users because phishing emails have always been around, but they're getting more sophisticated. Phishing emails used to take other forms like the classic email about the Nigerian prince who has $1 million that he needs to wire to your bank account in America. Will you accept the wire transfer? All he needs is your bank account information, and you will receive a fee for helping him to move the money.

Just as in grade school, if you're in doubt, raise your hand. Ask your IT partner for help. Help your IT partner train the staff to be more vigilant. When you're in doubt, don't take it upon yourself. Be on high alert. Absolutely, it can be annoying to have to include extra steps, however necessary they are.

These are some simple things that anyone can do to protect their business from phishing scams.

- <u>Number one</u>: if you're not expecting email from that person, don't open it. If the email is from someone who regularly emails you, examine the message and the sending address.
- <u>Number two</u>: when you're in doubt, pick up the phone and call to verify.

Look for anomalies in the emails you receive. If an email from a vendor with whom you deal regularly includes a link to click instead of the usual PDF acknowledgment of your order, follow up to make sure the new method is legitimate. If an email asks for updated shipping information today and you just spoke to that company three times yesterday with no mention of a shipping change, follow up.

UPDATE YOUR COMPANY POLICY FOR CYBERSECURITY

In addition to personal diligence, our firm recommends about 12 layers of protection against cybersecurity threats. Now, not every one of them is recommended for every client, and truthfully, most of our clients settle on about 6-7 layers of protection. Adequate cybersecurity protections are a cost of doing business today that pay back in peace of mind.

If I came to your office and placed a padlock on the front door and told you I would unlock it if you pay me $1 million, you would immediately recognize the threat to your business. You can't operate your business. Whatever is in there, the cybercrook doesn't care what's in there, but you'll have to pay him $1 million for the key so that you can go back to work.

Cybercriminals have become smarter and more sophisticated. You can't always stay a step ahead of them. Sometimes you are playing catch up. They are going to find workarounds to the best defensive measures. It's a cat-and-mouse game. One spam filter won't solve the problem. Five years ago, you could get away with a good antivirus, a good spam filter, a firewall, and a good backup. I would say a business today needs those four things at a minimum.

Now, however, every company also needs end-user security training, implemented regularly, and with regular user testing to locate the weakest links. Consider the number of emails each employee of your company receives daily. That is how many potential phishing emails your company receives daily that could jeopardize your network, your data, your finances, and your customer relationships.

How much do you think a business should be willing to lose to save time responding to emails?

About Wil

Wil Mangual is a dedicated and experienced IT professional with nearly 20 years of experience in the industry. With a strong focus on IT, Cybersecurity, and VOIP solutions, Wil is an innovative IT specialist who is continuously looking to remain on the cutting-edge of technology. As a driven and born leader, Wil prides himself on his ability to connect with his clients to address their technology needs – not only to grow and run their businesses efficiently, but to protect them from cyberthreats and disasters.

In 2005, Wil started his own IT consulting firm, Nerds "R" Us, Inc., based out of Lancaster, PA. As a client-focused IT consulting firm, Nerds "R" Us, Inc., specializes in Outsourced IT Support for Small to Medium-Sized Businesses, Cybersecurity, Cloud Solutions, and Managed IT Services. Prior to forming Nerds "R" Us, Inc., Wil held various IT support positions with local companies.

Wil received an associate's degree as a computer systems specialist from York Technical Institute in 2001, and he holds several industry certifications giving him nearly 20 years of combined practical and technical experience.

Wil's clients frequently point to his energetic, professional demeanor that makes their experience truly one of a kind. Wil's ability to answer questions clearly and succinctly is something that makes a difference for his clients.

Outside of his professional life, Wil enjoys traveling, reading a good book at home, volunteering for some of his favorite causes, or working out at the gym. Never one to shy away from technology, Wil is also an avid tech enthusiast who loves to try out the latest gadgets and gizmos.

You can contact Wil at:
- www.callthenerds.com
- wmangual@callthenerds.com
- (717) 984-2343
- https://www.linkedin.com/in/wil-mangual-b0266725/

CHAPTER 4

HOW TO PROTECT AGAINST VIRUSES AND MALWARE

BY DR. BRUCE EICHMAN

Ask yourself, when was the last time you were in a safe and public domain, whether it be your local coffee shop, a big box chain department store, or even your local gym? The first thing that happens when you enter the building and pull out your phone or device is that you are immediately prompted to join a public Wi-Fi internet network. Not knowing any better, you make a quick decision and willingly join the network. As a consumer, you trust and assume that this is safe for you to do. You don't think twice about joining, and then you immediately become a prime target for someone seeking out personal and private information. With just one click, you've allowed yourself to be exposed. Cyber attackers now have the ability to gain access to your email address and the information contained within your emails, which could include personal, financial, or client information.

Stories of organizations crippled by ransomware regularly dominate the IT news headlines, and accounts of six- and seven-figure ransom demands are commonplace. Almost three-quarters of ransomware attacks result in the data being encrypted. Of those, 51% of organizations were hit by ransomware in the last year. The criminals succeeded in encrypting the data in 73% of these attacks. 94% of organizations whose data was encrypted got it back. More than twice as many got it back via backups (56%) than by paying the ransom (26%). For those organizations that have insurance against ransomware, 94% of the time when the ransom is paid to get the data back, it's the insurance company that pays.

As times and technologies change, the people who want to steal your information change too, so they can keep up with the ever-evolving technological landscape. It is not just a matter of your computer being vulnerable. The virus, malware, and data breach epidemic has spread to portable laptop computers, tablets, and most notably, cell phones. This has resulted in a struggle to quickly and efficiently educate the public to help them ensure that valuable personal information is safe. This includes a broad spectrum of information from private conversations, social security numbers, birth dates, credit card information, bank information, passwords, data breaches, and other personal information that can be used for identity theft.

CALL IN THE PROFESSIONALS

This is where professional teams like ours come in. I'm a technology advisor, and I provide the information and resources needed to make sure that you, your family, and your business are adequately secured and not at a higher risk of these data breaches. Whenever your information is compromised, we act as a protection for you that alerts you and notifies you of the breach. Endpoint protection is no longer sufficient. Network security requires a layered approach, preventative measures, backups, and proper training to be educated appropriately. Viruses and malware are non-discriminatory. I am going to outline some of the precautionary measures you should take, including how to evaluate your risk factor and best practices that will need to be implemented depending on the size of your business and home computer.

UNDERSTAND: WHO'S AT RISK?

As cybersecurity grows more complex, criminals around the world are evolving along with it. Their methods leave you vulnerable, and many organizations are at risk. The simple truth is, the majority of criminal money is being made from SMBs in key verticals. Malware and viruses will target anyone. If you expose yourself to these attackers, they will embrace the opportunity and make off with your organizational data, extort financial gains, or gain personal information. No matter the size of your business, you are vulnerable to attack. Although, depending on the size of your business, you must take certain precautions tailored to the size.

SMALL BUSINESS SECURITY

SMBs are prime targets. More than 70% of cyberattacks target small businesses. Small and medium-sized businesses hold a dangerous misconception that hackers only target large organizations, when in fact, any business that handles personally identifiable information (PII), bank accounts, health data, and other sensitive information is vulnerable. For the most part, these hackers that deploy viruses and malware specifically target these businesses because of their overall general lack of knowledge about cybersecurity.

One common target is email. Small business owners tend to check their inbox daily, and one slip up, or one download through a virus containing email could be all it takes. Once the virus or malware has made its way into your system, you have already lost. Once the hackers are in, they scour your conversations for any traces of passwords, or credit card information, or correspondence that may be of value to them, including personal information. Many businesses tend to have very weak passwords to secure their data or bank and credit card information. It's much easier to use the same password that has been used for years and never update it.

You would be shocked to learn that companies are spending millions and millions of dollars a year beefing up their cybersecurity – but completely forget about the most obvious protection, passwords. It can be passwords that are easy to remember for the users but extremely easy for hackers to guess, some examples would include, password1, Welcome1, your birth date, and many other obvious password choices. These are not sufficient.

LARGE BUSINESS SECURITY

In a larger, more corporate setting, I have also found viruses and malware to be a major issue and player. Again, this is mostly due to negligence on the part of either the higher up decision-makers, or the employees simply not caring about securing data the way that it needs to be adequately secured, and not taking the precautions necessary. I have found through the course of my career that some of the higher-level executives have ignored training or not prioritized it to other aspects of their business. Cybersecurity, as well as proper teaching and maintenance knowledge training, costs a lot of money for these larger companies, and with the strong focus on profit margin, many times, cybersecurity measures become less and less of a priority.

Cybersecurity should be a top priority as these larger companies tend to have a gigantic collection of stored credit card information and stored user data, that many times is nowhere near as secure as you believe it is. Millions of people do business with these large firms and never even have a second thought about sharing their credit card information without reading the fine print, or making sure there is a backup security plan or service in place to protect you and your family. It is incredibly beneficial for you to have a company that knows what they're doing in your corner. The last thing you want is for your information to hit the dark web where it will then be sold, and your identity compromised.

SECURING YOUR HOME COMPUTER

The same principles that apply to businesses can also apply at home. Frequently these sectors overlap and create a massive data and financial risk. While many times intentions are good, they sometimes can result in a less than favorable outcome. For example, if employees have a work environment with a solid cybersecurity foundation in place, when they log in to their home computer to work, chances are, their home computer has nowhere near the cybersecurity protection. This is where business information is vulnerable. When care is not taken to ensure proper security measures and protocols are followed, customer and personal data are vulnerable.

One tip I always give people that have a work computer at home is not to let your children play games on your computer. You do not want your children to have access to the same computer on which you have banking and person filing data. Many times, children have no idea what sites they are visiting and will just click on pop-ups and agree to terms and conditions on websites that may not be safe for your home network. Before you know it, they have made your computer vulnerable to a virus or malware attack, and someone has remoted into your home network and now has access to all your private and personal computer data. This is compounded when the computer is also used for work, and client data has all of a sudden become vulnerable.

STAYING PROTECTED

Keep clean machines: utilize the latest security software, web browser, and operating system. These are the best defenses against viruses, malware, and other online threats. Set your antivirus software to run a scan after each update. Install other key software updates as soon as they are available. The biggest step to possessing well-rounded cybersecurity is having the proper education and following a set of protocols and utilizing a set of tools that will help better ensure your data is safe.

It is essential to realize that all your electronic devices are potential targets. The reality is that most people simply do not have the time or resources to always be on top of their cybersecurity and keep up with the latest and inventive new ways that everyday people are being targeted. Most of the time, cybersecurity measures are not at the top of the priority list for companies. It is additional time and financial expenses that many firms deem to be more useful elsewhere. This is simply not the case as it is causing massive issues for people who have entrusted their data with these large companies.

No matter the size or scope of the company, all can fall victim to a data breach through viruses and malware attacks. By the time it is noticed that the viruses have been spreading in the computer system, it is too late, and the data has already been compromised. Here is where a third-party web monitoring solution is so valuable. These services are able to keep tabs on all your data and information that may be compromised at any point and provide the best real-time monitoring and risk notifications.

Another fundamental principle to follow is to never do any business activity over an open public Wi-Fi network. This data can be easily accessed over an open network by somebody who can remote into your computer or phone and begin a brute force attack. All these attackers need is an opportunity to access all of your personal and business data. Many people tend to cross their business and personal email accounts, and that is a gold mine for people trying to steal data. By combining inboxes, hackers don't just have your information and email address, they have the email address of your clients, who may not be as educated and have very weak passwords that are easily broken. This is why user passwords are so crucial. A password followed by a text code, or two-factor authorization may mitigate some risk, but it is still not enough for the ever-changing and creative virus and malware data breach landscape.

KEY TAKEAWAYS TO STAYING SAFE

The only prerequisite for becoming a target is having something that hackers want, which puts all businesses at risk. Luckily, threat awareness and a proactive approach to security can go a long way in keeping your business secure. The right security layers can protect you from threats on all sides. As modern attacks continue to increase in complexity, and as attacks are automated at scale, your business will become more targeted. The best way to combat targeted attacks is to quickly and automatically remediate threats that do get through. Automated Detection and Response (ADR) solutions improve the accuracy of detection and speed of response, which is critical against attacks.

It is vital to make sure that all your computer mobile and tablets devices are as secure as they possibly can be. Make sure to avoid open-access wireless networks when possible; these include using the Wi-Fi at your local gym, restaurant, and even grocery store. These are not the places you want to be having business interactions and business emails. Constantly update your passwords, and make sure the passwords are complex, unique to you, and not stored on any of your other devices connected to your network. Once you leave yourself open to a remote entry virus or malware attack, none of your connected devices are safe. It is essential to take those proper precautions to ensure data security. The absolute best thing that can be done is to have a dedicated team, such as mine at TeamLogic IT, to monitor and notify you of potential cyber threats, and be proactive about your cyber health and security.

About Dr. Bruce

Dr. Bruce Eichman has over 20 years of IT support experience and currently owns and operates TeamLogic IT in Jacksonville, Florida. He is a 30-year Veteran of Naval military service, where he spent his last four years of service as the Director of IT financial services for the Military's Special Operations Command. After retiring in 2003, he was an IT Director for Oracle USA's support services leading teams of engineers and technical account managers to design, implement, and maintain customer technology environments.

Dr. Bruce has a Ph.D. in IT Organizational Management, a Master's in Business Administration, and a Master's of Science in National Security and Strategic studies. His academic/practitioner experiences bring a unique perspective to supporting technology, and his military background brings exceptional focus on process, policy, procedures, and controls.

He has more than 15 years of experience in risk management, compliance, and privacy with a focus on network security. Bruce has worked with businesses helping them identify solutions that make their businesses more secure, efficient, and easier to manage. He has managed information security governance, risk, and operations for state and local governments. Dr. Bruce provides niche expertise, helping small and medium-sized businesses to plan, streamline, and update security assurance processes. He has spent over a decade as a programmer with a focus on web applications and application security providing collaborative recommendations on cybersecurity controls aimed at protecting clients. Dr. Bruce Eichman is the author of the book, *HOW TECHNOLOGY CAN HELP YOU MANAGE AND GROW YOUR COMPANY.*

A proven security professional and leader of security teams and programs, he works within a Cloud Service environment, specializing in security education, program design and architecture, compliance, privacy, and vendor vulnerability assessments. An expert on the application of HIPAA, GLBA, SOX, GDPR, and PCI-DSS in tenant environments. He has a passion for helping the average person and new security professionals understand the why, what, when, and how of security. With a focus on prevention, he assists businesses in understanding how malware and network compromises happen and educates employees against social engineering threats.

Dr. Bruce is experienced in the art of communicating control responsibilities to customers and internal agents and agencies, preparing for audits, and accomplishing annual Service Organizations/Vendor assessments. He provides guidance to establish policy and technical controls to ensure information is appropriately protected throughout its lifecycle. Dr. Bruce is an expert in assisting smaller and mid-size companies in presenting their security posture to potential business partners, guiding them through the complex and sometimes daunting process of answering vendor security/posture questionnaires, developing a compliant security program, and remaining compliant with client demands.

Dr. Bruce Eichman is acutely aware of the need to improve the terminology and understanding of Information Security and all the issues and challenges this involves. He fully understands the importance of reliable information systems and how critical it is to get problems resolved quickly.

To connect with Dr. Bruce:
- Website: https://www.teamlogicit.com/jacksonvillefl915/
- Email: beichman@teamlogicit.com
- Phone: (904) 660-0001

CHAPTER 5

DON'T PANIC: WHAT TO DO ONCE YOU'VE BEEN HACKED

BY ANNE MORRISON

Think of your favorite action movie. When a major catastrophe happens, the action goes back seconds, minutes, and days to highlight all the small details that lead up to the moment when things went wrong. What you do in the event of a cyberattack will depend on what you do before it happens.

The scary thing is, even when you do everything right, you can still be vulnerable to an attack. To prepare for the worst, you will need to have a pre-attack plan in place that you have tested and updated regularly. In the event of a cyberattack, you are on your own facing an unknown attacker, not knowing what may come next. You need to marshal all your resources.

In most cases, companies will develop a business continuity plan or a BCDR – Business Continuity and Disaster Recovery Plan. When a natural disaster hits, they follow the business continuity plans to determine the best course of action. Sometimes, a company must follow directions or guidance from governmental agencies on when roads and services will be available. These are likely steps the company can take that are predicted and expected. This same sort of procedure can be applied to planning and preparing for a cybersecurity attack, and should be part of an organization's business continuity plan and involve many of the same parties.

The size and type of cyberattack will determine how many of the resources you will need to resolve the issue, but everything should be in place ahead of time. In this chapter, I will focus on what to do once the attack occurs, and the most efficient ways to recover. Before we dive in, we must discuss key signals that you've been attacked.

I. IDENTIFICATION

While some cyberattacks may be obvious, many others happen over time. You may log onto your system one day and find an ugly note that you must pay a ransom to get to your files. In other instances, it may take days to discover you have been attacked. The SMB (or Server Message Block) is a large target. In your computer network, the SMB is responsible for sharing files, printers, and serial ports on a network. Hackers will manipulate the SMB via a worm tool or other form of malware in order to gain access to your devices.

SIX WARNING SIGNALS YOU'VE BEEN HIT

Six key warning signals have been developed by professionals to help you identify when a breach has occurred. If any of these symptoms sound familiar – you've likely been hit.

1. If your browser redirects to a different website than you intended
2. If your team members are receiving emails that you did not send, especially ones that relate to payments or transfer of funds
3. If your computer shows pop-ups with urgent notifications to let you know that your computer is infected, and you need to run a tool that you're not expecting or familiar with
4. If your computer slows down immediately after clicking something on the Internet, emails or other programs
5. If your inbox is suddenly overloaded with coupons or junk mail to a noticeable degree
6. If your clients report they made payment to a new account, one that you did not create or are not involved in

If any of these sound familiar to you, please remember that the first step in any crisis is to remain calm. Once you've identified a breach, there are key steps you can take to save your client's data, their trust, and your money.

II. TAKING ACTION

FOUR ACTION POINTS TO RECOVER

Once you've identified what the attackers want – whether it's data, power, or money – you will be able to take steps to resolve the issue. There are four action points to complete to move forward in a timely and efficient manner.

ACTION POINT ONE: Document Everything

Before you do anything, gather the evidence so you can get help.

Once you've determined that you've been attacked, immediately take a photo of your screen, so your IT company or consultant can use this information to identify and remove the virus or malware. It's also important to document this for insurance purposes.

During the recovery process, be sure to document all steps taken. Keep a running diary and require that all members of your team do so. You may need to prove you took all necessary actions required by law for legal and insurance purposes. This is when you will also need to gather the inventory of all of your assets, along with the installation keys to access the software. Collect all system, network, and device logs and reports.

Part of your plan should be the documentation and imaging of your network. This would be much like a blueprint of your entire system, including software, software licenses, and the location of all hardware. This will assist when you need to re-establish your system post-attack.

Now that you've been able to document the issue, you can begin to identify the source of the breach and determine if the entire network is impacted, or if you can segregate the affected segment while maintaining the remainder of your operations.

ACTION POINT TWO: Bring in the Professionals

Whether you're great with technology or not, it's time to recognize when extra support is needed. Oftentimes, these breaches extend beyond just technology compromises. It's important to get the right counsel so you do not face legal or insurance complications post-breach.

Be sure your in-house or external counsel is up-to-date on laws governing disclosure. Fines and penalties may apply if you fail to meet your obligations before and after the attack.

Don't delay in contacting your insurance provider. There may be specific requirements. The company may want to have their representative involved in the mitigation, or they may consider hiring a company that specializes in detecting the source.

Internal or external communications personnel will be important in controlling public messages and addressing any requirements for notifying affected parties. See Action Point Four for more details on this.

Rely on the defined roles of each of the professionals that has been identified in your action plan. Empower them to implement their portion of the recovery, all the while documenting and communicating their actions. Some of the action points need to happen consecutively, and you will need to rely on a trained team to implement them.

ACTION POINT THREE: Hit the Pause Button

Unless your anti-virus protection provider advises against it, disconnect from the Internet until the virus/malware has been removed. Some software is built with artificial intelligence, and when a virus is identified, servers communicate with the software company to verify and help eradicate the problem. If in doubt, disconnect. Do not turn off the servers. They need to remain on so that your in-house team or the security professionals can use the information to determine the source and solution.

In the event you have backup servers, switch to them. Please note, the virus or malware may have been embedded some time earlier. Reloading your backup may just reactivate the virus. Be sure to run your antivirus program and have your IT consultant review your system before moving forward.

ACTION POINT FOUR: Critical Communication

Immediately after you realize that you've been hacked, you will need to control the information flow and craft the communications to various audiences.

- Audience One: Staff & Communication Tools

    Be judicious in communicating with staff. Keep the event on a "need-to-know" basis. If you have not already done so, have someone develop a list of alternate communications options (private cell numbers and email addresses) so that you can communicate instructions.

    Internal VOIP phone systems and email may be impacted. Make sure you have the contact information for your provider so you can redirect phones.

- Audience Two: Clients

    Depending on your industry, you may have obligations to notify your clients or patients. Follow the guidance of legal counsel with expertise in the laws governing your industry and jurisdiction. Some clients may have to be notified of new instructions on making payments. Make sure every client knows that any new payment instructions must be verified verbally with an employee known to them. As a protective measure, this should be the policy in place before the attack!

- Audience Three: Shareholders

    If you are a publicly-traded company, you may have obligations to report significant incidents.

As you begin to navigate communications post-breach, consider your reputation. To the extent disclosure is not a requirement for legal reasons or business continuity, consider restricting the information to a need-to-know basis. Clients may be unwilling to continue with a company that cannot protect their personal information.

But it's critical to be ready with a public statement regarding the event. The statement should include steps taken to mitigate the problem, how personal information will be protected, provision of credit monitoring if required, and what the impact on services will be.

III. MOVING FORWARD

Now that the issue has been identified, and you are taking steps to resolve it, there is one caveat that you might need to deal with. Some attacks occur because the hacker wants a ransom. There is a lot of conflicting advice about what to do when the hacker requests a ransom. Before deciding if you will pay, consider the bottom line, and what might happen during future attacks if you "pay off" the hacker.

WHAT TO DO WHEN RANSOM IS INVOLVED

Many advisors will warn that you should never pay a ransom, and for the most part, that is true. I recommend you consider whether or not your specific circumstances may make the payment necessary.

Consider this: if you make $1,000 per day in income and will need 6 days to repair the attack, you will lose a total of $6,000. If the hackers require a $3,000 ransom, paying the ransom may make fiscal sense.

Please be aware – I only recommend paying the ransom if you are prepared to immediately make changes that will protect against a second attack. If you do not have the proper tools in place, you will be compromised again, and likely for a higher ransom amount. Correcting any lapses in security is especially important once you have been attacked. Not only will there likely be a second attempt, but your vulnerability may also be sold to others to attempt a breach.

Once the attack is identified, HR staff may need to be involved. If a staff member has violated your policy on opening attachments or visiting a website, there may be a need for action, or at a minimum, additional training. It's important to make sure that the employee doesn't cause a breach again.

Use caution when relying on backups. It has been well documented that breaches may have occurred months before you realize it has happened. Hackers have adjusted the backup function so that you think you are backing up but instead may have lost days, weeks, or months of data. And keep a backup at an off-site and off-line location to be switched out on a regular basis.

Follow the 3, 2, 1 plan: 3 copies, 2 types of media, and 1 copy offline – not accessible via network or internet.

After you have identified your breach entry, you will need to address the reason for the breach. Most breaches are a result of phishing attempts. Review your personnel policies, institute a repetitive training regimen, and layer on additional levels of security.

It's also important to stay current – any of the guidance could change as hackers develop and expand their methods of attack.

IT HAPPENS

No matter what your company size is, what industry you're in, or how long you've been in business, you are vulnerable to attacks. It's important to prepare. Start developing your BCDR plan so you are equipped for the aftermath of an attack.

If you suspect you've been attacked, please review the six signals that you've been hit. If you have been hit, the four key action points will help you take the right steps to solve the crisis as quickly, safely and efficiently as possible.

Stay calm, contact your professional team, and think of all audiences who the attack might affect before moving forward.

In all cases, preparation and testing of the plan ahead of time is your best tool for recovery.

About Anne

Anne Morrison has an extensive career in building communities for families and small businesses, and supporting small to medium-sized businesses and organizations with IT support designed to meet their specific needs. Her passion for IT spans decades and can be credited to two pivotal people.

The first, a professor in her master's degree program, wanted each student to have a solid background in "all things computer." He took the class to a university lab that had preserved an original key punch machine and tasked them with making a functioning program from punched holes. This was just the beginning of Anne's journey in the tech industry.

The second, the Director of the St. Louis Housing Authority, then took a leap of faith and allowed Anne to write a computer program to organize important data, solving an ongoing problem with a service delivery program for the elderly. This not only saved the program, but it allowed Anne the opportunity to expand on that experience by building houses, as well as computer programs, for the community. Anne started with supervising a small rehab construction project and moved on to developing and financing larger projects, establishing asset management programs, and managing investments nationally. She was one of a limited number of female officers for a Wall Street firm. Over the years, Anne has developed databases, built out and managed a government agency website, and provided technical support for agency staff.

The project she's most proud of is a first-time homeowner project with Habitat for Humanity in Fairfax, Virginia. She identified financing for the project, then worked with future homeowners, White House staff, and county representatives to construct what was then the largest Habitat project in Northern Virginia. The community's short main street is named "Morrisons Way," and her personal copy of the street sign is proudly displayed in her office.

After completing a BS degree from the University of Tennessee, Anne earned a Master of Arts, Urban Affairs Degree, focused on federal policy, statistics, and research from St. Louis University. While in St Louis, she contributed research to a book on the history of one of the largest public housing failures in America. After graduating, Anne was selected for "Leadership St. Louis" where she was involved in several community-based programs before moving to Washington, DC. She was selected for and graduated from the Washington University Certified Public Manager Program. She volunteered with others to fundraise for the re-building of Eastern Market, and she served as Chairman of the Washington Area Community Investment Fund (WACIF) during the financial crisis and continues to serve on the board. WACIF provides technical and financial support to small businesses in the Washington, DC area.

Anne and her CMIT Solutions of Capitol Hill staff provide hands-on support to non-profits and local for-profit companies. They also co-manage IT infrastructure for larger companies by providing security overlay for operations. They serve clients in DC, Maryland, and Virginia.

CHAPTER 6

THE #1 THREAT TO YOUR NETWORK: UNTRAINED STAFF

BY DARRYL CRESSWELL

Award-winning Harvard University professor of developmental psychology and author, Howard Gardner, said, "If you think education is expensive, try estimating the cost of ignorance." Although IT and cybersecurity were not his areas of expertise, his words are an apt description of one of the primary problems plaguing businesses today and the number one cybersecurity threat: untrained staff.

WHY YOUR EMPLOYEE IS YOUR BIGGEST RISK

It used to be that hackers had to circumvent your firewall or passwords to gain access to your internal IT systems. Now hackers have your employees do it for them. Social engineering and phishing scams are now the preferred way to gain access to your network. Virtually every new office we visit lacks a security awareness policy and action plan to educate employees on what these scams look like. When employees do not know how to recognize a phishing scam or social engineering attempt, they blindly click on links and visit dangerous websites that bring untold amounts of malware into the corporate network. Your number one defense against cybercriminals is a well-educated, well-informed staff. We are consistently telling our clients they need to invest in their people in order to lower their risk. If your staff is well-educated and informed, they are significantly less likely to click on dangerous links or visit risky websites. We typically see up to an 80 percent decrease in successful simulated phishing attacks when we test employees who have been completing regular security awareness training.

Despite overwhelming data to the contrary, many business owners still balk at the suggestion that their employees put them at risk. The owner might tell me, "I would never click on that." Maybe not, but what about the rest of your employees, how confident are you they would do the same thing? I can virtually guarantee you they do not share the same level of security awareness as the owner of the business, and that's the problem.

WHY YOUR FIREWALL AND ANTIVIRUS ARE NOT ENOUGH

Typically, your firewall will block incoming connections that do not have rules defined. However, they do not typically prevent or filter outbound traffic. Therefore, it's a preferred way for cybercriminals to send a phishing scam email to your employees. Once your employee clicks the links, your firewall sees it as an outbound connection initiated by the user and thus does not scrutinize it in the same way as inbound traffic.

Essentially your employee just gave a big welcome invitation and did all the hard work for the cybercriminal. In the same way, traditional antivirus (AV) software is not enough to protect you. Many AV software programs are only as good as the last time you updated them, and the last time you ran a scan. Most phishing emails, malware and ransomware can easily bypass traditional antivirus software. We've seen myriad instances where an employee receives a legitimate-looking email stating, "Invoice Attached." It is commonly a Word document or a zip file containing a document. The attachment looks legitimate to the user, so they click on it and open the file. Before they know it, the file has pulled in a ransomware payload and encrypted all the files on the system. What's worse is the firewall and antivirus software did not even see it coming. To be adequately secured, at a minimum, you need next-generation endpoint protection, DNS filtering, security awareness training for your staff on top of your traditional antivirus and firewall. I hear this all the time from new prospects: "We have a firewall and antivirus software, so we are good," or my all-time favorite, "We are too small, we have nothing of value, nobody wants our data, so we are fine." No, you're not. I have yet to meet anyone who's had their data ransomed that told me after the fact their data was not valuable or that they were too small of a company. In fact, it's quite the opposite, but almost all these people thought they were "fine," were depending upon their antivirus and firewall alone to protect them. I always reiterate that these alone will not protect you from today's cybersecurity threats.

UNDERSTANDING DNS FILTERING AND WHY IT IS ESSENTIAL

Think of cybersecurity like an onion. It has many essential layers stacked one on top of another. Peeling back one of the essential layers is DNS Filtering, this is a critical layer of protection in your cybersecurity stack. DNS filtering works by acting as a sort of "middle-man" between what you are trying to access on the internet and what is known to be unsafe. It is used to block many categories of harmful or inappropriate content, such as malware sites, and other known dangerous corners of the internet.

While antivirus software is used to remove infections from your computer after you've downloaded them, DNS filtering serves to block your computer from encountering malicious content in the first place. If we can prevent a user from accessing a website with malware through DNS filtering, this dramatically reduces the chances of infection and the need for your antivirus software to try and intercept it. You can think of DNS Filtering as being proactive defense while antivirus software is reactive defense. It's important to remember, if your DNS filtering is blocking it, it's doing so for a reason.

WHAT IS SECURITY AWARENESS TRAINING?

Peeling back the onion layers even further, security awareness training is a critical measure to help keep your employees' security posture current and relevant. Typically, it is comprised of sending consistent short training videos, 4 – 6 minutes in length, that explain a cybersecurity topic in a non-technical, easy to digest way.

One round of training might cover phishing scams, while the next one explains CEO scams or malware. They are typically not very technical in nature and are explained in a simple way that non-technical users can understand. That's what makes them so powerful.

It is vitally important that employees receive regular ongoing security awareness training at least once per month. Security must always be top of mind; training should be done regularly at consistent intervals. Similarly, any time a new employee is onboarded, it's critical that they are made aware of the organization's stand on security, and that they agree and sign off on this security policy. It should be clear right from the start that regular and ongoing participation in the company's security awareness training program is a mandatory part of their employment.

Security awareness training is so crucial because employees learn common tricks and tactics they can use to identify a scam. We know that employees who have received consistent security awareness training fall victim to cyberthreats up to 80 percent less frequently than untrained employees. However, training is not enough. It's necessary to test the users by sending regular simulated phishing campaigns to identify which employees are at risk.

Training courses should focus on a variety of topics. You shouldn't expect to see different levels of training such as beginner, intermediate and advanced because we don't ever want this security awareness training to be so complicated that the end-user feels like they're being punished, given extra workload or going back to school for a degree in cybersecurity. It's very lightweight: short videos, four to six minutes at most. Anybody with a non-technical background can digest them because of the visuals and non-geek-speak examples that are used. They are audio and video, so they aren't being handed a book and told, "Here, read this, study it." It's very real-world examples, very non-technical in its description so that anybody at any level can digest it. After they've completed all the topics, then the employee will cycle back and reinforce the information that they've learned previously.

WHAT IS SIMULATED PHISHING?

A simulated phishing email is one typically sent to your staff by your IT department. It is designed to trick an employee into clicking on a fake link. When they click the link, it's common for them to be re-directed back to a security awareness training video to help them understand how they were duped. After a simulated phishing scam, it's common to generate a report showing the overall risk score of the organization, as well as identify the individual users who pose the most considerable security risk. I always advise business owners to ensure they use this as a tool to educate, not to discipline. It's important to remember that employees are the front line of defense. We want to help educate them and elevate their security posture. If simulated phishing identifies an individual as a risk, then additional training should be provided to bring their knowledge up to par with the rest of the office staff.

WHY IS IT SO IMPORTANT?

Today there exists an epidemic of cybersecurity threats, and no one's data is safe anymore. No matter how small or large your company, you cannot afford to overlook the significance of training your employees on industry best practices for cybersecurity.

Studies have shown that most of today's cyberattacks are attempts to exploit the human factor through highly creative and luring phishing emails. Human errors cause almost 90% of data breaches. Therefore, business owners must continue reinforcing the need for continuous employee education on cybersecurity.

Typically, employees should be considered as the weakest link in any organization's cybersecurity defenses. It is for this reason that, in most cases, the primary targets of cyberattackers are the employees. That's why we continue to see techniques and tools such as spear phishing, social engineering, ransomware, and malware, all targeting the employees and not the network directly. Think about it, why would a cybercriminal waste time by breaking a window to get in when your employee has left the front door unlocked and wide open?

How can an employee recognize, report, or eliminate a security threat if they do not know how to recognize it in the first place? They cannot. Despite firewalls and other security software, employees are still the most common entry points for cybercriminals. Online cybersecurity training is essential to help employees protect themselves and the company against cyber-attacks and threats. Training empowers employees with up-to-date know-how to recognize and mitigate a cyber-threat. By making employees able to identify and eliminate cyber-threats, you are strengthening the most vulnerable link in the chain. Cybercriminals are looking for the low-hanging fruit. If your organization has a well-trained staff and a good cybersecurity posture, cybercriminals will willingly move on to an easier target, that's a fact.

HOW EFFECTIVE IS SECURITY AWARENESS TRAINING?

Security awareness training plays a critical role in minimizing the serious cybersecurity threats posed to end-users by phishing attacks and social engineering. Phishing is the number one way in which malware, like ransomware, is delivered. In fact, Symantec found that a staggering 92.4 percent of malware is delivered as an attachment in a malicious email.

Mobile and voice phishing are also increasing, year over year. Phishing campaigns are becoming more complicated too. By removing the most common component of an attack, the untrained user, and by educating them consistently, they become your primary tool in thwarting cybercrime.

Cybercriminals take advantage of our natural human behavior. By doing so, they have made phishing the most successful of cyber-attack methods. One of the reasons that cybercriminals can trick individuals is because they have poor security awareness and are easy targets.

Since we know end users are the weakest link, countless studies (and this has been my own experience as well) have found that by using security awareness training and proper password management systems, you can reduce the risk of socially engineered cyberthreats by up to 80 percent. No matter which way you slice it – there is no compelling reason not to invest in proper and regular security awareness training for your staff.

TRAINING INCENTIVES

I recommend using some sort of training incentive for employees. We offer a certificate at the end of training that states they've completed the module; it has their name on it, and it proves that they completed the course with a passing grade of 80 percent or higher. Company owners can easily verify that their employees have taken the training. The employee has a certificate for the wall that is both a reminder of the accomplishment and a reminder to employ the principles learned in the training.

The best results are attained when the company has positioned itself with security awareness as a key performance indicator of its employees and a part of its IT policy. Once adopted, it must be known by all employees that regular security awareness training is mandatory and a condition of employment.

One final note. If the threat increase from untrained employees isn't enough motivation, your cybersecurity insurance might be.

Wait, your company does have cybersecurity insurance, right? This is not the same as errors and omissions or general liability insurance, and it's a whole other chapter on its own. If your organization does not have cybersecurity insurance, you need to get it <u>YESTERDAY</u>.

Regardless, insurance companies that write cybersecurity policies will need to know what safeguards are in place at your business. For example, it is common to be asked: Is ongoing security awareness training being provided? What type of ransomware protection is utilized? What antivirus is your company using and how often is it updated? Even if your company is not holding a lot of PII (Personally Identifiable Information), there's still the cost to the insurance company to have a cybersecurity breach remediated.

If your company were to be infected with ransomware, for example, your IT department is going to charge you the customer to remediate all that. The insurance company is going to be the one to pay for it, so the insurer has a vested interest to ensure you took all reasonable precautions before they agree to pay your claim, and you'd better believe they are going to do their due diligence.

About Darryl

Now a father of two amazing boys (6 and 9 years old) who have no clue how humanity survived without laptops, tablets, and interactive touch screens, Darryl Cresswell has watched computers go from toys for nerds to an everyday necessity that now fits in the palm of your hand.

Darryl is an entrepreneur and software engineer by trade. He has witnessed every big change in IT over the last 20 years. This unique perspective has allowed him to deliver highly-customized IT solutions and consulting services to his clients.

Darryl started MYDWARE at the age of 13 selling computer services and custom software to businesses and homeowners in the Greater Toronto Area (GTA), as well as the United States. In the early days, he wrote Batch files, C++, and Visual Basic programs to automate tasks for businesses and homeowners alike. Darryl wrote software to solve real-world problems and make life easier for his customers. Several of his software applications can still be found on popular shareware websites to this day.

Gradually, Darryl moved the company into the computer repair business, offering break-fix services to businesses and homeowners all over the GTA and Simcoe County. Noticing that it was difficult to pay the bills on computer repairs alone, he moved the company into Managed Services, first starting with website and email hosting, all the while providing ongoing computer maintenance services for business owners month-to-month.

In early 2005, Darryl discontinued residential services and moved the company to a fully-managed IT services business servicing business clientele only. A focus was put into ensuring MYDWARE could deliver a complete stack of IT support and services for its clients. Darryl ensured his clients would not need to self-manage multiple finger-pointing vendors every time something went wrong. Darryl knew that doing so would build client loyalty because it removed the technology burden from the client and empowered them to focus on growing their business.

Always innovating, Darryl noticed a huge problem his clients faced, which was skyrocketing telephone prices and costly on-premise phone systems that had very limited capabilities. Self-taught, Darryl began to develop his own customized Voice Over Internet Protocol (VoIP) platform and client portals that are widely used by his clients today. This offered clients monthly savings of over 40% while delivering high-quality voice and calling features.

Darryl knows that in order to stay relevant, the company must keep reinventing itself and adapting to the very fast-changing world that is IT. Noticing a massive influx of cybercrime, cybercriminals, ransomware, and dark web data breaches, cybersecurity became the next logical step for the company. Following this desire to provide clients top-tier IT support and services, Darryl made sure the company was linked up with industry-leading vendors, knowledge, and industry best practices. Since then, his company has been delivering a full stack of cybersecurity services and support to its clients.

You can connect with Darryl at:
- Telephone: 1-416-628-7107
- Email: darryl@mydware.com
- LinkedIn: https://www.linkedin.com/in/darryl-cresswell-mydware-it-solutions-inc

CHAPTER 7

20/20 VISION: THE IMPORTANCE OF A CYBERSECURITY CHECKLIST

BY RANDY MARTINEZ

What do you do before you turn in for the night? If you are like most people, you check the doors, and maybe even the windows around your home to make sure that there are no easy entry points for burglars. Is the garage door closed? Check! … the front door bolted? Check! …the patio doors secured? Check! …The security system armed? Check! That simple checklist gives you peace of mind because you know you have done what you can to keep the bad guys out.

Strangely, the same people who check window and door locks nightly often don't verify the cybersecurity of their business' computers or network, even annually. While checking to see if your home's doors are all locked is very simple, if you did not know where the doors and windows were located, that task might not be so simple. One in five small businesses will experience a cyberbreach this year. Of those cyberbreaches, 97 percent could have been prevented with current technology. There are fifteen important steps that will safeguard your company's computer network from cyberattacks.

You don't know what you don't know. When was the last security audit of your network? If you have not audited your security measures or have never audited, your systems could be at risk. It is time for a security assessment, so you establish the baseline for your systems and close any existing vulnerabilities. No baseline means you have nothing to measure against. So, how will you know if something in your systems has been compromised? What's more, a security assessment ensures that your IT provider knows what areas your company has already mastered, so that you can move forward intelligently to address the weakest areas first.

Advanced Spam Filtering will protect your email and secure your mail delivery, as most attacks originate there. Reducing spam will ultimately reduce your exposure to phishing emails that your staff has to determine are legitimate or fake. You can tweak the spam-filtering sensitivity depending on the industry. For a medical practice, for example, the sensitivity must be very high. However, if you're working with the adult entertainment industry—there are many in Southern California where I am—high sensitivity could block a lot of email that you need from legitimate vendors.

Passwords are one of the simplest ways to protect your business from cyberattack. Strong passwords—combinations of characters, letters, and numbers—are more difficult for cybercriminals to hack. The average employee has 10-15 passwords to remember. To keep employees from using the same passwords repeatedly, use a password manager to generate strong passwords, and keep track of them. Passwords should be changed at least every six months, as well as immediately when a high-level executive or a department manager leaves the organization. The new password should not have been used in at least the last five password changes.

Your employees are your last line of defense and your first line of offense. Security awareness training is critical for all users. It's always the employee that everyone thinks has been trained and knows better who ends up clicking on a bad link and compromising the system. Teach them about data security, email attacks, and your company policies and procedures. Web-based training solutions are highly effective in training employees in what to look for, and how to do their part in keeping company data secure.

If your business is still relying on anti-virus software for protection, you're behind the curve. Advanced endpoint security protects all your devices against attacks. These programs monitor how the computer is being used, and with artificial learning can predict when an activity is not legitimate. For example, does this user normally access human resources data. If that user generally does not perform such a task, the software sounds the alarm. Advanced endpoint security guards against the newer types of threat that are out there, which are far more sophisticated than previous iterations. Where previous phishing emails required that you follow specific steps, click a certain link, to launch a virus, the latest ones don't necessarily require the receiver to do anything but go to a website. An employee might receive an email that appears to be a legitimate correspondence from the bank telling them their statement is ready. The employee needs only click the link to get to the fake website for their machine to become infected. Even legitimate company websites can be compromised and ultimately infect every visitor to the site.

Multi-factor authentication should be utilized whenever possible on your network for banking websites and social media. It provides an additional layer of protection so that even if your password is stolen, your data remains secure.

Computer updates are to your network as vaccines are to your health; you periodically should ensure you are up to date. We recommend a critical update service to our clients to keep their operating system and applications up to date. Vulnerabilities are constantly being found by the bad guys, and they try to exploit them. Then, companies like Microsoft and Apple come back around and try to patch the vulnerabilities. Without those updates, the devices and data on your network are not safe. The same is true of your applications; the cybercriminals will probably know about a QuickBooks vulnerability before you do.

Updates don't apply only to software. Old computers, older than three years, and old servers, older than five years, cannot be adequately updated, and their performance degrades over time. Your IT team cannot adequately protect your business, your files, and your clients on ancient equipment. Three years for a computer is like almost 30 years in human years; it changes that much. Their age creates a performance issue without proper maintenance. If the operating system is very old, then it doesn't allow for operating system updates to occur. You keep adding patches and adding patches, and the performance starts degrading over time. At that point, the choices are either get a new computer or at least wipe the hard drive once during that three-year life cycle.

When an employee leaves the organization and a new one comes in, we will wipe the computer completely and reinstall everything fresh to extend the life cycle a little bit. However, after the three-year mark, it's time to upgrade.

Dark Web research allows you to be proactive in preventing a data breach by discovering which passwords and accounts have been posted to the dark web. Many IT companies are now scanning the Dark Web, specifically looking for stolen credentials obtained from their clients' domains.

Stolen email addresses, personal identifying information (PII), phone number, license, social security number, all those things that are stolen typically will end up on the dark web. The dark web is a trading post for criminals where they can buy tens of thousands of email addresses and personal information for pennies and then use that to start performing attacks and compromise those accounts. Cybercriminal organizations are growing by leaps and bounds. Even those wishing to learn to hack can go to the dark web to find tools to learn how to hack. Criminals no longer need to know how to program a computer – they can just buy a toolset that does it all for them.

SIEM (Security Incident & Event Management)/Log Management uses big data engines to review all events and security logs from all covered devices to protect against advanced threats and to meet compliance requirements. All servers have security logs, and if your industry is regulated, you will also need logging management software. This technology keeps record of internal and external attempts to log into any area for which they should not have access. Especially if your industry is regulated, meaning if you have to be HIPAA compliant, PCI compliant, any federal compliances, your business needs logging management software to efficiently review those logs and locate any anomalies. Issues that are recorded normally include numerous bad login attempts, multiple login attempts, or someone trying to access files for which they do not have permission. A SIEM log management system wades through those voluminous logs so a human component is unnecessary.

Internet security is a race against time. Web gateway security protects the online traffic in and out of your computer. Where are you going? What are you doing? Are you going to sites that are correct? Are you going to bad sites that are known to have malware installed on them? These cloud-based security options detect web and email threats as they emerge on the internet and blocks their access to your network before they reach the user, your employee. They also prevent your employees from going to sites they shouldn't be visiting. If you're a law firm, you would probably be going to county court sites, but you wouldn't likely be visiting porn sites on the office computer. Gateway security will block those sites because a lot of those sites are compromised.

Honestly, what company doesn't use cell phones and tablets to conduct business today? When an employee puts their company email on their phone, they have opened another door into your company's email and on to your network. Whether you provide the devices, or your employee does, if the device connects to the company network, it needs protection. Using Google Docs and One Drive on their phones creates another avenue to business information. Mobile device security thwarts cyber-criminals' efforts to steal company data or access the company network through your employees' phones and tablets. If your employee is going to be accessing work email from their phone, the device should be protected, or two-factor authentication should be enabled.

It is important to mention that as a business owner, you are responsible for every entryway into your computer system. You can ask your employees to use their personal devices to conduct company business, but you cannot compel them to install protections on those devices. Therefore, it's sometimes more prudent to provide devices you can ultimately control. Your IT advisors can install MDM (mobile device management) software on company devices. If a device gets stolen or lost, they can remotely wipe it so that no data is compromised.

How much risk are you willing to tolerate to offset operational costs? Companies regulated by the state and governmental agencies have no choice but to protect their devices. There are specific standards and heavy penalties to be paid in the event something happens, and records are compromised or if your company is caught during an audit. If your company is a small, unregulated business, then the decision comes down to risk. Are you willing to risk your company's reputation, company data, and client data because your mobile devices are insecure?

Every system should have multiple layers of protection—hardware, software, and human. A good firewall is the first layer of hardware protection. Think of it as the traffic cop that monitors and protects traffic in and out. Your firewall needs intrusion detection and intrusion prevention features. Detection sounds the alarm when someone/something tries to get into the system. Prevention blocks its entrance. Ultimately, the firewall should send log files to the SIEM with information about what happened.

Encryption makes it so that the data you use and store daily is unusable without a key to translate that data. All data needs encryption when it is at rest, in storage, or in motion, while being transmitted to somewhere else—as with email—and especially on mobile devices.

Each of the above checklist items helps to protect the most precious piece of the cybersecurity puzzle, your backups. If you're serious about cybersecurity, you'll be backing up your data in multiple locations. Backup local, backup to the cloud, and backup to an offline location monthly. Test those backups often. You never want to learn your backups have failed when you're trying to restore after a cyber-incident.

Even if the data becomes corrupted, at least you have backup in three different locations. And if your local hard drive crashes, which can happen, then at least you still have the backup that you have somewhere else and a backup in the cloud.

An IT company can assess and make recommendations on what needs to be done to increase cyber-security for a business. Then, the business must prioritize what things need to be done quicker than the others, based on their business model, their tolerance to risk, and if there are any applicable regulatory requirements. It is tragic for a company to lose everything because they tried to manage the security checklist on their own and assumed too much risk in the process. Hindsight may be 20/20, but it's a painful way to correct a company's vision.

About Randy

Randy Martinez is an Information Technology professional who is passionate about delivering enterprise IT solutions and services to small and medium-sized companies and organizations. For over 28 years, Randy has helped businesses and non-profits develop, expand, and streamline their Information Technology systems.

Randy is Vice President of Technical Services for IT Pros Management. As the head of the technical services team, Randy brings a "superhero ethos" to the company culture and service delivery to his clients. The "superhero ethos" of excellence, service, and ethics is the platform on which Randy bases his relationship with his team and clients. This ethos was developed and ingrained in Randy during his service in the US Army.

In the 80's, technology was a novelty for business; in the 90's, technology was a luxury for business; today, technology is a MUST for business. With the critical dependence on technology, small-to-medium size businesses and non-profits are on the front line of cybersecurity threats. While technology helps small-to-medium size companies, it also frightens them, as they cannot afford the infrastructure to actively adapt to the ever-changing threat landscape to defend themselves.

Unlike ten years ago, today's small-to-medium size companies and non-profits can have their very own "Managed IT Department" from IT Pros Management. They can have all the benefits of a large company's in-house IT force for a fraction of the cost. A team of IT professionals all working together to give your business or organization the security, support, and service you need to allow you to do what you do best – GROW YOUR BUSINESS.

IT Pros Management motto, "Focus on Your Business. We Got IT Covered." sums it all up.

Randy prides himself in providing personal service. There is no one-size-fits-all service. All his clients' IT needs are designed to be aligned with their business model and their budget.

"I am a business solutions provider that happens to focus on technology. I need to be creative to provide our clients services and solutions they want, as well as recommend and implement solutions they NEED," says Randy.

Unlike large IT chains, IT Pros Management's staff knows their client's business, their names, and their unique situations. IT Pros Management is not just another IT vendor, they are a strategic business partner for their clients, and Randy has become an invaluable member of their clients' management team in the role of Virtual IT Director or Virtual CIO.

Randy has an extensive background of real-world experience as an IT professional. He has held positions including network administrator, IT manager, IT director, and technical account manager. Randy has done news segments on local newscasts on technology and cybersecurity as well as presentations to non-profit groups on technology solutions.

Away from the office, Randy loves being with his family and being "Poppa" to his grandchildren. He is also a big fan of comics books and an avid marksman.

You can contact Randy at:
- randy@itpprosmanagement.com

CHAPTER 8

IS MY DATA SAFE IN THE CLOUD?

BY MARK BESTEL

Is your data safe in the cloud? Maybe.

I've spent a lot of time discussing this topic with my clients. They tell me, "Our data is in the cloud, so it's safe." For many clients, the cloud is an abstract concept that requires further discussion and clarification. For instance, what does "the cloud" really mean? Are you storing sensitive business data there? Are there compliance and regulatory considerations relating to personally identifiable information, credit card numbers, medical records, or European GDPR legislation?

Many people think data in the cloud is looked after and protected by some sort of magic. They don't even have to think about it. The reality is that the cloud is a marketing term that glosses over an enormous amount of complexity and possible risk. The products you purchase and access in the cloud are more often a set of tools to allow you to store and access data, but not protection, per se. The user is actually responsible to a certain extent for safeguarding that data. When we start talking to clients about moving some or all their data to the cloud, or about the safety of data that is already there, there are several factors we take into consideration.

I. Regulatory compliance

Security is talked about all the time, but we always suggest clients start by considering regulatory compliance. Compliance requirements vary dramatically depending on location and industry. Government departments must always provide a high level of data security and privacy. Businesses handling medical data in the United States must comply with strict Health Insurance Portability and Accountability Act (HIPAA) regulations. Those working in the European Union must consider the General Data Protection Regulation (GDPR) governing storage and movement of personal data. Australian companies need to be aware of the Notifiable Data Breach Scheme, which mandates reporting of data security incidents for medical practitioners and high-value companies.

Regulations can limit a client's choice of cloud service products, as many do not have the strict physical and logical access controls needed to comply – or may just be in the wrong location.

II. Location

Where is the cloud? Does the location matter as long as your data has a place to call home? Actually, it does. Depending on the type of data your company stores, the regulations outlined in the previous section may limit the options for where you can store data. If you are storing information relating to citizens or business operations in one country, it may not be appropriate or legal to store that data in another country where it is subject to a different set of laws. This is often referred to as "data sovereignty."

Speed and performance can also be reduced when data is stored on the other side of the world. If you need lightning-fast access to your email or files, you want it to be stored in the same city, or at least in the same country.

III. Financial stability

You should consider the financial stability of your cloud vendor. If they have been in business for a relatively short time, they may not be sufficiently well established to weather economic or other business difficulties. The number of years of experience (more than 10 years is recommended) and their market position are significant factors to consider. Consider a cloud service provider large enough to be listed on the stock market. Review their stock prices, earnings, and financial reports to help you decide whether your data will be in safe hands.

In early 2013, a local government office near London, UK, was told their sole cloud provider was bankrupt and going into administration. They were given 48 hours to get their critical business data and systems out and into a new environment. They were completely dependent on one provider, and estimated it would take 8 to 12 weeks to rebuild all their systems from scratch. Luckily, they were able to work with an existing supplier, and moved everything to their environment over one weekend.

IV. Service levels

It is essential to consider service levels when businesses have critical needs in terms of availability, response time, capacity, and support, which almost all do these days. Cloud service company Service Level Agreements (SLAs) should be reviewed and understood when choosing a provider. It is vital to establish a clear understanding of the contractual relationship between you and a cloud service provider. Particular attention should be paid to how the service relates to your regulatory compliance responsibilities that were outlined earlier. You need to be able to trust your cloud provider to do the right thing, and you need a legal agreement to back you up if something goes wrong.

V. Terms and conditions

Any time you install a new app on your phone or sign up for a cloud storage service, you have almost certainly agreed to the service provider's terms and conditions. Most of us click "yes" without giving them a second thought, but you might be surprised what you agreed to in the fine print. Take the time to check the terms and conditions and understand where the service provider's responsibility ends and yours begins. What limitations might you face in terms of privacy, capacity, and access? How do you get your data back if you decide to stop using that service? What compensation are you entitled to in the event of negligence or failure on the part of the service provider? Can they change the terms with little or no notice? If necessary, have the terms and conditions checked by an independent expert or your legal adviser.

VI. <u>Cost</u>

As we all spend more on digital services, it is tempting to minimize costs by using low-cost or free services. The least expensive storage options might be far from home and therefore, unavailable to your business due to performance or legal considerations. Free storage can come with terms and conditions that include a quid pro quo. One large cloud provider asserts the right to "host, store, reproduce, modify, create derivative works, communicate, publish, perform, publicly display and distribute" images stored on their free plan. They promise this legalese doesn't mean they will, but should you take the chance that your data could be used in this way?

VII.<u>Security</u>

Cloud and data security has been a hot topic for quite a while now, and rightly so. Long gone are the days when your backup was a stack of CDs on the corner of your desk or a couple of USB sticks. While these were susceptible to theft, disaster, or corruption, they were not accessible over the internet 24x7. Before a company or an individual stores their private data on one or more cloud servers, it is essential to understand the many factors that could contribute to the theft or destruction of that data. Awareness of the risks helps to inform a layered approach to security that will minimize the chances of catastrophic data loss due to corruption, theft, crypto-jacking, or other malicious activity.

Some points to consider include:

(a) Physical security

Make sure the cloud service provider you choose implements a robust set of protocols to protect your data from unauthorized physical access or natural and man-made disasters that might affect your data. Cloud services are hosted in massive data centers dotted around the globe. Is the facility able to withstand an earthquake in an area plagued by them? What measures do they implement to protect against failure of the power grid? Do they have strict rules governing authorization and logging of physical access to server hardware?

Check to see if the data center is certified for the data

IS MY DATA SAFE IN THE CLOUD?

security standards your compliance commitments require. At a minimum, we suggest ISO 27001 certification, but you may also consider HIPAA certification for US medical data, or PCI-DSS certification when credit card or payment information is stored.

(b) Access controls

It is a good idea for any business to develop an information security policy, and to define Role-Based Access Controls (RBAC) as part of that policy using the principle of "least privilege." Role-Based Access Controls clearly identify the data and access that team members need to do their jobs. Employing "least privilege" gives them adequate access to do their jobs, but no more. For example, your accounts department might have access to create, edit, and delete invoices, while read-only access may be sufficient for your customer relationship team.

Strong, unique passwords and multi-factor authentication should be enforced where possible. Research suggests that 81% of data breaches are caused by compromised, weak, or reused passwords. You should also understand under what circumstances your cloud service provider can access your data, if at all. What procedures do they have to track access, and who needs to authorize it?

These controls can significantly increase security and decrease risk. They protect against data theft, accidental data loss, or malicious damage caused by a disgruntled employee or external breach.

In 2010, an online healthcare services provider exposed the records of over 600,000 patients to the internet, after upgrading a cloud database but failing to apply security access controls properly. This resulted in a HIPAA fine of $1.7 million.

(c) Encryption

Experts agree that data encryption is a cornerstone of security. While many people have heard about encryption, it can be a difficult concept to understand as it applies to the cloud. Encryption protects the privacy of your data by ensuring that unauthorized persons are not able to view the content.

Ensure your data is encrypted "in transit" when it is moving between your computers and the cloud. It is increasingly common that this is done by default using the secure HTTPS protocol. This makes it very difficult for a third party to intercept your information in a usable form.

It is even more important to have your data encrypted "at rest" when it is sitting on your cloud service provider's systems. Your data will spend the vast majority of its time in this state, waiting to be accessed. Encryption makes the data indecipherable to anyone without access to the encryption keys, but when a cloud provider encrypts your data for you, administrators at the provider can potentially view your data. They may also be compelled by law to provide copies of your data to various governments around the world without notifying you. Encrypting your data with your own encryption keys before it leaves your network can prevent these scenarios.

A 2019 survey of cloud service providers showed 81.8% encrypt data in transit, 9.4% encrypt data at rest, and only 1.1% allows clients to manage their own encryption keys.

(d) Backups

If you want the ultimate in reliability, the cloud is far and away better, as long as you go in with your eyes open and know what you're looking at. The big players spend billions of dollars on servers, storage, networking, and security to ensure they can provide robust and reliable service. It is almost certainly more reliable than a server in your office, or an external hard disk. They use data replication to keep multiple copies of your data in different locations, protecting against data loss in the event of failure of hardware or an entire facility.

However, this is not necessarily the same as a backup. Most

cloud service providers implement a "shared responsibility model" for data protection. They protect against hardware failure, software failure, power outage, and natural disaster. The client is responsible for human error, malicious activity, hacking, and viruses or malware.

A few years ago, when most data was still stored in homes and offices, the cloud became a popular choice for backups. Now, as the cloud is becoming the primary storage for business and personal data, we are seeing backups kept onsite again.

Industry best practices recommend the 3-2-1 strategy: three copies, on two different media, one of which is geographically separate from the others. A single back up copy of your data is insufficient.

DO YOUR DUE DILIGENCE

Protecting against theft, loss, or damage should be a priority when moving your data to the cloud.

There are many cloud service providers and product choices available. The choices you make will determine how safe and private your data will be. It is probably a safe bet to go with one of the big names, but the devil is in the detail. If you're not sure which to choose, engage an IT consultant who can advise you on the best solution for your specific needs.

About Mark

Mark Bestel is the owner of an IT Managed Services Provider in Sydney, Australia, who helps small and medium business owners to sleep at night by ensuring the efficiency of their computer systems and the security business data.

Before starting his company, Mark worked for 15 years as a senior IT manager in the banking sector. After a successful career securing and maintaining the trading systems for one of Australia's largest banks, Mark now applies his enterprise experience to small and medium-sized business information systems.

In 2006, Mark earned the Certified Information Systems Security Professional (CISSP) qualification from (ISC)2. He continues to educate himself, his team, and his clients about all matters relating to security through training, client meetings, email alerts, and a monthly print newsletter.

You can connect with Mark at:
- www.netrev.com.au
- +612 8376 6234
- help@netrev.com.au

CHAPTER 9

HOW TO AVOID BEING HELD RANSOM

BY CRAIG POLLACK

INTRODUCTION

Ransomware continues to make headlines as it affects users, companies, and governments all over the world. This malicious software encrypts victims' files and then demands a ransom to decrypt them. Without the appropriate precautions in place, this presents a clear and present danger. In today's highly connected world - we live, work, and thrive utilizing tools, products, and services available online - ransomware is an existential threat to your business!

Having a healthy and secure network is one sign that your organization is trustworthy and reliable. It shows your current and prospective customers, clients, and partners that you take the security of their information seriously. This means taking precautions to prevent ransomware from affecting your business. Continually investing in the appropriate cybersecurity controls shows you not only "talk-the-talk" but also "walk-the-walk."

Because of this, more and more businesses are starting to recognize the value of aligning themselves with a Managed Security Services Provider (MSSP). The managed security services market is anticipated to grow up to 15% globally through 2025 and forecasted to top more than $18 billion in value.

WHAT IS RANSOMWARE?

Though there is no one singular reason why cyberattacks occur, we do know a common motivator is money. Most phishing, hacking, and ransomware attacks are perpetrated by individuals who seek financial gain. In this chapter, our focus will be on ransomware and how to avoid being held to ransom.

Ransomware can be devastating, wreaking havoc on individuals and businesses; in some ways, it's akin to being held hostage. You can think of ransomware as a technological form of blackmail.

Ordinarily, ransomware primarily infects in one of two ways: via phishing emails or by unknowingly visiting an infected website. The source is almost always an end-user who clicked on something they shouldn't have. We know that ransomware encrypts files on the infected computer network and then renders them inaccessible. The perpetrator then demands that a ransom payment be made (usually in Bitcoin) in order to regain access to the files.

For anyone, this loss of control with nefarious demands may feel overwhelming; and without the appropriate backup in place, nothing short of disastrous. For the organization affected, everyone may feel it in some way – whether by preventing business from occurring or creating stress and insecurity about the company, employees, and customers.

What can you do to prevent your business from being hit with a ransomware attack, and how can you mitigate the risks?

The answers lie in recognizing the threats for what they are and implementing the appropriate defenses ahead of time. Here are the tried and true ways that we've used to successfully protect and secure our clients and their computer networks, preventing ransomware so that you too, can keep your business safe and secure.

HOW TO PREVENT BEING HIT WITH RANSOMWARE

Simply put, prevention is the key to ensuring your business will remain safe and secure, and protected from the effects of ransomware.

Depending on your business and approach, there are numerous ways to boost your security footprint and safeguard against the prospect of being held ransom. For example: implementing effective end-point protection, adding the appropriate firewall, running a cybersecurity user-awareness training program, and monitoring for security breaches — to name a few of the ways to address cybersecurity risks safely and securely. Your IT Department can work closely with leadership to implement the right combination of these preventative measures for your organization.

The following steps outline how to build a culture of understanding and awareness around the risks present online, as well as various methods for protection. We refer to this as a "layered approach" to security. Utilize these tools and information to keep you and your organization safe from being held ransom. Consider coming back to this section or making a checklist to make sure you best leverage these effective ways to protect your business.

I. Building a "Cyber-Aware" Culture

One of the primary steps to avoid being held ransom in the first place is to create a "cyber-aware" culture within your organization. This entails approaching cybersecurity at an organizational level - starting with the leadership and then being propagated down to the rest of your staff.

Without a doubt, leadership plays a crucial role in building a "cyber-aware" culture. When promoting it to employees, the message on the importance of cybersecurity programs and best practices needs to come from the top. This requires buy-in from every leader within your organization; they should promote and nurture a culture that emphasizes cybersecurity safety, policies, procedures, and related initiatives.

The effects of this cultural shift create an advantageous environment for the development of new policies and procedures. These types of documents and strategies create processes and solutions for identifying and responding to threats before they become significant issues. In addition, while having the right technology in place is essential, keeping that technology as secure as possible requires more than just putting it in place and then assuming you're done. It requires regular maintenance, performing security updates, as well as simply knowing what devices are connected to your network.

Organizations with the best cybersecurity postures are those that regularly implement software and hardware audits and assessments. These ideal organizations also capitalize on the benefits of implementing employee training and enforcing comprehensive policies.

However, the reality is that cybersecurity need to be treated as seriously as a health concern: when someone visits a doctor, they trust that the physician knows what they're doing; rarely do patients diagnose themselves and then directs the health issues the physician treats. Of course, it's okay to get a second opinion from another healthcare professional, but you wouldn't diagnose things yourself. The same could be said for cybersecurity. It's critical that you align yourself with an experienced and competent professional. If not, key security components could be missed, and a dangerous security condition could spread throughout your system as a result.

II. Policies and Procedures

Having the correct policies and procedures in place is the foundation needed to ensure that your organization is covering all of its bases when it comes to its approach to cybersecurity. Implementing these in your business (regardless of size) drives the approach providing the appropriate level of protection. Some key policies and procedures are as follows:

- Acceptable Use Policy (AUP) ensures all employees are on the same page regarding data handling, security, and network usage, including how data is handled, transmitted, and stored.
- Business Continuity Plan (BCP) documents the approach needed to respond effectively to keep the business operational should a business interruption event occur.
- Computer Use Policy (CUP) helps businesses identify and address actions and activities that are appropriate for use with a corporate device.
- Disaster Recovery Plan (DR) will minimize downtime and get your business up and running in the event of a technology-impacting disaster including a cyberattack (see also: data backup).
- Email Policy defines the guidelines for what is considered acceptable or unacceptable in terms of the use of an organization's email system.

- Network Use Policy sets limitations and guidelines for employees and how they use the network from a workstation.
- Password Policy ensures that the integrity and security of an organization's data and other resources remain protected with outlined rules pertaining to password security standards.
- A policy of Least Privilege defines the minimum amount of access rights necessary for users to access data and other resources to minimize risk.

III. Building a "Layered Approach" to Protection

Here's THE most important takeaway from this chapter:

There is NO one, single solution that you can implement that will provide you with a totally secure computing environment.

The best way to achieve the level of defense needed to avoid being held ransom is for your organization to implement a layered approach to cybersecurity. Many businesses choose to use a Managed Security Service Provider (MSSP) to help them secure their systems, detect intrusions, and recover quickly in the event of an attack. Regardless of who you partner with to make it happen, layers of protection are needed and start with the following:

a. Backup & Disaster Recovery Solution (BDR)
A complete and comprehensive backup solution is the greatest difference-maker in your ability to recover from a ransomware attack - period, end of story. It's imperative that your backup solution is based on full image backups of both your data files as well as all of your servers.

b. Firewall with Intrusion Protection Services (IPS)
Next, in terms of priorities, is to ensure that your network is protected by an enterprise-level firewall that is correctly configured, continuously monitored, and includes up-to-date Intrusion Protection Services (IPS) analyzing every packet of data that's going in and out.

c. System Patching and Updates
Implement a methodical and disciplined patch and upgrade procedure so that all workstations and servers are updated with the latest security patches provided by the vendors. Also,

make sure to keep the firmware up-to-date on all network devices as well (switches, routers, and firewalls). This is an often-overlooked recurring maintenance task that increases your risk vulnerability.

d. End-Point Protection

End-point protection is two-fold: anti-virus protection (like ESET or Webroot) and anti-malware protection (like Malwarebytes). It's important to ensure all computers on the network (as well as remote ones) are protected and kept up-to-date at all times. The best way to ensure this is to make sure all machines are monitored and managed on a consistent and ongoing basis.

e. Internet Threat Protection

One of the more recent (and highly worthwhile) protective measures that we and our clients have had great success with is something called Internet Threat Protection. This is a layer of software that prevents users from going to "bad" websites. This is done by checking the link that a user clicks on against a list of known bad websites, and if it's on there, it prevents access to it. This giant database is crowdsourced, leveraging the internet to continuously get better over time.

f. Dual-Factor Authentication

Multi-factor authentication or dual-factor authentication (MFA or 2FA) protects your systems by using a second source of validation, like a cell phone or token, to verify user identity before granting access. This strengthens login access significantly – another "must have" in our book. 2FA is an effective way to protect against many security threats that target user passwords and accounts, such as phishing, brute-force attacks, credential exploitation, and more.

g. Specific Group Policy Objects (GPOs)

Group Policy Objects (GPOs) are a key component of Windows Domain management. They are great for implementing security policies within your network to secure things like locking down user rights or removing local Administrator-level rights from given users. Configured correctly, these can specifically prevent ransomware from running because the program simply doesn't have the needed rights to do so.

h. Cybersecurity End User Awareness Training

While technology is an incredible resource and provides a great deal of advantages for businesses, technology is still simply a tool. It isn't the end-all, be-all of cybersecurity solutions, and it isn't going to magically fix all of your problems or close your security gaps. You can have the best technology in place, but if users still open malicious emails and click on links, attackers are going to find ways to get in. You MUST consider the human factor.

The strongest defense to avoid being held ransom is using technology (such as the preventative measures detailed above) paired with education and training at the user level. The more "cyber-aware" your end users are, the more protected your network will be. In a nutshell, cyber user awareness training is a program that not only trains users on how to identify threats but also how to prevent issues from occurring in the first place.

Not only is end-user security awareness training vital to increase users' capabilities, but it's equally important to test users on a recurring basis. And one of the most effective ways of doing this is through pseudo phishing attacks. This allows your users to learn what phishing is all about, how to best react to a seemingly innocuous email, and keeps them honest over the long haul.

IV. Human Weakness vs. Human Firewall

The unfortunate truth about cybersecurity in our digital world is that more breaches occur because of people than because of technology. While it's critical to do everything we can to improve the security around our technology, if we ignore the human weaknesses of security, we're leaving a gaping hole in our defense for hackers to exploit. Too often, users demonstrate ignorance about safe online practices and the threats poised to attack. At the same time, many simply don't take cyber threats seriously. Employees have more of an effect on network security than most realize, often falling into the role of the "weakest link."

This can be addressed by companies creating a culture around building a "human firewall." This relies on four critical components:

1. baseline user testing
2. user training
3. automated and recurring phishing testing
4. managing and retraining based on results

Think of these stages as a way to build a truly effective human firewall: a literal "wash, rinse, and repeat" – giving your organization a chance to educate, test, refine, and repeat based on what you learn and where weaknesses arise.

IN CONCLUSION

These days, ransomware is an easily preventable security threat you have to take seriously and address with a layered approach. Regardless of your industry, your security is a key component of your technology footprint and a key component of the ongoing success of your business. In today's online global marketplace, having a healthy and secure network is not only a sign that your organization is trustworthy and reliable, but also shows your clients, customers, and partners that you take the security of their information seriously. And this means you have to take all the necessary steps to prevent ransomware from ever appearing in the first place.

In this chapter, we've outlined how to build a "cyber-aware" culture, how to create a "human firewall," and how to prevent ransomware through a layered approach of protection. It starts with your policies and procedures, training and testing your staff, and a number of cybersecurity solutions.

Keep in mind, no one preventative measure, solution, or strategy can stop every cyber threat. And certainly, the more complex your technology environment, the more you'll need to pivot to include various solutions to increase the level of cybersecurity protection. This is why your business must have a defense that contains a multi-layered approach. Refer back to this chapter as needed to ensure that you've done everything you could to keep your organization from being held ransom – because the life of your technology AND your business depends on it.

About Craig

As Founder and CEO of FPA Technology Services, Inc., Craig Pollack, a Technology and Business Advocate, has created one of the most preeminent IT Service Providers in the greater Los Angeles area. With over 30 years of technology and business experience, Craig has become one of the area's leading authorities on how small to mid-sized businesses (SMBs) can leverage and secure their technology most effectively to achieve their business objectives.

With a background in business systems design and application development, Craig now provides the vision, strategy, and leadership for FPA's unique, one-of-a-kind business culture, with the underlying purpose of redefining what it means to be an IT Service Provider, delivering technical solutions with the highest level of professionalism. FPA delivers "IT The Way It's Supposed to Be!" — providing advanced technical solutions with a service level unheard of in the industry. In addition, Craig also acts as a key trusted advisor for a select number of clients — providing expertise for FPA in the Investment Counsel, CPA, Business Management, Manufacturer & Distributor, Insurance, Legal, and Non-Profit vertical markets.

Craig has been on the forefront of delivering cybersecurity services through the Managed Security Services Provider (MSSP) model long before it was fashionable. As Craig likes to say, "Cybersecurity best practices must be baked into every client engagement. If you're not, you're simply shortchanging the client by not looking out for their best interests. Cybersecurity isn't a 'one and done' solution, but rather an ongoing journey to ensure constant vigilance. And within the IT Service Provider industry, we should all be helping our clients understand the business value of properly secured technology."

Craig is an active thought leader in the IT Service Provider community sharing what he has learned over the years having created a successful IT Services business. Craig hosts the "Business Before Technology" podcast focused on sharing knowledge and promoting other thought leaders to help business owners grow their own businesses. Craig has had numerous articles published in industry trade magazines including *ChannelPro* Network magazine and *Channel Executive Magazine*. In addition, Craig has also been a guest on numerous podcasts including *MSP Voice, The BrightGauge Podcast, Frankly MSP,* and *From Founder to CEO*. Craig is also an active speaker sharing cybersecurity best practices with the local Southern California business community.

Craig holds a Bachelor of Science degree in Computer Science with a focus on Business Systems Design from California State University - Northridge. Craig began his professional career developing custom financial applications, modifying accounting packages, creating custom reports, automating workflows and integrating websites and web-based applications.

Craig is married with three kids and, when not working on the business or on personal development, he enjoys spending his free time with his family as well as playing guitar, tennis, chess, and wakeboarding.

Contact Information
Craig Pollack — Founder & CEO
FPA Technology Services, Inc.

- Email: craig.pollack@fpainc.com
- LinkedIn: https://www.linkedin.com/in/craigpollack/
- Twitter: @craigpollack
- Blog: https://www.fpainc.com/blog
- Web: https://www.fpainc.com
- Phone: 818-501-3390

CHAPTER 10

KEEP YOUR KIDS SAFE ONLINE

BY PAUL VILLANUEVA

We all know how important it is to keep our children safe online. If this is true, why do so many of our children fall prey to the schemes of the internet? The answer to this question is a combination of not understanding how high the risk is, and not knowing how to eliminate that risk.

Growing up in the Bronx, we avoided certain areas, certain streets, and certain blocks, because our parents knew the "bad" areas of town. They wanted us to stay out of dark alleys and avoid potentially dangerous situations. Today, cell phones and the internet are the new dark alleys, and parents need to teach their children new ways to stay safe.

A children's internet usage study conducted by the Center for Cyber Safety and Education reveals several important statistics that may shock you. Forty percent of children surveyed said they had friended a stranger online or had chatted with a stranger online. After chatting online with a stranger, some had gone further and chatted with the stranger via text or voice on their cell phone. From those that had chatted with strangers online, 45 percent told the stranger their age, 10 percent said they were adults, 25 percent gave the stranger their phone number, and 6 percent gave the stranger their home address. Twenty percent of these children searched for adult topics, and sixty-two percent of those proceeded to the adult-oriented sites. Some children in this group admitted to using the internet to visit sites with sexual photos or videos, sites with weapons, dating sites, gambling sites, and alcohol sites. Some children even stumbled on adult websites accidentally.

It is difficult to keep our kids safe without knowing the threats they face daily. Frankly, for a parent, talking about these risks with a child or teen can be uncomfortable, which is one reason some parents would rather pretend the risk doesn't exist. Sexting is one such subject.

Sexting is the sending or receiving of explicit messages or images of oneself using mobile devices. According to the *Journal of the American Medical Association* (JAMA), over 40 percent of youth studied have participated in sexting. Some say that sexting is a predictor or indication of other unhealthy behaviors. You have to educate your children about this issue way before it happens. It also helps to have your kids use devices or computers in your presence. Children must understand that the potential for harm is great. They can be expelled from school. They can get into legal trouble. If compromising pictures make it to the internet, they can possibly be there forever. It is easy for a young person to be lured into this, and the potential for damage is great. Forwarding these messages or pictures can lead to child pornography charges. The legal consequences of sexting can include being labeled a sex offender and having to report your presence to the neighborhood. This might be a good point to mention now, that your child's cell phone if you allow them to have one, and their tablets should have a password or passcode that is only known by you and the child. This will help avoid the types of problems that can occur when your child's friend grabs your child's phone and decides to send content from his or her phone that is inappropriate.

Cyberbullying is bullying that takes place over digital devices. Cyberbullying can occur anywhere people can share content. For example, it can happen via text messages, apps, social media, forums, or during online gameplay. Cyberbullying includes sending, posting, or sharing negative, harmful, false, or unkind content or information regarding another person. Any child can be the victim of cyberbullying, and any child can be a cyberbully. According to stopbullying.gov, some warning signs that a child is being cyberbullied or is cyberbullying others are that there are noticeable increases or decreases in device usage or that they are exhibiting emotional responses such as laughter, anger, or being upset with regards to what is happening on their device. A child may also hide their screens when others are close to them, and they may avoid discussion about what they are doing while using their device.

You may also notice that they have closed social media accounts or that they have opened new ones. You might notice that your child has become withdrawn or depressed and that they have lost interest in people and activities and may have started to avoid social situations that they enjoyed in the past. Remember, to help a child in this situation, the parents need to keep communication open and to use the tools at their disposal to gather information. Look to others for support and make sure to report problems to the proper authorities. The person that is bullying your child may be bullying others, and getting help from the proper authorities may help put an end to the problem.

What else can we do to protect our children? The single most important thing to do is speak with them, have conversations, teach them, and explain to them. But do not do this once. There needs to be ongoing dialogue to reinforce the importance. When I was a kid, the threats were different. Drugs were the big problem at that time. I remember a police officer who came to my 5th-grade class and taught us about different drugs and what they do to people. When I was a teenager and had the opportunity to try these things, I refused even to try, and I attribute this to proper education at an early age. This may not be everyone's experience, but it was mine.

When children are toddlers, parents often place their play areas within eyesight so that the parent can get things done but still glance over to see what the child is doing. A similar approach can be employed to monitor your child's online activity. Place the computer they will use in a common area where you can easily see what they are doing, perhaps the kitchen or living room, wherever you are most. When my son is on the computer, he sits in the kitchen where my wife can see him, or he sits in front of me in the living room where I can see him. Our job as parents is to protect him. He is our most valuable asset, and we must protect him from all threats. Some of the things on the internet are exactly that, a threat. Also, when possible, consider using a desktop computer instead of a tablet or cell phone for your child's internet access. They cannot walk away with a desktop computer while you are distracted. Also, do not allow them to take cell phones and devices to bed. One study shows that many kids are online on school nights after 1:00 am while their parents are likely sleeping.

There is a saying that people respect what you inspect. Inspection is very important. What should we inspect? Make sure you are checking their web browser's history and their deleted items. They might be clearing this data, in which case, you will need parental control software, which will log the information into a system in the cloud to which your kids do not have access. Check their social media accounts. Know their passwords. Start this practice when they are young. It does not mean you do not trust them. All people are subject to submitting to temptation. You are basically acting as your child's accountability partner and helping them resist the temptation of starting down paths they should not follow. *While we are on the topic of social media, please let them know that whatever they put online may haunt them when they get older.* Kind of like a digital fingerprint, some of their online activity can affect them adversely when looking for employment, establishing credit, or renting an apartment.

Protect your computers and devices from malware with strong anti-malware software such as Malwarebytes. We recommend Malwarebytes and use it on hundreds of computers we manage with few issues. If you plan to use it as part of your home security solution, use the paid version. The free version does not run actively, which means it does not look for threats until you activate it. Make sure you install anti-malware on all your devices, including phones and laptops. Remove unused apps from computers, tablets, and cell phones. Less is more. Every app adds to the potential risk to your child.

As a parent, parental control software will quickly become one of your favorite tools for monitoring and protecting your children. Once you get parent control software loaded on all your devices, you will be able to filter adult content in real-time, block pornography or other undesired content categories, receive alerts about online activity, manage screen time and give yourself peace of mind. There are many products that provide these services, such as Net Nanny. This one has been around for many years and has a good feature set, but you should look at a few before making a final decision so that you get what works best for you.

When evaluating parental control software, make sure you get a central console from which you can log in securely and review usage across all your devices, whether Apple, PC, Android, or Kindle. You want to make sure you can block whatever apps you want to block and see what apps your children are using. Another great feature that many of these products offer is the ability to see what websites they visit, how long they spend on the website, and at what times the website was accessed. You will want the ability to block websites or apps either by name, time frame, or by categories such as pornography or drugs. Finally, look for parental control software with GPS location tracking so you can track your child's location via their cell phone or tablet and feel confident they are where they say they are.

Today, our children have access to abundant video content from sources like YouTube, Amazon, and Netflix, to name a few. One website that I love is vidangel.com. I love it because it filters out profanity and inappropriate content in movies. This greatly increases the number of movies I can watch comfortably with my kids. This service connects to your Amazon and Netflix accounts to pull the movies then displays them on your computer or TV without the parts you do not want your kids to see. Parents can limit their kids to using kid-friendly search engines like kiddle.co, which is powered by Google. Using Kiddle instead of Google will greatly reduce or eliminate access to inappropriate content.

YouTube has a nice option for kids at youtubekids.com, which gives some control over what they can see on YouTube. Similarly, Amazon Prime Movies has some parental control features, as well, that can be found under the settings section. In general, you will find that many apps have parental control and can be easily found if you do a little hunting. Make sure to check under settings because that is where these controls are most often found.

For many children, cell phones are their primary window to the virtual world. Cell phone providers, too, offer options to protect children. For example, Verizon has features that allow you to limit access to calls, texts, and data. They also have tools to block access to inappropriate apps and websites, monitor usage and activity, block unwanted contacts, view your child's text and call history and control your child's online experience—whether they are using Wi-Fi or your data plan—and track your child's location. Some of this may overlap the parental control software mentioned earlier, but keep in mind that security experts will recommend applying security in layers to increase your protection. A security guard at the front door and in the living room would be better than just one security guard at the front door. Please also note that this option will only cover your child's cell phone, not tablets, and computers, so you still need parental control software. Avoid letting your kids download their own apps. Some apps create hidden back doors and places to hide information from unsuspecting parents.

Whenever possible, you should use multi-factor authentication. Multi-factor authentication makes it harder to compromise devices and online accounts. Please, please make certain your child is backing up files regularly. Losing years of homework, pictures, and music can be a disaster. Remember the old saying, *"It is not if it will fail, but when it will fail."* This is still true today.

Regarding your home network, make sure your router is up-to-date with current firmware and that you have changed the default password. Some routers have content filtering that your child, or a friend, can turn off if they know the password. Use WPA2 encryption on your wireless network, and do not have any open networks without password protection. Speaking about Wi-Fi, teach your kids to avoid public Wi-Fi, and never to use public Wi-Fi to transmit important or confidential information. At home, you are likely your own IT company, therefore, you need to protect your home network just as your IT company would at the office. Keep all devices and computers up-to-date and updated regularly. That makes it harder for hackers who take advantage of software issues to gain access to systems and data. Treat every device on your network— Alexa, Wi-Fi enabled thermostat, security camera, baby monitor, and the television—as a portal someone can use to get to your children.

You can keep your children safe online. Stay abreast of the risks. Your child's school will often have information about the latest threats, newest problem apps, and current online obsessions long before your child mentions it to you. Forewarned is forearmed.

About Paul

Paul Villanueva has been helping businesses design, deploy and manage technology-based solutions to business problems in New York for over 20 years. Paul was born and raised in the Bronx. From his father, who came from Puerto Rico in the '60s, he acquired an extremely strong work ethic. His father also taught him to deeply appreciate and pursue higher education and knowledge. Because of this, Paul is an avid lifelong learner who has developed a mastery of many things. Thank goodness Paul developed an interest in information technology at an early age.

Over the years, Paul has earned Microsoft Certification, Cisco Certification, an Associate's Degree in Electronics Engineering and a Bachelor's Degree in Technical Management. He has also taken many other classes he has applied to his work – such as Database Design, Project Management and Systems Analysis and Design. He also taught himself PHP, XML, HTML, JavaScript, SQL, and more. Paul is a proud graduate of the Goldman Sachs 10,000 Small Businesses, where he competed with other businesses to win the opportunity to learn about entrepreneurship and business development with experts from Babson and the Wharton School.

Paul worked for several businesses like IBM, where he provided system support services for midrange systems and supercomputers to many large companies in Manhattan. He also held IT management positions in the banking and consumer lending industries and was an early leader in securing the systems under his management. Before this, he was a field engineer who ran around NYC solving computer, network, and printer problems for businesses in the garment district. He remembers when Windows was first used, and recalls saying to himself, who needs a mouse when everything can be done faster from the keyboard – a comment he now smiles about.

His vision was that he would take all his big IT experience and use it to provide creative IT solutions that solve business problems, provide a competitive advantage, reduce costs and increase business efficiency. Slowly but surely, when business owners met with Paul, they quickly saw that he was the asset they needed to help move their technology and businesses forward.

Having become an expert in information technology and cybersecurity, Paul left his position in 2006 to start an IT services and consulting business, Intelligent IT Designs. Here he leads a team of technology professionals who share his vision of providing excellent and secure IT services to small and medium-sized businesses. Together, the team of experts at Intelligent IT Designs work together to manage, support, and secure the information technology systems of businesses all over New York. Under Paul's leadership, Intelligent IT Designs provides small businesses with creative and innovative solutions to their business challenges and opportunities. Intelligent IT Designs understands that many businesses struggle with keeping up with technology and security, and their goal is to remove that burden from businesses so that they can better focus on their real objectives.

You can connect with Paul Villanueva at:
- www.IntelligentIT.net
- 877-914-3577 x701
- Expert@IntelligentIT.net

CHAPTER 11

TIME IS MONEY: WHY A GOOD BACKUP IS CRITICAL TO A BUSINESS

BY STEFAN HELLERSPERK

On a scale of one to ten, ten being the best, how secure do you believe your business data files are? Write that number down; we'll come back to it later. If you are in business long enough, I can guarantee you will experience some sort of failure with the potential to adversely affect the valuable data your business needs to function.

Any one of the five primary risks to data can take a business to its knees in minutes:

- **HARDWARE FAILURE**
- **OPERATING SYSTEM FAILURE**
- **MALWARE or VIRUSES**
- **RANSOMWARE**
- **A NATURAL DISASTER**

It is essential to understand each risk and how it might affect a business.

1. **Hardware Failure** is the loss of the hardware on which the data is stored, such as a hard drive with a bad sector.

2. **Operating System Failure** occurs when the computer itself on which you store the data, or the software that lets you interface with it, fails.

3. **Malware and Viruses** infect data and keep the user from being able to retrieve it or destroys the data outright.

4. **Ransomware** is a specific variety of malware that gets into your system and encrypts your files to hold them hostage. The perpetrator of the ransomware attack typically then asks for money in exchange for the encryption key so a business can unlock its files.

5. **Natural Disasters and Weather Events** destroy businesses, and the data housed within them, often without warning. Tornados, fires, lightning strikes, sinkholes, and hurricanes are just a few of the natural events that might stand between business owners and their valuable data needed to operate the business.

Ransomware has been a hot topic of late. Companies, large and small, and increasingly, hospitals and municipalities, have been under cyberattack specifically for the data files a cybercriminal can ransom. If you hear about a company or municipality forced to pay a ransom for their breached data files, they either didn't have good backups, or their backups didn't work. The best-case scenario when disaster strikes is that the company has good backups of its data so it can get back up and running in a matter of hours, not days. In the case of a ransomware attack, backups allow an IT company to roll back the system to a place in time prior to the ransomware attack with little to no loss of data. This way, the business doesn't have to worry about paying a ransom.

It's a misconception that a small business is a small target for cybercriminals. Small businesses have a big bullseye drawn on them. Hackers know that many smaller businesses don't protect themselves because either they think they aren't a target, or they don't have the resources to put appropriate barriers in place. Add to that some hackers simply want to disrupt businesses. They watch some YouTube videos on hacking or creating a bug or something, and they just go out and find a computer that's vulnerable. They're just happy that they're causing havoc in the world. Their satisfaction comes from infecting a system and causing data loss. If the data is important to your business and you don't protect it, the impact on you is the same whether the hacker profits or not.

What is the value of the information you store? If you are a small business that does $1 million a year and has $100,000 in receivables stored in

QuickBooks, the value of that QuickBooks data exceeds \$100,000. If ransomware locks down your AR files and you don't have a good backup of that information, you could lose the opportunity to bill for the work you have already done. Maybe honest customers would understand your plight and pay what they owe. What if they don't? How many additional human hours would be spent trying to replicate that information? That proposal your staff has painstakingly spent weeks preparing and is nearly ready to submit, could be gone in the blink of an eye, and with it, the business it might have brought.

Whether a business wants to protect its data from ransoming, to preserve accounting data and emails, or to comply with government regulations, the best defense is a good offense, and that begins with backing up data. Redundancy is a good thing when it comes to data security. A business should have multiple methods of backups stored at different locations. No two businesses will have the same configuration for their backups. A good cybersecurity provider will offer backup solutions tailored to the data needs of the specific business and its budget. Backup options should include a combination of cloud storage, local storage like a hard drive or flash drive, and network storage. Backing up all data to one large hard drive is not enough.

An external hard drive kept somewhere safe that gets backed up prior to a storm hitting, for example, can be carried to a safer location. Even with a verified backup offsite such as in the cloud, an additional backup to an external drive can help the business set up quickly from another location should the business headquarters take a direct hit. If the business is forced to relocate temporarily or internet access isn't available for a few days, a good backup to an external drive can be reconnected to a system in an area with power and internet.

There are two concerns with backups:

1. **Do you have a usable copy of important data?**
2. **And how quickly can you get up and running again if something happens?** To that end, we try to mix in file backup with imaging software. Software now can image an entire computer into one file that can be stored offsite or on an external hard drive. Then if something happens to that hardware or if something happens to your business, you can get a new set of hardware quickly or find a

computer that you can use as a spare. You can dump that image onto the new computer, and it's right back up and running just like it was before whatever happened. So, it's a quicker way to get the business operational. Our recommendation is to backup files daily during the week to either offsite or a local drive. Then, once a week, image those drives to offsite storage.

Software imaging is especially important if you use multiple programs in your day-to-day operations. It saves critical time not to have to download each program manually since backup data is useless without a computer with which it can interface. Just think about how cumbersome it is to set up a new computer and download all the different software. When you purchase a new computer, you expect to spend time setting up. If the computer crashes, all that software must be reloaded, and the licenses reset while in the middle of a crisis.

I had a new client for whom we created backups, and additionally, I suggested imaging for them. Thankfully, they opted to do the imaging. Inside of a week after that, they took a direct lightning hit to their server room. When I walked into that room, there was still smoke. There was one orange light that was flashing on the server, and that's all it would do. We took the virtualized image we had created the week prior on a backup drive, plugged it into one of our spare computers and launched it virtually. We brought that computer back to them about an hour and a half later. Their business ran off that computer through the virtual image for about two weeks while we got the new server in place. With just a backup, they would have been protected, but without the imaging, they would have lost two or three days of productivity while we got their various locations pointed back to the server.

Sometimes despite the best cybersecurity measures, a system will get hacked. If you back up to a local hard drive and don't encrypt the data, the backup is directly accessible through that computer. If that computer gets a bug, the infection will go looking for those backups and can easily access them. Now, the computer and the backup are locked by ransomware. However, if you encrypt that data when you store it on the hard drive, then the bug might infect the computer but be unable to access the backup data without an encryption key. The same is true for an offsite backup.

Verifying that the backup is running is not enough, your business needs to test the backup, too. I have had customers that verified their tape backups were functioning. They were diligently checking their tape backups as prescribed; however, they did not ever attempt to retrieve the files that were supposed to have been saved. When they did that, they found out the tapes were blank.

A backup failure equals going to the bank to withdraw money from your emergency fund only to find out someone has drained your account. Every business should have a plan to test its backups at least monthly. The test should utilize whatever method would be used to recover those files in the event of a disaster, ensure that the retrieved files are viable, and verify that the data expected to be there is there.

It is interesting that many businesses have no problem paying for insurance, but when it comes to protecting the information most important to their business, they think the worst-case scenario won't happen to them. Encrypted backups housed in multiple locations and tested regularly are insurance for your business. An experienced IT advisor might sound a bit like the Grim Reaper foretelling doom-and-gloom when he or she asks questions or makes recommendations for your business. The right specialist will be up-to-date in the standards and regulations affecting the industries he or she serves. It's not enough to know how to create a backup. Does your business need archived copies of data in addition to the regular backups?

How often do you swap out the hard drives to which you back up data? What happens if somebody breaks in and steals your server? What if your building burns down and the only backup you had was in that same building? Each situation is different, and that's why it's helpful to have somebody from the outside coming in to assess your operation, what you're trying to accomplish and what you're trying to protect, then design a solution that's custom-tailored to how you operate.

No business can predict with certainty when or what type of disaster might befall it. An undertrained employee might click a link in a phishing email or visit an inappropriate website, and suddenly, malware or ransomware gets into your systems. An older computer could crash, rendering it useless and the data housed on it inaccessible. A wildfire could destroy the office without enough lead time to grab the server loaded with customer contact records and accounting files. Time is money. In each of these cases, at least two good backups, encrypted to keep the data secure, could be the difference between business as usual and business down the drain. Now, on a scale of one to ten, how would you rate the security of your business' data?

About Stefan

Stefan Hellersperk has been serving clients and protecting networks in Carteret and surrounding counties since 1997. Three days after High School graduation, Stefan was standing in Parris Island, SC, earning the title of US Marine. After six years working as an Avionics Technician, he received an honorable discharge and started serving his local community first as a Police Officer and then as a Deputy Sheriff. After six years of service, he decided to pursue his dream of owning his own business and started ACS Computer Services.

Over the years, Stefan has positioned himself as a trusted expert in Cybersecurity. He has used his expertise to advise and assist his clients in keeping their networks operating smoothly and securely. Along with many industry-specific certifications, Stefan also has a Bachelor of Science with a focus on Information Systems Management from Kaplan University and a Master's degree with a focus on Information Systems Security from American Military University.

Stefan prides himself on being the go-to person to help current and prospective clients make the right decisions—from establishing their initial infrastructure to running their computer networks and systems. Understanding the dangers that businesses face and designing solutions to help them stay protected are a significant focus of his business. Establishing effective gateway protection, workstation monitoring and security, and encrypted offsite backup solutions give clients the peace of mind that they are protected from the threats both today and in the future.

You can connect with Stefan at:
- www.acscomputersupport.com
- (252) 240-3399
- stefan@acsit.biz

CHAPTER 12

REDUCING CLOUD BACKUP DISASTERS

BY AKIVA GOLDSTEIN

UP IN THE CLOUD

We backed all our data
up into the cloud
We'd found a great storage
That made us feel proud

We put up our data, our passwords,
and numbers
Into this new place
Filled with mystery and wonder

Our business was great
And no backup was needed
We felt almost guilty
To the system we cheated

But danger was lurking, spreading like flu
Did you know that a virus could be uploaded too?
That's right; this huge problem could happen to you
Just look at my cloud, the ransomware zoo.

If only Dr. Seuss were around to help us navigate the web the same way he fearlessly maneuvered through Seussville…

Take *The Cat in the Hat.* A feline with the enviable ability to make things that disappeared, come back again. We all wish that type of magic could be replicated in the cloud, but as the owner of the IT consulting firm, **OnsiteIn60**, I'll be honest, it can't. No one person or company can guarantee the restoration of family photos, hard work, or valuable personal assets that haven't been properly stored and protected.

According to the research and advisory company Gartner, through 2024, a majority of businesses will continue to struggle with appropriately measuring cloud security risks.

Organizations tend to put too much faith in the cloud service, simply trusting that their information is backed up and safe. In reality, while the cloud has a number of benefits, including cost savings, ease of usability, and the capability to work without Internet, it is not enough. It doesn't matter if you have 3-terabytes of storage for your company or 64-gigabytes on a smartphone. If the data isn't duplicated with an offsite backup, one malfunction, flood, or IT failure could result in a total loss. Additionally, there is human error. Gartner's research shows that through 2025, 99% of cloud security failures will be the customer's fault. That said, the good news is that consumers can take action to reduce risk, and as I will show you in this chapter, the steps are fairly simple, straight forward and important to execute in the right way.

DON'T BE A VICTIM

One of the largest Service Providers for online data backup uses the phrase, "set it and forget it." That is such an easy trap for a consumer to fall into. Wouldn't it be nice to set a backup and never have to worry about it? I hate to be the bearer of bad news, but the only thing you can forget about if you use this approach is keeping your data secure! It's insanity. I'll let you in on a little secret… this particular company only sells to resellers, which I believe is by design to prevent them from getting sued. It makes sense because, with this plan, it is fair to assume people frequently lose data.

Considering that a business's greatest asset is its data, there's no reason not to actively protect it in the safest possible way. According to the National Archives and Records Administration in Washington DC,

93% of companies that lost their data as a result of a disaster, filed for bankruptcy the same year. Trust me, everyone thinks they have a backup plan in place, but when I ask specific questions such as, "What exactly are you backing up?" and "What are you protected against?" Most times, the answer is, "I don't know." The majority of people don't want to hear it, but believing your files are "safe in the cloud," is irresponsible. **In 90% of the companies I walk into, I discover a hole in their backup strategy.**

Part of the reason consumers get lulled into a false sense of security is the misconception that the cloud is a cozy infinite universe. In reality, the cloud is just a bunch of servers racked in a data center. If you use a computer, you use the cloud. It is because of the cloud that we have the ability to access our information remotely. Imagine all of the documents you may have saved to Google Drive (Google), OneDrive (Microsoft), Box, or Dropbox. Don't forget about your emails in Gmail or Yahoo or photos uploaded to Facebook or iCloud. They are not secured on a personal hard drive. They are on a public cloud server, and they are all vulnerable to getting deleted accidentally by the users themselves or corrupted.

It is important to understand the difference between a public and private cloud server. At OnsiteIn60, we design a hybrid solution leveraging both public and private cloud storage to ensure data is kept safe. Private cloud solutions are more flexible and customizable due to the small scale and personal interactions that public hosts can't offer. Numerous businesses originally choose public cloud storage as their default solution, but taking the private route increases security, provides faster recovery time, and makes accessing files faster and easier.

In addition to solely relying on public cloud backup, and falling victim to ineffective options like the "set it and forget it" plan, there are a number of other traps consumers fall victim to when it comes to protecting their data.

Here are four of the biggest cloud backup mistakes:

1. Synchronization
Syncing and backing up are two different things. Syncing takes a file on a server or desktop and allows it to be shared with other

devices through the cloud. Yes, the file is now saved in multiple places, but if it is lost or damaged in one, it is lost or damaged in the other. In the case of a virus, the bad file simply overwrites the good one.

2. Ignoring a Test Restore

Businesses need to be aware of what their coverage is and how to access files should disaster strike. In the case of a fire, flood, or virus, if a business is unclear whether its backup is safe or not, it's already too late. Managing backups is one of those things that's easily overlooked because it's not critical... until it is. Testing to see if files can be pulled up two to three times a year is a good rule of thumb. Anyone can back up personal items, but for a business, this is something that a professional should handle and stay on top of.

3. Putting All Your Eggs in One Basket

The cloud provides one level of security. True data-loss prevention means pursuing multiple strategies to create redundancy. For example, external hard drives, which are fairly inexpensive, can serve as another level of protection. Having encrypted external hard drives on hand and utilized in a rotation (similar to the way tapes used to be used) is an easy and highly recommended solution to add additional protection at a very minimal cost.

4. Being Presented With, And Accepting, One Plan

I always advise customers that when it comes to security, don't be lazy. If you are a business owner, do not leave storage decisions completely in the hands of a tech team. Take responsibility, get educated, and be involved. Contrary to popular belief, the customer has options when it comes to choosing plans and accepting pricing. Knowing what those options are is key to making informed decisions on proper backup implementation.

THE SECRET TO SAVING ON STORAGE

When it comes to storage solutions, you get what you pay for.

Typically, upon meeting with a client, the first thing we discuss is the potential loss of data or RPO (Recovery Point Objective). The faster the recovery time and the closer the RPO, the higher the cost. Most consumers don't realize that choosing a storage solution is more a business decision than a technical one. In the same way, one would arm themselves with figures for comparison when walking into a car dealership, and a similar tactic can be applied to data backup. Too often, techs will provide companies with one quote or plan for private storage, eliminating any ability to compare and contrast options. That is bad practice.

As a consumer, when looking over a quote, consider how much risk is acceptable and search out the best possible deal. For example, a medical practice or financial institution generally cannot afford any type of loss, while an advertising agency, public relations firm, or construction company may be willing to sacrifice up to a day's worth of data. The less often you back up, the less storage you require, and the less you have to pay. Most companies I meet with tell me they can't afford to lose anything – until I explain that they can save a good chunk of change if they are willing to part with a few hours' worth of data (e.g., they are not performing continuous backups, but performing them at acceptable intervals of time). Then the conversation inevitably changes.

THE BEST APPROACH TO A SECURE SYSTEM

The next determination to make is the method of backup. A backup is basically a safety net, and as with any support system, it's impossible to have too many. I compare this to disability insurance. You don't want to purchase it, but when you do need it, you're really glad it's there. There are natural disasters, theft, and breaches, and unfortunately, with a breach, it's not a matter of if, but when. Hackers are coming up with new ways to access private data all of the time, so in addition to the ransomware we know about, there are plenty of attacks coming down the pipeline that no one's even heard of yet.

Implementing a plan with both "onsite" and "offsite" backups is the most effective defense against total loss of data.

1. Onsite backups entail periodically storing important data on a local storage device such as an external hard drive. It's a low-cost solution that doesn't require internet access, and offers the consumer immediate access to data, maximizing their RTO (Recovery Time Objective).

A new threat right now with ransomware is that it has the ability to attack backups by hijacking files, creating multiple versions of them, and encrypting them over and over again, making the possibility of a full restoration unlikely. Cloud backups simply cannot restore indefinitely. A cost-effective way to create an onsite backup plan is to simply keep multiple external hard drives on hand and manually swap them out. It takes minimal effort, and they only cost about $100 per drive. The issue is hard drives are not indestructible, which is where offsite storage comes into play.

2. Offsite cloud backups house data on remote storage via the Internet. Cloud backups in an offsite facility give you peace of mind that your documents are securely stored at a remote location, and protect against catastrophes such as fire, flood, theft, and even cyber-attacks. Files can typically be restored on local or cloud servers fairly quickly. The downside is efficiency, as having information stored elsewhere means it is not always easily accessible.

This is why a hybrid solution, consisting of an offsite cloud backup and onsite hard drives, makes the most sense. If there is an issue on one side of the equation, it can be offset by recovery on the other. This plan is not just suggested for big business. A home plan for personal files is very similar, just on a smaller scale. Simply back up the files in your home office to the public cloud and, in addition, purchase a small hard drive and back data up to it at least once a month. Back up every week, and the most you're going to lose is a week's worth of data. It's that easy to ensure a system is about 99% protected. Just as effective security is about discipline, good behaviors, and being mindful, the world of data storage is no different.

If you utilize Amazon Web Services (AWS), Amazon's cloud computing division, or a similar service, you'll find IT staff will often run backups of all different kinds. Unfortunately, ask them how many AWS accounts they are using, and they will admit they use just one. So, in essence, if your cloud servers/environment is breached and can be deleted, why wouldn't the data backups be in the same boat? If you aren't crazy about the local backup plan, at least have a second cloud account that does a backup and not a synchronization. Even if this situation is in the minority, we can create another low-cost safety net for this scenario. There's no reason to assume even a 1% risk if you don't need to.

CONCLUSION

According to Mozy by Carbonite Online Backup, 140,000 hard drives crash in the United States each week. So the question really comes down to this, "How much is your data worth?" Just as it is a good rule of thumb not to walk a tightrope without a safety net, it is necessary to be protected in the often unpredictable world of the Internet. Having a combination of both offsite and onsite storage solutions not only offers peace of mind, but could be the answer to avoiding regret, and ultimately, saving your own work and, quite possibly, your business.

About Akiva

Akiva Goldstein is the CEO and founder of OnsiteIn60, an outsourced support company that is dedicated to providing IT consulting and services for SMBs throughout the East Coast. His knowledge of the industry comes from over 25 years of experience in the IT field, as well as a lifetime of entrepreneurship as a fourth-generation business owner. When he was just 14, he began fixing window screens for local apartment buildings, all on his own. He expanded his business each spring, and after four summers, young Akiva had found his unique strengths and affirmed his destiny. He knew he had been bitten by the self-employment bug.

In college, he started a small T-shirt design company and fell in love with business software such as Microsoft Excel and Access. As he experimented with different business ideas, he continued to embrace emerging technology that gave him the power to manage day-to-day operations more efficiently. He was formally introduced to the IT support field when he was given a job by his computer professor to manage the college's computer lab, albeit with zero experience! In 1997, Akiva earned his Microsoft and Cisco certifications and began working for small consulting firms. In addition to learning about networking and tech support, he began to recognize common issues and complaints from his employers and their clientele. Too often, IT companies lost clients and struggled financially due to poor communication methods and slow response times.

In 2001, Akiva started marketing his IT services on the side. The pitch was simple. For the first time ever, Akiva guaranteed a 60-minute response time, which he knew no established competitor could match. Additionally, he offered a free 2-week trial period. As a result, Akiva closed his first corporate deal. He called his new business OnsiteIn60 to describe his commitment to providing in-person support with unprecedented response times. Furthermore, his commitment to security and fair pricing has rewarded him with loyal customers and dedicated staff.

Today, nearly two decades later, OnsiteIn60 continues to support companies with all of their IT management needs. By listening to clients and being willing to evolve, Akiva Goldstein has greatly expanded OnsiteIn60's service offerings beyond core network maintenance and desktop support. Over the years, OnsiteIn60 has added services such as office technology relocation, new server room design and setup, complete network cabling installations, cloud backup and disaster recovery, and scalable database solutions.

One of Akiva's greatest skills as a businessman and CTO is the ability to bridge a client's business needs with their IT and cybersecurity requirements. Most recently, Akiva launched OnsiteIn60's "Ask a CTO" feature on the company's website. The page can be used by clients and non-clients alike. "Ask a CTO" is a free service designed to answer user-submitted questions, which range from basic tech support topics to higher-level IT strategy.

You can connect with Akiva at:
- www.OnsiteIn60.com/ask-a-cto/
- 212-763-6582
- agoldstein@onsitein60.com

CHAPTER 13

CYBERSECURITY ISN'T JUST AN IT RISK (OR PROBLEM) IT'S A MAJOR BUSINESS RISK

BY IAIN ENTICOTT

Ask any business owner how they build their business, and most will tell you they establish relationships with their clients. Those relationships are carefully constructed on trust. The customer entrusts the business to deliver products or services that the customer needs with as few headaches as possible. The customer entrusts the business with information—often extremely sensitive information—and expects the business to be good stewards of that information.

Abuse that trust and the business relationship, so carefully constructed, crumbles like a house of cards. Any business that maintains records containing personal information about their clients sits precariously on a house of cards. That house stands one cybersecurity breach away from utter decimation.

Each record containing personal information is a liability for the business storing that information and a meal ticket for the cybercriminal, hoping to gain access to it. Although the sensitive information held varies by industry—my company works heavily with accounting firms—the inherent risks are similar in all industries. If a business operates anywhere in the digital realm, it has something to protect from a cyberattack.

There are several misconceptions around cybersecurity, which I will

119

discuss below, but before that, let me introduce you to what I refer to as the "The Security Dilemma." I discuss this with clients, and this is becoming more relevant as businesses further embrace the cloud, and the "edges" of the traditional corporate network continue to shift.

At the top of the Security Dilemma triangle is secure; the second side is usable and the third is cheap. You can only have two of the three sides, as illustrated below.

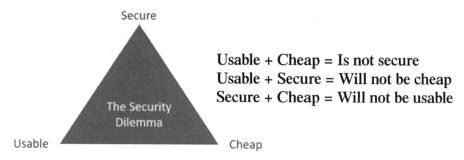

Usable + Cheap = Is not secure
Usable + Secure = Will not be cheap
Secure + Cheap = Will not be usable

As the Security Dilemma triangle shows, you need to invest in security ("Usable & Cheap" is not Secure). The security landscape is one that is continuously evolving, hence the need for continual investment. The question now becomes: where do you invest in getting the highest return (the best security you can afford), and how do you determine your return on this investment?

THE FIRST MISCONCEPTION – CYBERSECURITY IS AN <u>IT</u> ISSUE

There's a misconception among business owners that cybersecurity is strictly an IT issue, and risk can be eliminated by purchasing a piece of technology. So, what is the difference between Information Technology (IT) and Cybersecurity?

1. Information Technology (IT) focuses on hardware, software, and networks. This includes things such as routers, firewalls, networks, anti-virus, windows patching, and backups.

2. Cybersecurity focuses on people, processes, and policies. This includes staff awareness (i.e., human behavior), legal risks, regulatory compliance, business continuity, incident management, and operational frameworks and policies.

Put simply, IT has a "fix-it mentality," while cybersecurity has a "secure and monitor" mentality.

Certainly, the addition of up-to-date technology aids cybersecurity protection. Information technology focusing on hardware and networks is not all there is to cybersecurity. Ninety percent of cybersecurity breaches are caused by human error, not IT systems. Human behaviors, risks, compliance, operational framework, and policies are all factors, as well.

THE SECOND MISCONCEPTION – WE NEED TO PROTECT EVERYTHING

The next misconception is that we need to protect everything. Since trying to 'protect everything protects nothing,' companies need to set and follow priorities regarding what data assets to protect, what threats to defend against, and where to spend their money on cybersecurity countermeasures.

When we are working with accounting firms, it is especially important to determine where their data is, who has access to the data and who can access the data from where. It is about identifying the "digital crown jewels" of the firm, which is more important than ever when operating in the "Cloud."

But protecting every bit of data equally isn't a viable strategy, as no business has unlimited funds for security measures. You need to start by identifying what you are trying to protect. This can include, for example:

- **Your website**
  Some hackers live for the pure joy of stopping a business from doing business. How long, do you think, your company can survive without the revenue from its e-commerce site or the leads from its well-written landing pages?
- **Documents on your server or in the cloud**
  What is there and to whom is it valuable?
- **Accounting applications**
  It's fair to assume that your business wouldn't be able to revert to ledgers and calculators in the event a cyber attack disrupted access to your accounting applications.

- **HR Applications**
  If it is critical to managing your employees, it is critical to your business.

Your business must maintain an up-to-date data asset registry. This is a list of every application, the data it stores, where it is, and who has access to it. Identify and establish which data assets are linked together and how they interact. Ask questions specific to your business, such as:

- Where can I access each file from?
- Can I access any corporate networks from the guest Wi-Fi?
- What are my most valuable data assets, who can access them, and from where can they be accessed?
- If an attacker compromises the CEO's user account, what else can they access?
- Do all your Cloud Applications used in your business have and enforce Multi-Factor Authentication?
- What are the security statements and protocols from your Cloud Providers?

It is incredibly common for businesses to think they have certain access controls in place, but there is a misconfiguration or a complete lack of security protocol in place. This could be a simple oversite, or even worse, it was requested because the security that was in place was too hard for the user (remember our Security Dilemma triangle). Make sure you manually test every one of the answers to the questions above. *Assuming that everything is in order can prove to be a costly mistake.*

THE THIRD MISCONCEPTION – INDUSTRY STANDARDS ARE ALL YOU NEED

Another misconception I often hear from business owners is that they are compliant with an industry standard (i.e., NIST Cybersecurity Framework), so this means they are secure. Being compliant with an industry-specific set of control standards (e.g., PCI DSS for payment card processors) is not equivalent to having a robust and effective information security posture.

You need to look no further than the massive credit card data exfiltration at Target a few years ago. Target was certified as being PCI-compliant at the time their breach occurred.

Cybersecurity standards are about compliance, but hackers are cunning and devious, always looking for ways to penetrate business defenses or lack thereof. The key here is that compliance does not equal security, nor are they the same thing.

Compliance is a regulatory, one-size-fits-all, point-in-time snapshot that demonstrates you meet the minimum, security-related requirements of specific regulatory standards like PCI or NIST. Security is the whole unique system of policies, processes, and technical controls that define how your organization stores, processes, consumes and distributes data.

A key difference between compliance and security is that compliance requirements change slowly and predictably. The security and threat landscape is in a *perpetual* state of change, which often means compliance is a few steps behind current threats. Just checking those compliance boxes won't cover all your security needs and can leave your data and systems without adequate protection.

THE FOURTH MISCONCEPTION
– UNDERESTIMATE FUTURE RISK

Everyone has their own definition of risk. Some people will go sky diving, while others will consider a day at the beach as risky. It is difficult for people to assess its true level. People tend to underestimate long-term risks and overestimate short-term risks.

Have you ever wondered why people still smoke? Or why climate change is so hard for some people to accept? It is because we tend to underestimate long-term risks. We focus on the news of today, tending to be concerned with what is happening now, and see only what is directly in front of us.

Take, for example, the BYOD movement in workplaces. Employers think it a win for them to have their employees bring their own device (BYOD) to the office. After all, by allowing or encouraging the employee to provide their own laptop or cell phone, the employer avoids the expense of providing those items, and the employee may be more likely to work from home, putting in more hours for the company. Employees probably do not have the same level of security on their personal devices that a company device would have, thereby making it easier for a hacker to compromise the corporate system while the personal device is connected to the network. Saving $1000 on a laptop in the short run can lead to cybersecurity issues in the long run, resulting in downtime, loss of revenue, and potential fines.

Many businesses forgo employee cybersecurity training to avoid the expense. They rationalize it by saying, "My staff would know not to click that link." However, that same staff member will do exactly that if they think the email is from their boss. That tendency goes back to the employee's understanding of risk; they see the risk potential as somewhere down the road, not an immediate threat.

On the flip side of the coin, employees do see a risk in questioning their bosses. The risk of disappointing the boss is immediate, and the retribution swift. The employee who just opened a hacker's email will defend his action by saying, "It had my boss's email address. It had my boss's name on it. I believed it was my boss instructing me to do something, and it's not my job to question it."

Complicating the issue, employers tend to trust their employees. "My employee would never do that," they say. However, one company had to pay ransom to a hacker not once, but twice, because of the negligent actions of the same employee.

This is not about personal trust (which society depends on), but about digital trust. Digital trust refers to the connections between people, data, and networks. How are you doing this in your business?

<u>So, trust your employees, but never underestimate the risks.</u>

THE FIFTH MISCONCEPTION – NOT PLANNING FOR DISASTER

Companies map out the trajectory of the business in six months, one-year, and five-year increments. They plan for all the positives but fail to plan for failures. When cybersecurity threats manifest, they have no business continuity plan in place. Once that employee opens an email containing a ransomware payload, there is no control-alt-delete to stop the process. The only way out for your business is through it.

The clock is ticking. A business continuity plan is a comprehensive guide to protecting your business from known cybersecurity threats, as well as a recovery plan for the aftermath of the unthinkable. Just like our Fourth Misconception (Underestimate Future Risk), most businesses underestimate the amount of time a recovery can take. What's the plan if you cannot recover?

SUMMARY

Cybersecurity, at the end of the day, is about balancing people, processes, and technology, like the house of cards. With a finite set of resources—a 52 card deck—you can choose to construct a tall house or a wider, more stable one. You may remove a card to reposition it, as long as you are aware of the weakness its removal creates in the structure. And you must have a plan for when the unexpected breeze wreaks havoc, and you are forced to rebuild.

About Iain

Iain Enticott is the founder and director of Technology For Accountants. Technology For Accountants is Australia's only IT provider uniquely dedicated to serving the needs of accountants with technology solutions, support services, and security guidance.

Iain's background within the IT and Accounting industries spans more than 20 years, including roles with Ceedata and Solution 6 as a Systems Engineer, before identifying a need for specialized IT support to the accounting profession.

He has worked with firms of all sizes and different practice management software over this time, aligning their technology with their business goals. Iain firmly believes that while "technology may run your firm, you're not in the business of running technology."

Iain is a regular presenter over the years at Accountants' Technology Showcase Australia (now called Accountech.Live) as well as a "recommended speaker" for CPA Australia. Iain is a professional expert contributor to various publications such as Accounting Technician Magazine, Accountancy Insurance Newsletter, and various other online websites on Cybersecurity, Cloud Computing, and Technology Planning.

You can connect with Iain at:
- W: www.technologyforaccountants.com.au
- P: 1300 765 014
- E: ask@technologyforaccountants.com.au

CHAPTER 14

DANGERS LURKING ON THE DARK WEB AND HOW TO AVOID THEM

BY ERIC STEFANIK

Are you familiar with the Dark Web? How much do you know about it?

When I ask these questions, most have heard of the Dark Web, but few can define what it is with any accuracy.

The Dark Web is the black market of the internet, a clearinghouse of ill-gotten information. It is a hidden universe contained within the "deep web". This universe is a sublayer of the internet that is hidden from conventional search engines like Google, Bing, Yahoo. These conventional search engines can only search about .04% of the Dark Web. It is estimated to be 550 times larger than the regular web and is growing. The Dark Web is the cybercriminal's playground because it can operate anonymously and hidden to authorities. This is where email addresses, login credentials, compromised personal information, and more are harvested from people and businesses large and small and sold to the highest bidder. The Dark Web is accessed through Tor browsers that provide anonymity to cybercriminals, and payments are typically made in bitcoin, a web-only cryptocurrency that operates independently of a central bank—and the value fluctuates.

No matter what metrics you analyze, 2019 was a devastating time for data security. In 2019, the number of cyberattacks increased by 219%

over the previous years. In the 2019 Cost of Data Breach Study, the cost of data breach reached $3.92 million—an all-time high—and 12% increase in just five years. According to Verizon's 2019 Data Breach Investigations Report, 32% of all data breaches began with phishing attacks. An astonishing 76% of businesses reported being a victim of these phishing attacks.

In July, a former Amazon Web Services software engineer hacked into Capital One's servers, ultimately compromising the personal information of 100 million people. The cybercriminal bragged about her activity online and left a trail of clues, indicating that she wanted to be identified. The episode was embarrassing and expensive for Capital One, costing the company as much as $150 million – *"What's in your wallet?"* All the compromised data from these attacks will end up on the Dark Web. Generally, when I ask clients about the Dark Web, they begin laundry-listing all the safeguards they have in place:

- "My company has this antivirus software."
- "Our IT department keeps up with all that for us."
- "Our employees can't access the dangerous websites."
- … or the very common, "We are too small to be a target for that."

Wonderful. Do you know how much of your information is already on the Dark Web?

Eight out of ten times that I run a free report for a client's domain name, it turns out the CEO's or one of the high-level executive's information is on that report. Although it's good to know the status of your company's information on the Dark Web, prophylactic measures such as changing passwords won't remove credentials or personal information once it has been posted to the Dark Web. Once information is on the Dark Web, that means it is up for sale. That information will get copied and distributed through trading or re-selling to numerous cybercriminals who are all in the same business—to make money. It is generally implausible to remove data that has been disseminated within the Dark Web. If your personal identifiable information (PII) is found out there, we highly recommend investing in identity and credit monitoring services ASAP. In short, there is no such thing as removing information from the Dark Web.

Information harvested during a cyberattack will be used for years after the initial theft. On the dark web, the chop shop of stolen credentials, the whole is not greater than the sum of its parts. The parts can be sold to multiple entities, including to the individual and/or the organization from which it was stolen.

The minute a cybercriminal posts information to the Dark Web, he's working it from multiple fronts. First, he attempts to negotiate a payment from the very company from which he stole the data. Secondly, failing the first attempt, or even simultaneously, he'll try to unload that list to another criminal through the Dark Web. Sometimes cybercriminals try to extort money from the person whose email they hacked. The email usually says something to the effect of, "I caught you on your webcam, and I know what you were doing. Here's your username and password. I've got this information. You have exactly three days to pay X amount in bitcoin to this address. If you don't do this, I am going to post these photos to your Facebook, contacts, and all over your social media." That criminal is working three different angles simultaneously, trying to make money.

A cybercriminal might market a list for sale on the Dark Web for a dollar a name. They might offer to sell the whole list for a set amount. They might encrypt part of the list and charge an additional fee for the encryption key, of course. Another criminal will buy the list for their own uses. That purchaser might sell the information individually. The Dark Web is where collateral from cybersecurity breaches—identity theft information and stolen credit card information—end up being sold to the highest bidder among the network of cybercriminals.

Sometimes, clients do not understand why they should be concerned about their personal information on the Dark Web. They comprehend why a social security number floating around is a bad thing, but why should they worry about their medical records, aside from the personal numbers like driver's license or social security number associated with it? Well, the short answer to that question is that a cybercriminal's livelihood is based on finding ways to use acquired information nefariously.

If that cybercriminal has all the procedure codes from a compromised medical record, they know what the person's diagnosis was and what procedures were done. They will first sell any information acquired like social security numbers. What is worse is, what if the patient has an illness about which they don't want their coworkers or boss to know? The cybercriminal might just ransom that information back to the person to keep it from getting out. Have you received anonymous calls on your cell phone? Most likely scam calls? Where do you think your phone number got compromised? The phone company did not sell your number to criminals, there are laws that protect you from that happening. It most likely came from a Dark Web compromise of PII – personal identifiable information.

When we monitor the Dark Web and discover a new breach or compromise of our client's domain, the date showing on this report is most likely not when the actual compromise took place. Information we most often see is a username or email address that was compromised. Typically, we see the password associated. Sometimes the Dark Web record discloses the origin of the data, but not always. Even though the information may not be disclosed on the Dark Web, you can bet the cybercriminal has all the information. The cybercriminal will post the information on the Dark Web and try to profit from it.

You may ask, how did they get my information? They get it from compromising sites that you frequently visit, not necessarily from hacking you directly. Most everyone has created an account online for some website. You keep information in that account, like your name, address, phone number, log on ID, account password, etc., you get the idea. So, if you shop online and you save your credit card on a site for the ease of checking out in the future, they have it, if you have your cell phone number, they have it, driver's license, they have it. But if you never save your credit card, they don't have that... only the data that is saved is compromised. Again, cybercriminals are in a profit-making business. They will find any and every way to sell your information in pieces, sell it three times, or perhaps ten times, as the more they can splice it up and sell it, the more money they can make per compromised account.

Cybercriminals are detectives. The original target might not have been a business, but once they get access to a personal Gmail or Yahoo account, it might direct them to a business account. If they can hack one business email address, they gain access to the global address book that leads to email addresses for other employees. They get a few credentials, pop into the company domain, and start digging for more information. It might lead them to accounting, then to the CFO's email, then to an email from the CEO. Both of those executives have plenty of personal information in their signature lines of their emails. Worse, the criminal can copy the email signature and create as many phishing emails as he wants to for obtaining access to more information.

A cybercriminal is hoping to find victims who use the same password or different variants of their password. For example, let's take a victim's favorite sports team like the Philadelphia Eagles football team. A victim might use a password on Site #1 of Eagles#1. That seems somewhat secure. Then on Site #2, they use a variant like 3agles#1, or Eagl3s#1 or 3agl3s#1, or even worse where the victim is using the same one password variant for many sites. You get the picture. Cybercriminals look for a pattern. If they see the same password used over several sites, then chances are they can give it a crack at any site—Facebook, Twitter, LinkedIn, Indeed, Monster—by entering the email address and trying the different variants of Eagles#1 hoping that one will work. Once they log on, they change your password and then sell the information to another cybercriminal who wants to use this information. Now your compromised credentials just became more valuable.

It is often said to keep your friends close and your enemies closer. Dark Web monitoring combines human intelligence with the search capabilities of sophisticated software and applications. It identifies what is on the Dark Web, based on domains and the information sought. Dark Web monitoring works tirelessly 24/7 x 365 days a year, listening in hidden chat rooms, watching private websites, investigating peer-to-peer networks, and internet relay chat channels. Having Dark Web monitoring in place allows you to act—changing emails and plugging network holes—before significant damage can take place. We monitor over 500 distinct internet relay chatroom (IRC) channels, 600,000 private websites, 600 twitter feeds, and execute 10,000 refined queries daily. We monitor the Dark Web and the criminal hacker underground for exposure of our clients' credentials to malicious individuals.

A quick glance at a dark web monitoring report for the past month reads like a who's who of failure to protect business data. One of our manufacturing companies with 1500 employees had 734 compromises in 30 days. A small business with 50 employees had 106 compromises in that same 30-day period. One construction company has 60 employees and had 183 compromises. That's three compromises per employee! How many do you think your organization has? Would you like to find out?

Please, do not try monitoring the Dark Web on your own. It's high risk to the average user, like walking through a minefield. Government agencies continually monitoring the Dark Web don't know if you're in there looking for your stolen data or trying to buy a truckload of military weapons. Too many people think if they have a bit of a tech background that they can watch a YouTube video and figure out how to navigate the Dark Web. That is like assuming if you have taken basic first aid, you can watch a video and figure out how to perform open-heart surgery. The last thing you need is the government knocking on your door for suspicious activity on the Dark Web where you were just looking. It is best to call in the properly trained, certified and experienced professional with the right tools for the job.

In addition to Dark Web monitoring, businesses, and individuals, you need to recognize that the enemy most often comes from within. Businesses need protection from their employees' bad habits, some of which are sanctioned by the business itself. Take frequent business travelers, for example. The boss thinks it's great when the employee is logged on and working in those minutes they spend waiting for the flight to board. The employee logs onto the airport's public Wi-Fi, ignoring the warning that says their credentials may be visible to anyone. Little do they know that there is a hacker sitting in that busy airport with special software used for "sniffing" to harvest credentials from nearby travelers' laptops. The same risk applies to public Wi-Fi at your local coffee house, restaurant, or sporting event. Worse, using your own hotspot to share internet access with a business colleague or family member is a massive security breach. Cybercriminals love when they see this. They will compromise your connection, be hidden and surf your systems, yes, and all the systems including gaming machines, to gather information. Have you played a game console? They all have a username and a password tied back to an email address.

The individual is the first line of defense to most of these attacks. Small fixes yield significant results. Using a password vault or generator application allows you to create long, mixed-up, more secure, and different passwords for each site as well as "remember" the password for you. This relieves the use of the same password multiple times. Additionally, turning on two-factor and multi-factor authentication provides additional safety by requiring verification from either an email address or a code that is texted to a cellphone. There are applications you can set up to generate a code that will cycle a new code every 30 seconds to use for access to an account. Adding these tactics along with employee education will give a business the confidence that less of its information will end up a statistic on a Dark Web compromise report, at least until the cybercriminals find another way.

About Eric

Eric Stefanik is a U.S. Navy Veteran. He enlisted in the U.S. Navy right out of high school. He served on the USS Nimitz (CVN-68) in the Persian Gulf during The Gulf War of 1990 – 1991. His experiences as Tower Supervisor working directly for the Air Boss incorporated the use of computers, technology, and confidential information. After 1991, he completed a minor in Physical Fitness and a major in Business Management. Then in 1993, he started a Personal Training business focused on helping others achieve healthy and fit lifestyles. It is in Eric's nature to serve, help, and protect others.

In 1996, he started learning mainframe server's hardware to the fullest. He provided Fortune 1000 companies with the HP 9000, HP 3000, and Sun Microsystems Unix mainframe servers and peripherals. Servicing the enterprise-level clients 100% remotely and working with large enterprise budgets, Eric saved them thousands of dollars on their IT budgets. At the time, most of Eric's clients varied from hospitals and healthcare providers to manufacturers and retail stores.

Helping many organizations through the turn of the century 2000 date scare and experiencing the end of the dot-com era, Eric noticed Windows servers increasingly replacing mainframe servers and wisely formed Elliptic Systems Corporation to help meet that need. Guided by his deep passion for helping and serving others, he built his company with a strong emphasis on education of IT trends. Eric tired of watching small businesses suffer from lack of funds, expertise, and knowledge of the IT Industry while larger organizations prevailed. Between 2005 and 2008, he built a Managed Services department solely focused on empowering small businesses with technologies on point and on budget. By 2010, Eric was proactively providing most of his clients with protection from data loss and disaster. His certified technical staff readily provides remote resolution of issues over the phone quickly, efficiently, and securely. These services have streamlined IT processes for many small to medium organizations who use them.

Quarter 1 of 2019 saw the most significant increase of ransoms by cybercriminals, a devastating blow to data security. Eric instinctively implemented a new Cybersecurity service, capitalizing on his knowledge of the Dark Web, the cybercriminals' playground. His monitoring and alerts of the Dark Web compromises allow him to educate clients that they are never too small to be a target of a cyber-attack. Eric and his team educate and serve the Everett to Seattle business community. They consistently track industry trends and has adjusted Elliptic Systems Corporation's managed services focus and solutions to becoming the best Managed Security Service Provider (MSSP). He has done this by keeping the best solutions, protections and knowledge at the fingertips of small and medium-sized businesses. These businesses range from, but are not limited to, Healthcare specialty providers, Legal, non-profits, general contractors, architecture firms and finance industries.

You can connect with Eric at:
- Eric@EllipticSystems.com
- (425) 441-9500
- www.ESCOffer.com

CHAPTER 15

KEEPING YOUR IDENTITY SAFE ONLINE

BY JEAN-MARC PAMPELLONNE

We all know identity theft happens. We've seen the news; we just assume it will happen to someone else. The statistics are sobering. According to ITRC (the Identity Theft Resource Center) in 2016, in the United States, a whopping 791 million identities were stolen. In 2015, 4 million accounts were taken over, when thieves gained access to accounts and changed the passwords so that the account owners can no longer access them, leading to losses of over $2 billion. In the United States, identity theft represents 13 percent of criminal complaints recorded by the Consumer Sentinel Network. In the United Kingdom, CIFAS (the Credit Industry Fraud Avoidance Scheme) reports that almost 500 identities are stolen every day in the UK alone.

Despite awareness of the statistics, our daily lives often include cybersecurity risks that we don't realize. People who engage on social media have a 46 percent greater risk for identity theft than people who don't use social media. CIFAS found that men are statistically more at risk than women, 62 percent of men versus 38 percent of women. Those age 55 and older who were traditionally more at risk for phone and email scams are now also experiencing a growing rate of identity theft, according to a 2017 report from the Australian Payment Network. Even children's identities are at risk, with 3 million children's identities stolen in the last year. In the United States, half of all Americans think that identity thieves will not be interested in them because they have poor credit. More than half of all small businesses do not invest anything in cybersecurity, and a third do not take any active precautions at all against cybertheft.

Our demand for instant access, too, puts our identities at risk. Thousands of public unsecured Wi-Fi hotspots are available all over the world. You'll find them in airports, shopping malls, restaurants, the subway (or The Tube - as we call it in London). These hotspots allow you to get connected without a password. It's so convenient, right? Here's a way to get online without having to worry about tapping into our mobile data tariff. My kids are always looking for places to get online, and public Wi-Fi is a great way to eliminate the worry of extra data charges from your mobile provider.

Be cautious of public Wi-Fi. Throughout any business traveler's life, there is going to come a time when an unsecured, free, public Wi-Fi hotspot is the only connection available, and the work simply must get done right away. Understanding public Wi-Fi risks will ensure your important business data does not become just another hacking statistic. Wherever you can, use secure Wi-Fi and look for WPA2/AES encryption.

Keep Wi-Fi off when you do not need it. Even if you have not actively connected to a network, the Wi-Fi hardware in your computer is still transmitting data between any network within range. There are security measures in place to prevent this minor communication from compromising you, but not all wireless routers are the same, and hackers can be a pretty smart bunch. If you are just using your computer to work on a Word or Excel document, keep your Wi-Fi off. As a bonus, you will also experience a much longer battery life.

The problem with unencrypted, open hotspots is that they're also wide open to hackers. No one polices these hotspots, which leaves the user open to attack.

Man-in-the-middle attacks occur when hackers can intercept every piece of information, including usernames, passwords, credit card info, or the time of your next meeting.

Malware attacks involve attackers using cleverly engineered malware to activate a microphone, webcam, or access files and photos. Malware is a tiny program that lives on your computer, until discovered, with the potential to report back to the hacker with stolen data. You probably thought your device was safe.

Hackers also create bogus hotspots that appear to be a genuine, public Wi-Fi hotspot, as in the local coffee shop, but is it? These networks can be installed by attackers to trick you into thinking they're genuine. Once connected, you'll be vulnerable to their attacks.

Phishing and Scams threaten both businesses and individuals. Companies need to protect their business records and the personal data included in those records that can lead to identity theft for their clients.

In these scams, the criminal contacts you, posing as a genuine supplier and asks you to change the bank details typically used to pay them. It's not hard for criminals to investigate invoice details, even down to payment dates, to make their approach look more convincing. The message will often have a sense of urgency and ask you to act immediately.

The fraudulent letters and emails they send are well-written, so the fraud is difficult to spot if a business doesn't have secure operating processes and controls. Email addresses are easy to spoof. If a PC is infected with malware, criminals can access genuine email addresses and take over existing email conversations. Requests made in writing often come on paper with a company's letterhead to make them look convincing. In what ways can you help circumvent such attacks?

When your company gets bank account details by email or a letter about making a payment, paying an invoice, or as part of a notice telling you about a change of bank details, always verbally confirm changes by calling a known contact at the company to confirm the request is genuine, using details you have on file and not the ones in the message. If you receive a personal email from a company with which you regularly do business, especially if you have not initiated anything new, contact them to verify that what you are being asked to do is legitimate.

Businesses should build a process to check new bank details on invoices. Have a clear procedure for making payments in your business and make sure that all staff knows how these scams occur, particularly those responsible for making payments. An individual that feels pressured or anxious should take their time and ask for assistance.

Criminals can access or alter emails to make them look genuine—hacking real email addresses is increasing. Do not use the contact details in an email. Instead, check the supplier's official website or documents you know are real. Keep essential security software up to date to help protect your company's devices from viruses and hackers.

If you mistakenly click on a phishing link, you could be taken to a spoofed webpage that looks like the homepage of a bank or financial institution. But when you enter in your account information, you'll be sending it to the scammers behind the phishing attempt, not any bank, credit union, or credit card company. Before clicking on suspicious links, hover your cursor over the link to view the destination URL. If it doesn't match the financial website you use, don't click.

Given the risks out there in the ether, how can a person protect himself or a business protect its records, thereby helping to protect its clients from identity theft? It begins with taking responsibility and ends with monitoring in case something does go awry.

Take an active role. Fortunately, there are plenty of ways to protect your identity online. Know what to look for when you receive emails. Before you open an email, look at the sender of the email. If it is from John Smith, you want to make sure that the email is John Smith's genuine email address, and you're not just looking at his name and surname. For your business, train employees to be more discriminating when opening emails, so they don't inadvertently open a suspect email and launch an attack.

Use a VPN. A virtual private network (VPN) connection is a must when connecting to your business through an unsecured connection, like a Wi-Fi hotspot. Even if a hacker manages to position himself in the middle of your connection, the data here will be strongly encrypted. Since most hackers are after an easy target, they will likely discard stolen information rather than put it through a lengthy decryption process. Surprisingly, although using a virtual private network is a proven way of protecting online activities and defending against identity theft, 75% of people do not use VPN.

Use SSL connections. You aren't likely to have a VPN available for general internet browsing, but you can still add a layer of encryption to your communication. Enable the "Always Use HTTPS/SSL" option on websites that you visit frequently, or that require you to enter credentials. Remember that hackers understand how people reuse passwords, so your username and password for some random forum may be the same as it is for your bank or corporate network, and sending these credentials in an unencrypted manner could open the door to a smart hacker. Most websites that require an account or credentials have the "HTTPS" or 'Secure' option somewhere in their settings.

Websites that are not secured by SSL can have malware installed on them by a cybercriminal or fraudster. This means that they can gain access to the communications between the user and the website. Hackers can then obtain sensitive data on website users. SSL ensures that users cannot do this by preventing intruders from tampering between a website and its users.

Turn off sharing. When connecting to the internet at a public place, you're unlikely to want to share anything. You can turn off sharing from the system preferences or control panel, depending on your OS, or let Windows turn it off for you by choosing the "Public" option the first time you connect to a new, unsecured network.

Stay protected. Even individuals who take all the possible public Wi-Fi security precautions are going to run across issues from time to time. It's just a fact of life in this interconnected age. That's why it's imperative to keep a robust Internet security solution installed and running on your machine. These solutions can continuously run a malware scan on your files and will always scan new files as they are downloaded. The top consumer security software will also offer business protection solutions, so you can protect yourself while you're out and about, and your servers back at the office, all at the same time.

Install security updates. If you're on a Windows machine, make sure it's fully up-to-date in terms of all the security patches that have been released. Make sure that anti-virus and anti-malware software is installed and up-to-date as well. Likewise, with any of your devices, make sure you are running the latest version of the software, and your apps are current.

Privacy Recommendations. Limit info you share on social media.

Criminals can browse through this data to see where you went to school, your mother's maiden name, your best friend, where you work, and when you go on vacation. Better still, make your social media accounts private, so few people have the option of trolling your account for information.

Create strong passwords. Consider using a password manager such as Dashlane, which works across all your devices. It will remember a different password for every site. This prevents the use of insecure passwords or, worse, using the same password on multiple websites: the same one for Amazon Prime, Netflix, banking, or anything else to which they sign up. All it takes is for one of those organizations to be breached. If the cybercriminal acquires your username and password to that one organization—you ordered pizza, and you use the same username and password you do for everything else—they now have access to your username and password for everything. The cybercriminal will try those credentials against everything and, ultimately, they could potentially access something more important than your pizza order.

Turn on two-factor authentication. It might have an awkward name, but two-factor authentication (or 2FA, or MFA for multi-factor authentication) is a way of adding an extra layer of security to your accounts. When you log in, you get a one-time passcode sent to your mobile phone, or even better, to an authenticator app such as Google or Microsoft Authenticator.

Even if an account has been hacked, two-factor authentication will keep the hacker from accessing the account because the hacker won't be able to access the authentication code. You may also receive a notification of a login attempt. If someone tried to log into your email, you'd be notified on your mobile device, where you have the option to approve or deny the logon attempt.

Go password-less. Two-factor authentication plays a big part in this. The same technology can allow you or your business to get away from passwords altogether. When an employee puts in his username, it recognizes that username and links back to the app on that employee's phone. They approve the sign-in directly, so it doesn't need to ask a password. Not asking for a password is beneficial because even if there were a man-in-the-middle attack with a packet sniffer on that device, all the hacker would see is a username, not a password.

142

Switch search engines. Most search engines keep tabs on what you're looking for so they can target ads to your tastes. If you don't like the idea of your search history being used to sell you things, DuckDuckGo is the search engine for you. The site doesn't track any of your personal data, so you can search without anyone watching over your shoulder.

Use Breach Monitors

Breach monitors give a person a heads-up that their information has been compromised in some way. Sometimes that early alert is enough to allow a person to change their passwords and keep further details from getting into the wrong hands. When you sign up for breach monitoring, they monitor all the breaches that have been reported online. For example, when you sign up with a Firefox breach monitor, you put in your information, and it reports back, "I can see that your username has been breached at your cable company during a data breach in 2019." The same is true of Credit Karma. Credit Karma will flag anything that is suspicious in terms of your credit record, or anything in which your identity has been used if it doesn't look like it was genuinely you. Both of those services offer that information to you. Two of the most popular breach monitors that I recommend are https://monitor.firefox.com/about and https://www.creditkarma.com/id-monitoring/.

As if there wasn't enough risk to personally identifiable information daily, crises bring additional cybercriminals out of the woodwork. New scams arise every time a significant event occurs—natural disasters, pandemics, and even the census—criminals are on the move trying to get personal information and finances. Fake census takers knocking at the door hoping to con parents into releasing information about their children, for example, and for which the United States Government would never ask on a census form, such as for your social security number. Fraudulent telemarketers will call seeking credit card donations for relief efforts. Follow the steps to protect your identity online and off but be extra vigilant during times of crisis when new threats emerge. The first step to protecting your identity always begins with personal responsibility.

About Jean-Marc

Jean-Marc Pampellonne is the Managing Director of Atlantec, an MSP that helps his clients use Microsoft technologies to optimise business efficiency while improving their security posture.

Born and educated in the UK, Jean-Marc grew up in an era where communication via video phones, flying cars, and trips to Mars was a concept limited to science fiction. OK, so we're not there quite yet, but still, it was amazing to think of how else technology could enhance the lives of every human! Fast forward through the 80s and a Commodore 64, Amstrad PC and ZX Sinclair spectrum and Amiga 2000, Jean-Marc went on to graduate from the University of East London in 1996 with a BSc (Hons.) degree in Distributed Information Systems. He began his career supporting the IT needs of the Department of Health and the Department of Social Security until 2005 when he set up his company and became a freelance consultant.

Jean-Marc still lives in London with his wife and two children, and continues to work through his company Atlantec, expertly designing and delivering innovative solutions to his customers. Microsoft has also published a case study where he championed the rollout and adoption of new technologies at a local school to better engage students with anytime, anywhere learning. (https://www.atlantec.co.uk/s/4-St-John-Fisher-Case-Study.pdf)

He has contributed key technical insights to support the strategy and planning, and the resolution of challenges arising from poorly implemented IT systems for a number of globally-recognised clients (large and small), such as The Ministry of Justice, Visa, Bank of America, BNP Paribas and Oxfam International as well as the SMBs with fewer than ten staff.

Jean-Marc is passionate about equipping small businesses with the right tools, knowledge, and support they need to thrive in the digital world.

You can reach Jean-Marc here:
- www.atlantec.co.uk
- jmp@atlantec.co.uk
- https://www.linkedin.com/in/jpampellonne/
- https://twitter.com/AtlantecUK

SPECIALTIES...
Cyber Security, MSP, Business Consulting, Client Engagement, Contract Negotiation, Sales & Marketing, Budgets | Revenue, Organisational Change, Stakeholder Management, Technical Innovation, Microsoft Azure, Microsoft 365

CHAPTER 16

HIPAA COMPLIANCE

BY WES STRICKLING

In May 2019, Touchstone Medical Imaging, a Tennessee diagnostic medical imaging services company was ordered to pay the Office of Civil Rights, the enforcement division of Health and Human Services, $3 million and to adopt an action plan to settle a breach that exposed over 300,000 patients' protected health information in violation of HIPAA. (https://compliancy-group.com/hipaa-fines-directory-year/).

For practices like Touchstone, three million dollars in fines could wipe out executive bonuses and employee salaries for a year. It is nearly impossible to monetize the reputational damages. How many of those patients whose records were compromised were women who had received a mammogram because they felt a lump, an octogenarian getting a bone density scan, or a child having an X-ray after a soccer injury? Will they, or their families and friends, still trust their care to Touchstone? Or, will they instead take to social media to blast Touchstone's reputation for making them endure years of credit monitoring and fears of identity theft?

HIPAA is the 800-pound gorilla in the room, no one really wants to talk about it, and fewer still want to pay to bring their practice into compliance. I get it. However, for a healthcare provider, a violation could mean – at the least – embarrassment from negative publicity and a breach of trust with patients, but at worst, could include massive financial damage, as it has with Touchstone, as well as in the most egregious incidents, criminal prosecution.

FINANCIAL AND REPUTATION RISKS

If Touchstone's penalty seems steep, it is helpful to understand how that number was calculated. HIPAA violation penalties are broken into four tiers. First Tier violations apply when findings indicate the covered entity did not know and could not reasonably have known about the breach. First Tier fines range from $100-$50,000 per incident up to $1.5 million. Second Tier violations are applicable where the covered entity knew, or could have known, by exercising reasonable diligence, that a security breach was possible; however, they acted instead with willful neglect. Fines for the Second Tier range from $1,000 to $50,000 per incident up to $1.5 million. Third Tier violations apply when the covered entity acted with willful neglect, but corrected the problem within 30 days. Fines for a Third Tier violation can be $10,000 to $50,000 per incident up to $1.5 million. A finding of willful neglect and failure to correct within a timely manner is needed for Fourth Tier violations, which can include criminal prosecution.

Reputation penalties are much less formulaic. Consumers impacted by a breach tend to not trust an organization after an incident. According to an October 2019 survey from Ping Identity (https://www.pingidentity.com/content/dam/ping-6-2-assets/Assets/Misc/en/3464-consumersurvey-execsummary.pdf), 81 percent of consumers would stop engaging with a brand online after a data breach, which – at a minimum – could mean your practice must handle more phone calls, due to fewer patients being willing to use online scheduling features. Worse still, as many as one-third of consumers indicated they might stop using a service altogether after a breach. Aggravating matters, the Office of Civil Rights publishes a "Wall of Shame," a permanent registry of entities that have experienced HIPPA breaches. There are no second chances.

In order to understand how Touchstone ended up paying $3 million in fines, let's explore the rules they should have been following.

HIPAA 101

Put simply, HIPAA (Health Insurance Portability and Accountability Act) was created in 1996 to ensure patients' health information was legally their own, and that they would always be able to access it, regardless of the circumstances of any individual medical or insurance provider (called Covered Entities by the legislation).

Per HIPAA, Covered Entities are really just the custodians of their patients' protected health information (PHI) in any format, electronic or otherwise. PHI is defined as any item (document, electronic record, image, etc.) that has both patient identifiable information together with their treatment(s) and/or diagnosis. In practice, a sign-in sheet showing that Ms. Smith has an appointment at noon is not PHI; however, if it showed Ms. Smith has a glaucoma checkup at noon, it would be considered PHI.

HIPAA is overseen by the Department of Health and Human Services, and enforcement is carried out by its Office of Civil Rights division for non-compliance. HIPAA regulations incorporate privacy, security, and breach notification rules and have evolved since the original 1996 legislation to keep pace with technological changes.

The HIPAA Security Rule, created in a 2005 amendment, provides specific protections for electronic Protected Health Information (ePHI), including ramping up enforcement and fines for violations. ePHI is an electronic form of PHI, including words, images, and voice files on any media. From an IT perspective, the HIPAA Security Rule is the standard by which to safeguard and protect ePHI, whether in use, at rest, or in transit.

The HIPAA Security Rule is used to protect health information and is divided into three categories:

1. **Administrative safeguards**
2. **Physical safeguards**
3. **Technical safeguards.**

   o Administrative safeguards are the procedures and processes that govern the way information is handled. They include information access management to keeps those without the right to view PHI from handling it. Security incident procedures cover breach management, security awareness and training to ensure employees handling PHI understand how to prevent data compromises.
   o Physical safeguards encompass things like facility access controls, workstation use, workstation security, and device and media controls.

o Technical safeguards include access controls such as unique user identification, emergency access procedures, automatic logoff, encryption, and decryption; audit controls; integrity; person or entity authentication; and transmission security.

The Breach Notification Rule establishes guidelines for handling a breach. In January 2013, the HIPAA Omnibus Final Rule changed data breach law so that proof of harm is no longer required. If a breach occurs, harm is now assumed, and the Breach Notification Rule is triggered.

In addition to the above requirements, HIPAA IT requirements cover facility access rules regarding the physical security of any technology used to store, access, or transport ePHI.

COVERED ENTITY AND BUSINESS ASSOCIATE RESPONSIBILITY

Covered entities include providers that bill electronically, such as doctors, hospitals, dentists, chiropractors, physical therapists, nursing homes, pharmacies, and labs. Covered entities also include payers like Medicare and insurance as well as records clearinghouses.

Business associates are not covered entities, but through their relationship with covered entities, come into contact with PHI and ePHI, and therefore, must safeguard it and follow all the same rules. Business associates include companies such as shredding companies, paper records storage, IT companies, copier vendors, EHR vendors, attorneys, accountants, and even collection agencies. Business associate agreements also fall under HIPPA's IT requirements and cover hosting companies, software developers, and SaaS providers. A 2013 amendment to the legislation now charges data centers, online backup companies and Cloud vendors with the task of protecting ePHI if they "maintain" data in any way, even if it is encrypted and they never look at it.

SECURITY RISK ASSESSMENT – SRA

To protect your practice from any variety of breach, you must know your risk. Covered entities are legally required to perform a Security

Risk Assessment (SRA). SRAs proactively uncover a practice's potential security risks. SRAs, similar to the ones we conduct for our healthcare clients, ultimately become the covered entity's blueprint for their compliance strategy and any necessary remediation. Keep in mind: once an issue has been identified and documented, it must be addressed. Ignoring it after identification opens up Fourth Tier penalties, including potential criminal prosecution. SRA methodologies and formats would encompass their own chapter. National Institute of Standards and Technology (NIST) provides guidance on this process (https://nvlpubs. nist.gov/nistpubs/Legacy/SP/nistspecialpublication800-30r1.pdf). There are also many reputable companies that provide this service. The bottom line is: however you approach it, it is legally required to have been completed and will serve as your guide to ensure compliance in your practice.

COMPLIANCE

Rather than viewing HIPAA compliance as an expensive burden, covered entities should view the process as a competitive advantage through which they can streamline and secure their practice. Compliance with the HIPAA Security Rule requires the implementation of security policies and procedures that can reduce risk from malware, including ransomware. This includes enacting a security management process that incorporates the SRA to discover threats and vulnerabilities to ePHI and implement security measures to mitigate or remediate those risks. Covered entities must implement procedures to protect against malicious software, train users to identify and report potentially malicious activity, and enact access controls to limit ePHI to only those with a legitimate need to it. These actions are examples of ways to prepare your practice to respond to security incidents, decrease the potential for security breaches, including ransomware attacks, as well as punitive damages after a breach.

From an IT standpoint, pursuant to HIPAA, your practice must document how many endpoints (i.e., laptops, desktop PCs, tablets, phones) access, interface or communicate with patients and their health-related information. All of these endpoints must have certain protections such as virus, malware, and spyware protection. They must also have their software automatically patched and updated. You must ensure that all devices are protected from spam, malicious and phishing emails, keep a log of all individuals in your organization who access ePHI, and ensure those machines are included in your comprehensive backup disaster and recovery protocol.

DANGERS! RANSOMWARE, INCIDENTS, AND BREACHES

Healthcare is a target-rich environment for cybercriminals because providers sometimes have limited technology resources and budgets, and may feel forced to cut corners with security. Therefore, they become a relatively soft target.

HIPAA defines a breach as the acquisition, use, access, or disclosure of ePHI/PHI in a manner not allowed by HIPAA Rules. Any impermissible use of PHI is presumed to be a breach unless the covered entity or business associate can prove otherwise. Data breach incidents include any potential loss or unauthorized release and may be reported by anyone. All such incidents should be investigated quickly. Lost devices are considered breaches unless they are recovered, or forensic proof indicates that no data was accessed.

Ransomware is growing exponentially in healthcare. Q4-2019 saw a **350%** increase in attacks from Q4-2018 (https://www.beckershospitalreview.com/cybersecurity/ransomware-attacks-on-healthcare-facilities-spike-350.html). *Ransomware is a computer virus designed to hold your computer hostage.* Imagine if someone came to your practice overnight and changed all of the locks. That's ransomware. According to updated guidance from the Department of Health and Human Services (https://www.hhs.gov/sites/default/files/RansomwareFactSheet.pdf), a ransomware attack is considered a HIPAA breach unless proven otherwise. Breaches are most often caused by ransomware and include loss of unencrypted devices containing ePHI, improper disposal of PHI and ePHI, PHI sent to the incorrect patient, theft of patient data to defraud payers, selling of patient data to personal injury attorneys, posting ePHI on a public website, and snooping around patient records.

BREACH RESPONSE AND NOTIFICATION REQUIREMENTS

As soon as a breach is discovered, the entity must activate its security incident and response reporting procedures. The National Institute of Standards and Technology provides an excellent resource for the creation of security incident procedures (https://nvlpubs.nist.gov/nistpubs/SpecialPublications/NIST.SP.800-61r2.pdf). Remediation begins with an initial analysis to determine the scope, the origin of the attack, whether the incident is finished, or the additional incidences have been propagated, and determine how the incident occurred. This is best accomplished by a professional technology forensics company.

The HIPAA Breach Notification requires covered entities and business associates to report breaches of PHI to impacted individuals and the Department of Health and Human Services. Data breaches of more than 500 records must be reported to the Office of Civil Rights within 60 days of discovery of the breach, and reported to OCR in an annual report. In California, you have only five days to report after discovery. You must notify patients directly or through media if direct is not possible. The burden of proof falls to the covered entity to demonstrate that all required notifications have been provided. This is an arduous, expensive, and embarrassing process that also has the added penalty of being under the continuing scrutiny of OCR going forward.

EXAMPLE OF AN EXEMPLARY RESPONSE

In July 2018, May Eye Care Center in Hanover, PA, was the victim of a ransomware attack during which sensitive patient information became encrypted, including electronic health record system data. The ransomware had been downloaded on a server that contained ePHI, including patients' names, dates of birth, addresses, diagnoses, insurance information, and even some social security numbers. They received a ransom demand but did not make any payment because they were able to restore all of the encrypted records from backups with no data loss.

A knowledgeable computer forensics company investigated, following HIPAA breach requirements, while an IT firm reviewed the security system, protocols, and improved security to prevent future attacks.

Finally, May Eye Care Center informed all patients that were impacted by the breach and reported the breach to HHS and OCR when all forensic activity had been completed.

As a provider, you might have told patients, "an ounce of prevention is worth a pound of cure." Take these three steps to ensure you never find your practice at risk of a HIPAA breach or violation:

1) **Have a thorough SRA performed.**
2) **Remediate any and all processes, procedures and security protocols found to be lacking.**
3) **Repeat this process annually.**

About Wes

Wes Strickling is the CEO of CodexIT, a Healthcare Technology Services Provider that is leading the way in virtual CIO and Technology Support services. Under his leadership, the company has become a leader in Healthcare Information Technology and Cybersecurity. He worked as IT Director for a regional retail chain before starting his business in 2004. Over the last 16 years, he has grown his company to provide services across North America. With employees in 8 states, he offers a unique model that delivers both onsite and virtual services with the best technology support and compliance solutions in the country.

Wes is active in the Central Ohio entrepreneurial community, serving as a mentor at the incubator Rev1 Ventures and as an investor in local startups. He also provides expertise for multiple non-profit initiatives focusing on expanding STEM education in Central Ohio. Serving as a judge and sponsor for the inaugural Philanthropitch (shark tank for non-profits) in Columbus, he is working to connect the traditional service organizations in Central Ohio with the Startup Community.

When not working or helping his community, Wes is an avid adventurer. His adventures include climbing Kilimanjaro, diving and sailing the Caribbean, riding his motorcycle throughout the country, and running. Wes trains year-round to pursue his passion for trail running and competes in Ultramarathons across the country. Wes lives in Columbus, Ohio, with his family.

You can connect with Wes at:
- www.codex-it.com
- 614-439-5232
- wes@codex-it.com

CHAPTER 17

SECURITY FOR MACS IN YOUR SMALL TO MID-SIZED BUSINESS

BY TIM NYBERG

People value Apple products because their platform provides seamless integration between hardware and software, and that integration allows for greatly enhanced security and performance. Government agencies, hospitals, airlines, and the motion picture industry all choose Macs for their quality, longevity, performance, and enhanced security. All that is true, but when it comes to cybersecurity, Mac users do not have a free pass, they are by no means off the hook.

A lot of Mac users say, "Well, I'm on a Mac, so we're not going to have any of these problems," and historically that has been somewhat true. For many years the Mac world enjoyed relative freedom from many of the security issues that have plagued the Windows world, and many of the businesses we've worked with let their guard down as a result. Mac or PC, your small business network is at risk, cybercrime is at an all-time high, and you need to create a culture of security in your business.

SOCIAL ENGINEERING

As a small business leveraging Apple technology, you need to be as concerned about security as any network of Windows-based systems. Many of the attacks your business will face may not be as simple as Malware or Adware, but could take the form of a sinister social engineering attack. Be sure you know who is coming and going at your office, keep your network gear secured, and be sure to check the ID of any service staff that comes to your office wanting to access anything connected to a cord. We have worked with several businesses that have been compromised, including a few that allowed access to their network gear to an "internet service provider's employee," only to get a knock on the door months later from the FBI who tracked down their IP address because their network was being used to launch various attacks and downloading illegal materials. These kinds of attacks do not show preference to the kinds of computers you are using, so companies using Apple Technology are as susceptible as any other to social engineering attacks.

Despite their safety from viruses, Macs are not impervious to all threats. The other risks to a Mac involve human error in one way or another: poor passwords, phishing attacks, or social engineering attacks. This is technically not a problem with the computer hardware or the type of computer as much as the person using it. Social engineering is big business.

What is social engineering? Figuring out who you are and then using that information against you to trick you into providing access to more information or to your computer itself with the purpose of gaining access to credit card information, passwords, social security numbers, or critical company information and ripping you off. The number one threat to your small business security is your untrained employees!

We recently got a very distraught phone call. The person on the other end of this call had been tricked out of $2,500 in a multi-front social engineering attack. It began with an email (and so many do). The email, disguised as a message from Apple, said there was a problem with their computer, that it had been compromised by hackers, and they needed to call right away to set up a phone support call with Apple support. Worried, they quickly called the number and trusted that because they were the ones making the call and the email looked real so that it must be legitimate. The hackers posing as Apple support answered, "This is Apple Tech support, thank you for calling," took some basic information and "confirmed" the caller was being hacked. They then instructed the business owner to purchase Apple gift cards so tech support could figure out how the hackers are trying to get onto their machine. After losing $2,500, they called me for help.

Another version of this plays out like this: "We'll need to get your credit card; this support call will cost $49." People feel comfortable with this, remote support is common; it is a reasonable cost, and seems likely enough – and they are scared, so they make unreasonable decisions. What they actually do with your credit card information later is another thing, however.

These schemes do not depend upon the kind of computer you're using, Mac or Windows; it is about being tricked by a highly trained and skilled hacker. Up against your untrained staff, you don't stand a chance.

ADWARE/MALWARE

Viruses aren't a threat to Mac OS or other UNIX -based operating systems the way they are to PCs, so it's unlikely you will need to spend seven hours in front of your Mac trying to remove viruses the way you would need to on a PC. However, in the Mac world, you are not off the hook. You can get Adware and Malware, which are introduced primarily through a web browser. These nasty little cousins of viruses might cause some performance difficulties with your machine or prevent you from getting to the right webpage, but to date, I have never seen Adware or Malware that could delete things off the hard drive or destroy your data like a virus can. Most often, users run into these issues because they are untrained about how to avoid these things and their machines are unmanaged, so they are downloading bogus software or "free" fonts that often carry a payload that includes the Adware.

The FBI's most wanted hacker back in the '90s and now one of the world's top penetration testers, Kevin Mitnick, was using a Mac the last time I saw him. Maybe he knows something about the security of Apple's products we should be paying attention to – give that some thought.

EMPLOYEE ACCESS AND USE OF TECHNOLOGY

Perhaps because they trust Apple technology so implicitly, business owners often leave employees with a sense of entitlement about how they use "their" computers, specifically Macs. There are usually two main reasons that this happens: businesses have no IT support at all, or their IT technician knows nothing about Apple technologies, so they turn the computers over to users and hope for the best.

As a business owner, you need to take control of your computers and technology by implementing maintenance and security practices that ensure your company's data has not ended up in the wrong hands. If you don't take control of your network, someone else will, and I can promise you will not be happy with the results.

What are your employees doing with your computer hardware when they are at home? Are their kids doing homework on the same computer that provides your employees with access to your company's CRM or financial documents? Your employee might be aware of what not to click on, but will that employee's child know better? Trust me, after 20 years of doing support I have seen it all, from lost files to jelly-covered DVDs in the optical drive at the breakfast table. Good intentions or not, what your employees do with those computers should be outlined in a policy and monitored.

Employees working from home or at remote locations create new risks. Those computers are not at the office protected behind firewalls and standard security protocols; you have no idea what is going on with your company computer, much less the data on it. As the business owner, you can be held responsible for any data breach from those roaming computers. We recommend a strict policy that no personal data is allowed on any company-owned computers. For Macs, that means employees should not be logging into these systems with their personal Apple IDs, Dropbox accounts, or other cloud sharing services, and should avoid allowing their kids to do schoolwork or play games on company computers unless properly configured to ensure your company data is protected. What data might that be? It could be the credit card your employee uses to pay their department's monthly expenses or a client list. It only takes a second for a lot of work that you have paid for to be lost to an innocent button click.

MANAGING APPLE IDS, DATA AND RISK MANAGEMENT

What information does your business store that you would not want someone else to see? Wire transfer numbers? Bank account numbers? Client contact information? Pricing sheets? The same goes for your iCloud account; once a hacker has your information, they can see every text message you send. What kind of information have you texted your spouse while in a hurry—knowing you should not—like passwords?

I have untangled more than one mess in which clients were sharing their Apple IDs with their staff so they could share a calendar, oops! The staff learned more than they wanted to know about their boss's relationships before he realized that everything on his personal Apple devices was linked to the Apple ID he shared. A skilled Apple consultant will know how to manage those Apple IDs, DEP, Apple Business Manager and your Apple Custom Store Portal, intricacies a Windows-based IT shop will likely know nothing about.

BACKUPS AND SECURITY

As a company leveraging Apple technology it is important that the backup tools you deploy are Mac-friendly tools designed for use with Apple technology specifically. Using backup software that was made to work with Windows and then retrofitted to work with your Apple file systems and data will most often not end well. You can avoid a lot of headaches by hiring a Mac-specific IT advisor to design your backup system.

MANAGING UPDATES

Updates are another overlooked security risk that should be properly managed. Thoughtlessly applying patches comes with risks like the High Sierra root bug found in a macOS update, for example. This patch made it possible for hackers to gain access to the settings on Macs without using a password. It is unlikely that staff downloading their own updates would know about such a risk. Therefore, Mac-specific managed IT support is imperative in a small business setting.

An important aspect of a managed IT support model is that it relies on device-management software that, when properly configured, implements security policies that reduce your risk. If you have ever worried about an employee losing a company device containing confidential data, device-management software can eliminate those concerns by automatically enabling FileVault on your Macs or enforcing non-trivial passcodes on iOS devices. Lost devices can even be locked or wiped remotely from a central management console. Remote management of computers has become a must; if you're trusting your network with someone and they are not leveraging these tools, I would question their qualifications.

PASSWORDS

What about passwords on your Macs? Although Apple makes it much easier for the user to choose a strong password using Apple's Password Assistant, passwords are still one of the weakest links. Poor passwords leave data unprotected. Few people can remember a good password, much less 50 different passwords. How many passwords like this one do you think you can keep in your head: TzZusqxB!Bf@uXt9zZHiFFg8k? That is what a good password looks like; notice the word puppy or kitty is not in there anywhere. Password managers are available to generate secure passwords and remember them for your team, eliminating the temptation of using easy passwords like "Kitty2020" or using the same password on multiple sites.

MOBILE DEVICES – BYOD

Don't forget about all the iPhones, iPads, and other mobile devices that are creeping into your office, commonly called BYOD, Bring Your Own Device, or BYOT, Bring Your Own Technology. If these devices are used to access company data, then they should be secured. Are they? Can you remotely lock or wipe those devices to secure company data on them in the event the device is lost or stolen? Even Apple's amazing hardware cannot protect your company data if those devices do not require a passcode, or do not automatically lock after a few minutes, or when people get lazy and set their computers to automatically log in after a restart. Any of your employee's or visiting guest's devices should be managed and kept on a network separate from any company data.

Have you considered the risk associated with all the devices your staff connects to the computers and network? Siri patiently waits in the wings for you to command, "Hey, Siri!" Not only your computers, but all the technology on your network are always listening: TVs, smart thermostats, internet-based cameras, and home "smart" interface devices that control your lights. These devices may be alluring to bring into your office, but when unmanaged, can invite trouble.

All these unmanaged devices and software working around your IT systems are called Shadow IT and this is a big risk to your security. If you don't know what is under your employees' desks or what they are connecting to your network, it will be hard to secure it. Daily there are reports of these devices being compromised and people being spied on by hackers. Look around at your employees' desks and see what they have brought to and connected to your company's network, unprotected, and ready to be brought into service by a hacker.

Another big risk that is commonly overlooked on all these smart devices is the camera. Anyone that you allow into your building can use their unmanaged device to take photos of your company's secrets, text or email those images anyplace in the world, or post them to social media before you have any idea what happened. No one thinks twice about someone gabbing on the phone or sending a text message these days, but what if that message contains your company data?

Your business will benefit the most if your time as its leader and business owner is spent providing vision and direction versus learning new IT skills. Likewise, letting your well-paid office manager learn how to do IT support takes them away from more valuable, revenue-generating endeavors. What is one client worth to your business? What is one missed call worth? I bet if you or your office manager are handling IT tasks, you are missing more than one call from more than one client. A skilled Apple consultant will ensure your Mac technology works harmoniously with the other technologies your business relies on in and out of the office while minimizing the cybersecurity risks.

SHOULD CYBERSECURITY BE HANDLED BY AN OUTSIDE IT ADVISOR?

Don't feel bad for not knowing how to secure your company's network or computers. Time-deprived business owners should spend time working on their business, not troubleshooting IT issues. However, you are ultimately responsible for all the data on your network. Whether your business operates in a Mac or PC environment, an IT advisor will mitigate the cybersecurity risks to your business so that you don't have to worry about how thin the ice is between you and the next cyberattack.

About Tim

From the days of the Apple II, Tim Nyberg was known as "The MacGuy" because he could confidently fix any Apple computer. Tim kept the name, opened The MacGuys+ in 1991, and today he and his team are still obsessed with all things related to Apple. His everyday passion is to help small and medium-sized businesses in the Minneapolis Twin Cities area grow through better IT, and a seamless network infrastructure. As a Certified Apple Consultant and a trusted member of the Apple community for over 20 years, Tim is the go-to authority who will ensure your network is secure and your Apple technology works as it should, to support your business goals.

Tim knew early on that education, training and hands-on experience were all essential if he was going to provide a far greater level of service and support to his clients. That commitment began with two Associate in Science degrees and a Bachelor of Science degree. In fact, he is currently working on his MBA degree so he can better serve his clients. Beyond his education prowess, Tim proudly holds certifications in today's most prominent computer software, including Linux, Windows and macOS as well as supporting certifications in networking, Wi-Fi and security.

While Tim Nyberg's passion and expertise for technology is clear, it's his drive to help clients enhance their business that sets him apart in the IT industry. As a result of his years of experience working with small to mid-sized businesses as a trusted advisor, he has become an important part of their successes. By providing the right tools, technology and business-accelerating strategies and advice, Tim has helped countless clients execute a better business plan.

Many of Tim's clients have described him as focused, diligent and dedicated. Throughout his years, he has demonstrated a unique ability to resolve the most complex challenges, develop long-lasting business relationships and lead cross-functional team members toward organizational goals. He has always had an ability to see the big picture, evaluate potential obstacles and create solutions that align with his clients' business vision.

While Tim loves his business, his family and friends complete his life. His two boys bring greater value to his life, and he enjoys being a Boy Scout leader for them. When he's not at the office, Tim power lifts for exercise and loves traveling and spending time with his family.

Always striving to share his vast knowledge, Tim Nyberg dedicated months to put his ideas and advice on paper. The results culminated in this very book: *On Thin Ice.*

You can connect with Tim Nyberg with The MacGuys+ at:
- on-thin-ice@themacguys.com
- 763-331-6227
- https://www.themacguys.com/
- https://www.linkedin.com/in/nybergtim/

CHAPTER 18

CYBERSECURITY FOR FINANCIAL SERVICES

BY SCOTT HAGIZADEGAN

Every 12 seconds, a business is attacked by a cybercriminal. To put their prevalence into perspective, there are 15,900 automobile accidents per day every year in the United States, or one every 11 seconds. Your business could be compromised before you finish reading this page. The average loss per cyber incident has risen to $369K, with 43% of online attacks now aimed at small businesses; and according to insurance carrier Hiscox, sixty percent of these go out of business within six months of being victimized. Equally worrying for modern executives, it's also set to cost businesses $5.2 trillion worldwide within five years, according to Accenture.

Cybercrime is a risk to any business, but the stakes are significantly higher in the financial services vertical. Ransomware, which locks down a company's network and files until a ransom is paid to the criminal, represents the biggest threat. Phishing schemes run a close second. Phishing emails are sent to company employees hoping to convince them to act on whatever is requested in the email, usually a request for sensitive information or the transfer of sums of money.

Financial services firms acquire sensitive data, including financial and personal information for their clients and business clients. Those individuals and corporations entrust that sensitive data to the financial service firm with the expectation that is will unquestionably be safeguarded. The direct cost of a data breach includes IT expenses to locate and neutralize the threat, loss of revenue during downtime, loss of customers, and loss of the financial firm's reputation. Indirect costs include the threat of lawsuits and the associated legal fees, even as the financial services organization believes they have managed the situation well.

Think about the typical information retained by a CPA or financial services firm: clients' personally identifying information such as name, gender, birth date, contact info, social security number, W-2s and other tax documents, and bank account information and routing numbers. For their business clients, they hold company information, employee tax documents, EIN number, social security numbers, and employees' beneficiary and partner contact information.

All that personal information can be used by a cybercriminal to create fraudulently-filed tax returns, damage client relationships, and lead to legal battles with those clients over damages. All of that can happen after a single employee's email credentials have been compromised. Industry data indicates that small to mid-sized CPA firms are just as vulnerable to cyberattacks and data security breaches as their larger counterparts, maybe more so. Hackers have been known to target smaller CPA firms because they tend to have outdated networks, unsecured email accounts, and less cybersecurity awareness, all of which make them the low-hanging fruit of financial organizations for the cybercriminal.

A few years ago, a California CPA firm discovered a data security incident involving their clients' tax records. With the help of their IT consultants who secured their network and a third-party forensic security firm that assessed the breadth of the breach, the CPA firm learned that in the course of a week, nearly 50 fraudulent tax returns had been filed using their clients' stolen personal information. The hackers had obtained identifying information about individuals and entities. The IT company discovered and removed malware on a hard drive that had created an open door for the hackers to make internal software system management changes. Due to the large potential exposure, the CPA firm had to recommend that clients review their bank accounts, brokerage statements, and credit reports for changes then alert the credit bureaus to place a fraud hold on their credit reports.

DIRECT COST OR DOWNSTREAM LIABILITY, IT'S STILL ON YOU

No client wants to be informed that the fiduciary they have entrusted with the most important information about themselves has been compromised. No business wants to be the bearer of that bad news. CPAs and other financial services organizations face a one-two punch of direct costs from a security failure and the downstream liability of potential hacks to their clients.

Trust is the cornerstone of financial services; shatter the trust and the relationship crumbles. The financial services organization's reputation is built on that trust. Logically, a data breach could cost a financial services organization its reputation. According to a recent IBM data breach report from https://databreachcalculator.mybluemix.net, firms that experience a data breach are more likely to lose clients to their competitors. How much more likely? Sixty-four percent indicated they would leave a firm if their personal or financial information was stolen. Worse still, ninety-four percent of those would also file lawsuits against that firm, amplifying the cost of the breach. How does a firm ever recover from that?

In addition, the risk of downstream liability is huge. For example, you have a CPA firm with 15 accountants, that manages hundreds of businesses, or several thousand clients. The cybercriminal hacks into your network and locks everything up, and gains access to all the sensitive financial data of those clients. Now, it's not just your business being exposed because the hackers have access to client files. If the business doesn't pay up, that makes the price tag higher than that of the average Joe that gets hit.

Secondly, the downstream liability is exponential. If the business doesn't pay for any reason or even if they do pay, the cybercriminals can go after the clients directly.

CYBERSECURITY RECOMMENDATIONS

Cybersecurity protection begins with a system audit. During the audit, we look for vulnerabilities and test a company's team members by sending them fake phishing attempts. The goal is to determine how many employees will open the email and how many will then respond with the information requested in the phishing email. The results are often shocking.

Cybercrime defense falls into two categories: proactive and reactive. It's a dance between acceptable risk and overkill. If you don't mitigate as much possible damage as you can, what will happen? So, you perform your due diligence and understand that an ounce of prevention is worth a pound of cure.

Our firm utilizes industry-leading tools to begin with an assessment of a firm's current vulnerability. Are their usernames and passwords for sale on the dark web? That allows the firm to prioritize protection because they immediately know what email or data, if any, have been compromised and need to be changed immediately. From that point, the client can move forward proactively. Despite everyone's best efforts, a firm still might be compromised. For those instances, it's imperative that any financial services firm be covered for cybercrimes under its insurance policy.

Many insurance companies still don't offer cybersecurity protection, or if they do, it's minimal. Do not assume that the insurance agent will know that your firm needs this coverage or that they will know it is available. Understand what the basic coverage is and also the coverages one, two, or three steps up from the basic coverage. You wouldn't insure a $100,000 Maserati with $15,000 collision coverage. Financial firms cannot afford to short their cybersecurity coverage either. This is the firm's last defense against total ruin in the event of an attack. Even with the most current cybersecurity measures in place, a business isn't bulletproof.

The key to success long-term is the right strategic partnerships. When a business has been compromised, often the owners or principals feel overwhelmed – how did it happen, what data was affected, and what is the next step. It is possible that even their long-term IT provider does not know how to handle a financial services data breach.

When I approach a company about their cybersecurity, I frequently share with them the information about their company that is readily available on the Dark Web. I share that information to demonstrate their vulnerability. Sometimes, the owner thinks I have hacked into their network, but long after a security breach, the information is still out there. Worse still, if they have been hacked and paid $300,000 in ransom, I must show them that after all that, they are still vulnerable.

If a company's cybersecurity measures fail, then financial services companies should be aware of what is required of them after a breach. The previously mentioned CPA firm breach perfectly illustrates what happens in the aftermath of a breach. Immediately after the discovery of the attack, the firm contacted their IT consultant to secure the network and brought in a forensic security firm to investigate the breadth of the exposure. The IT company then removed the malware from the computer, made internal software system changes, and ascertained that all network firewalls, computers, and security protections were working appropriately. How do you think their business and personal clients felt when they received letters informing them that their personal information had potentially been shared with the dark underbelly of society?

CPA firms are a top target for hackers. Upfront costs for protection almost always cost less than the accrued cost after the fact. Hire the best people for the job who will utilize the greatest technological safeguards. Make sure those safeguards are up to date, as well. Remember, too, that there's the potential for cybercriminals to come up with a work-around for the best protection. For that, cybersecurity insurance is a solid investment. Too many companies pass up that protection because they think the premiums are cost-prohibitive, but the cost of forensics, mailings to clients, additional IT repairs, and damage to a company's reputation will far outweigh the premium expense.

For smaller to mid-sized firms, the expense of a breach is catastrophic, but they're a common target. Industry data indicates that small and mid-sized CPA firms are just as vulnerable to cyberattacks and data security breaches as larger organizations. Lately, smaller CPA firms have become targets for cybercriminals. Hackers know that smaller firms tend to be easier to infiltrate with their outdated networks, unsecured email accounts, and easier to phish, undertrained employees. A small business using an outdated operating system such as Windows XP are sitting ducks because Microsoft no longer provides the patches to keep them secure. Web-based email products are ubiquitous and flawed. Those vulnerabilities are well-known and easy to compromise even for an inexperienced hacker. Hackers have been known to use Google Maps or

Yelp to locate independent CPA firms and scan their networks searching for vulnerabilities.

If the cost of proactive protection still seems out of reach for your CPA or financial services firm, consider this. The average cost for a lost or stolen record is $242.00, nearly double what the cost was a year ago. Multiply that by the number of files you have—not just from the last year, but the archived records as well—then, add on the potential legal fees associated with a data breach. Are you prepared to spend that money, plus the additional marketing dollars you would have to spend to regain your reputation or replace the clients that you lost?

How long did it take you to read this chapter? Remember that cybersecurity attacks happen every 12 seconds. Was your firm one of them? If you don't feel confident in your answer, connect with your IT company or MSP. You have probably spent years building your client base, your reputation, and your place in the community. A couple of minutes in your network is enough time for even an average hacker to level your business like a house of cards and expose it to lawsuits.

Instead of burying your head in the sand or hoping your firm won't be the next target, make data security a top priority of your business and use that to position yourself as the CPA firm that prides itself in data security. From the top-down, embrace security as part of the firm's culture and invest in the infrastructure and education to make it so. An ounce of prevention really is worth a pound of cure!

About Scott

Scott Hagizadegan is a speaker, entrepreneur, marine captain, and philanthropist. Prior to founding his current company, Shield IT Networks, Scott was the co-founder of Ignisis for over 20 years. He uses his 25 years of extensive experience with helping clients, who range from startups to Fortune 500s, including such well-known clients in the financial and retail industries as Ernst & Young, FPA, Guitar Center, VF Corp, Vans, LAPD, 4 Wheel Parts, and Don Roberto Jewelers, with the design, implementation, and maintenance of next-generation networks.

Using a philosophy that design drives outcome, combined with his character and competence, Scott continues to earn high praise and trust with fierce client and team loyalty of over six times the industry average of 2.5 years, whereas his currently runs at 17+ years.

Scott is also very passionate about giving back via a hand-up, not a hand-out, and has led philanthropic projects raising funds and gathering teams to build computer labs at orphanages around the world (Zambia, U.S., Honduras, Dominican Republic, Mexico, etc.). He is a volunteer leader at his daughter's AWANA class for the past nine years and has served on the Board of Retail Orphan Initiative - Zambia. He continues this deeply held belief in his business life via a "Profit with Purpose" approach that simply means we earn profit with the purpose of reinvesting it into the needs of the world around us as a "Serving Leader."

His favorite hobby is adventuring the islands and waters off the coast of California on his boat *Yippee Ki Yay* with his family, friends, and clients. As a licensed Captain, he also operates one of the top chartering businesses in Southern California.

You can connect with Scott at:
- scotth@shielditnetworks.com
- 818-489-9877
- www.ShieldITNetworks.com

CHAPTER 19

SURREPTITIOUS MARAUDERS

BY RICK THOMAS

Safeguarding technologies in today's ever-changing interconnected world is no easy task, particularly within the healthcare space. Cybercriminals are keenly aware that digital crime involving identity theft and financial fraud pays very well – and even greater when healthcare-focused. Cybercrimes originate from both domestic and foreign locations where bad actors are hard at work with new and creative ways to pillage the treasure trove of Protected Health Information (PHI). With an extraordinary net worth, this information has become a sought-after commodity on the Internet, specifically on the Dark Web—where PHI may be bought and sold with untraceable digital currency and other means of exchange.

The difficulty with tracing and investigating these underground marketplaces is forcing the Department of Health and Humans Services (HHS) to take notice and place the responsibility on the organizations that house such data. Taking a proactive approach to safeguarding the data is truly the only effective method. However, less than six percent of IT budgets are currently allocated to cybersecurity, according to the Healthcare Information and Management Systems Society. As cybersecurity risks rise in both frequency and amplitude, many healthcare organizations may have a wake-up call to reassess their IT budgets, specifically with regards to cybersecurity. This is particularly evident with smaller healthcare systems in which IT budgets have not grown proportionately to their technology and staffing requirements.

Earlier this year, I had the opportunity to interview Nancy, the CEO of a 25-bed hospital, considered a smaller healthcare system in the grand scope of things. During our conversation, Nancy expressed concerns that her hospital system might be vulnerable to a data breach and did not know where to begin with addressing this gut-wrenching feeling. When asked why her IT department had not made this a top priority, her response was that their day-to-day activities of supporting the numerous departments within the hospital system leave them little to no time to prepare for a breach. "You see," she described, "a hospital system is a lot like a shopping mall where you have a variety of stores all located under one roof, and they all accept the same forms of payment; however, they have dissimilar systems for their transactions." Nancy's parallel couldn't have been more 'spot on'. In fact, a hospital may have any number of patient services with unique and often disparate technologies that operate on a multitude of servers.

My curiosity around Nancy's anxiety of a breach led me to ask, why now? She responded that with all the recent accounts in the news media warning of ransomware and phishing attacks being on the rise—especially in healthcare news outlets—it's only a matter of time. The reality is that healthcare organizations are subject to phishing and ransomware attacks, much like any other organization. However, due to the potential value of the data, the stakes are higher, and the bullseye significantly larger. Phishing attacks are by far the easiest to carry out by cybercriminals, and healthcare workers are easy prey as they are givers by nature. Through an exchange of emails, text messages, or even phone calls for the most brazen of attacks, sensitive information may be inadvertently forfeited, sometimes without ever raising suspicion.

A study at Carnegie Mellon University revealed that women are more likely than men to click on phishing links and subsequently enter information on phishing websites as compared to their male counterparts. The study concluded that training and awareness proved effective in leveling the playing field between genders, however, was not the cure-all for the sexes. With women making up the bulk of the caregiver labor force, the results from the study may suggest that a greater threat vector exists within healthcare organizations that have not incorporated security awareness training as compared to those who have. The cases are plentiful, with attacks becoming ever craftier as cybercriminals wait patiently for the right time to strike.

The Federal Bureau of Investigation reports that cyber-intrusions are becoming more commonplace, more dangerous, and more sophisticated. Malwarebytes witnessed a 235% increase in threats between 2018 and 2019 aimed at organizations from enterprises to small businesses, with ransomware as a major contributor. The report further indicates that healthcare is particularly at risk likely because of legacy infrastructure, outdated software applications, and lack of security funding. Unlike private organizations, who can drive their own profit margins and make unilateral decisions on funding, financial backing for healthcare is often driven by governmental policy and political climate.

The reality that less than 50% of organizations surveyed are fully prepared to deal with cyberattacks may prove costly or even catastrophic for smaller organizations who are ill-prepared to respond. According to VelocIT Solutions, a Managed Security Services Provider with a focus on healthcare, being on the right side of the statistics requires organizations to build up layered defenses. Consider a moat, draw bridge, and walls as the proactive defense to protecting the technologies and data within the keep. The firewall acts as the draw bridge allowing safe passage into the inner castle after inspection, while security solutions such as packet inspection, anti-virus, anti-ransomware and artificial intelligence (AI) technologies, secure the perimeter from invaders—just as the surrounding waters and high stone walls of a castle perform their roles.

Practitioners provide a myriad of care needs in any number of departments, which results in enormous volumes of electronic data. The data ultimately becomes the responsibility of the hospital system to safeguard. The patients also expect that their data is being protected at all costs. This data becomes part of the patient record, and in some cases, may be shared externally with other organizations, provided that it has been deemed necessary and authorized. Let's return to Nancy for an example of the potential ramifications of inadequately fortifying the castle keep. During a recent healthcare conference, one of her employees had in her possession a hospital laptop that was stolen from her hotel room. When the employee reported the missing laptop, it was discovered that the hard drive was unencrypted; to add insult to injury, patient data was admittedly saved to this computer.

Nancy's healthcare system was now faced with a reportable event that was neglectful, as interpreted by HHS. The hospital had an immediate fiduciary duty to notify HHS, providers, and the three hundred patients impacted by the loss of their Protected Health Information. Had the breach exceeded five hundred records, HHS specifically mandates that prominent media outlets must be notified of such incidents, which in turn would have created a further loss of confidence in the healthcare organization with their patient population. Of course, avoiding such a problem in the first place is the ideal scenario, albeit at a cost, it is one of predictability, compared to unexpected capital outlays due to bad publicity, HIPAA fines, and the likelihood of patient-related lawsuits.

While HIPAA fines can knock any healthcare system on its laurels, there is a silver lining. Under the new 2019 HHS HITECH Act interpretation, breaches are assessed and penalized using a four-tier system. For "Tier 1" violations in which the affected party had no knowledge of, nor culpability in, the privacy breach fines are capped at $25,000 per year. On the other side of the spectrum, "Tier 4" violations will continue to amass up to $1.5 million in fines per year caused by willful neglect and inaction to correct identified areas within a timely manner.

Metaphorically speaking, when all else fails from a proactive security approach, and marauders have breached the walls of an organization, the archers and swordsmen must be called upon to react. The solution – breach detection and response – comes out fighting to rapidly sever compromised systems at the network level while maintaining electrical power to any infiltrated machine. Maintaining power is essential for instances where a forensic study of the compromise and attack vector is sought by law enforcement agencies, and may additionally prove helpful where a Cyber Insurance policy is called upon to offset monetary damages.

"When all else fails?" Nancy perked up in her seat and asked with a furrowed brow, "What will it take to keep my hospital from failing? We don't want to be attacked!" So, just how does a healthcare organization react to the gluttony of guidelines beginning with the 1996 HIPAA act, followed up by the HITECH act of 2009 and most recent Cybersecurity Guidelines of 2018 with an already overburdened IT department? The answer may be tasking the existing IT staff, hiring additional IT talent, outsourcing, or a combination of internal and external resources working together to tackle the problem.

Recognizing where the problems lie is a fundamental first step for developing a relevant action plan in risk mitigation. According to VelocIT Solutions, the top three areas for risk in any modern-day healthcare organization are:

1. **PHI leakage**
2. **Electronic Medical Record (EMR) disruptions**
3. **Extended organization-wide unplanned downtime**

Internal IT departments might consider "at a minimum," beginning with the HHS Security Risk Assessment (SRA) Tool that can be downloaded free of charge to identify and assess risks and vulnerabilities of the confidentiality, integrity, and availability of PHI. The software does not transmit information back to HHS and is designed to run locally from a Windows-based computer. It's important to consider examining all technologies (cloud and on-premises systems) when conducting the security assessment. Be forewarned that there is a significant time investment for completing a risk assessment, and this will vary dramatically from organization to organization based on the services provided. Allocate appropriate time for the assessment to be successful or consider outsourcing.

Leverage an MSSP if the in-house IT talent does not have the time or meet the necessary criteria for the job at hand. Keep in mind that what an MSSP performs is vastly different from what an IT support department provides to an organization. Be transparent with your IT department, if their resumes don't reflect the skills necessary for the job, think twice before bestowing such a responsibility. You'll find, in most cases, outsourcing to an MSSP has cost savings advantages through a holistic approach – being equipped with the tools, software and purpose-built equipment of their trade, intrinsically reduces the costs of creating the job role internally.

Former Acting Deputy Director for HIPAA at HHS, Iliana L. Peters, recommends that organizations partner with solution providers that can perform comprehensive risk management, specializing in security practices, compliance, and countermeasures. While it's not mandatory to outsource, doing a thorough and professional risk analysis that will stand up to a compliance review will require expert knowledge that could be obtained through the services of an experienced outside professional.

If acquiring in-house cybersecurity talent is truly desired, recognize that it comes with its own set of obstacles. Consider hiring two individuals, reducing the knowledge gap should one leave. Consider the cost to retain, train and keep your cybersecurity team effectual, and lastly, consider the costs associated with the tools, software, and equipment necessary to sustain an effective security posture for the organization. At the very least, consider developing a staff training program with a cadence interval of no more than ninety days between simulated phishing attack campaigns along with awareness training for those identified at risk for taking the bait. Given that most settlements are related to risk management, organizations are fundamentally incentivized to engage in IT security best practices and training.

A healthcare system's reputation and its leadership will undoubtedly be tarnished if marauders compromise the integrity of any system that is intended to protect and deliver patient health information to those that need it when they need it. The decision to outsource, build out an internal cybersecurity team, or leverage a combination of the two should be apparent by now, as inaction is surely to be a future reaction. As Nancy's interview with me ended, I said, "You know, there's a cost to doing this." Her candid response was, "Yes, but what's the cost of us not doing it?"

References:

Lorrie Faith Cranor
https://lorrie.cranor.org/pubs/pap1162-sheng.pdf

Malwarebytes
https://resources.malwarebytes.com/files/2019/08/CTNT-2019-Ransomware_August_FINAL.pdf

The Office of the National Coordinator for Health Information Technology
https://www.healthit.gov/providers-professionals/security-risk-assessment-tool

About Rick Thomas

Rick Thomas is the co-author of *On Thin Ice* and founder of ProTechnical, a Managed Services Provider (MSP) and its subsidiary, VelocIT, a Managed Security Services Provider (MSSP) with offices located in Reno, Nevada and Portland, Oregon. Combining cutting-edge technologies with a highly talented technical team, each organization offers up a truly holistic and unrivaled complement of services and support.

Beginning in Silicon Valley, Thomas quickly learned his tradecraft working for companies such as Palm, Knowledge Universe (parent company of LeapFrog Toys), Caesars Entertainment, State of Nevada, and Tahoe Forest Hospital in Northern California prior to the 2009 launch of ProTechnical. With a 30-year tenure as an IT professional, he has assembled a formidable team of Subject Matter Experts who complement and contribute to his vision, and Rick is recognized for his "Go-Giver" nature of giving back to great causes through charitable events, sponsorships, and volunteer work. ProTechnical delivers brilliant and innovative IT services to the healthcare industry and was independently ranked in the top 500 Managed Services Providers worldwide.

In this book, Rick Thomas addresses rising cybersecurity threats in healthcare. His candid interview with Nancy, the CEO of a 25-bed hospital, uncovers the immediate cybersecurity needs of her organization. It's an epidemic that must be treated with a balance of technology and talent to secure electronic Protected Health Information (ePHI) from falling into the wrong hands. With the high value of ePHI for sale on the Dark Web, the healthcare threat landscape couldn't be riper for the taking through vulnerabilities and exposure.

Rick Thomas holds a Bachelor of Science in Information Technology with a specialization in Information Assurance and Security. He is regularly engaged as the HIPAA Security Officer for clinics and healthcare systems. His many years of IT experience, awareness of current threat landscapes, and ability to manage security challenges make his writing both informative and highly relevant to IT professionals and healthcare leaders alike.

Rick Thomas can be reached by:
- Email: onthinice@protechnical.com
- Phone: 844.784.3330
- Website: www.protechnical.com

CHAPTER 20

SOCIAL ENGINEERING ATTACKS

BY TERRY ROSSI

What do Abe Froman (the Sausage King of Chicago), Frank Abagnale Jr. and Thomas Crown have in common? They were all characters in movies with great examples of social engineering. They demonstrate how we can simply be fooled by a teenager like Ferris in *Ferris Bueller's Day Off*, a con man like Frank Abagnale Jr. in, *Catch Me If You Can*, or a criminal like Thomas Crown in, *The Thomas Crown Affair*. On some level, we want to believe in their good intentions.

Make no mistake, there are real cybercriminals out there looking to take your money, steal from you, destroy your reputation, and bankrupt you and your businesses. Cybercriminals use a technique broadly called social engineering to trick you into giving up confidential information. Their goal is to make you reveal your username, password, credit card information, and banking information or to entice you to click on something that will allow them access to your computer. From there, they can then install malicious software that gives them access to anything they want.

Believe it or not, it is much easier for a criminal to exploit your natural inclination to trust than to break into your bank account or hack your personal information. Today, this is mostly accomplished with a specific technique called phishing (pronounced "fishing"). A phishing attack works because the attacker, usually through an email, will cause you to act. I'll give you a few examples.

You get an email you think is from a trusted source. This could be someone in your address book, a customer or supplier you deal with. Phishing attacks commonly come from Verizon, eFax, American Express, and other well-known companies. They will often ask you to log into your account by clicking on a link in the email. But what people often don't realize is, it is really a fake webpage, and just like that, they have your account information and can start impersonating you.

The goal of one well-known phishing email, involving eFax, was to steal banking information. In the eFax phishing email, the perpetrators convinced the victim to open a Microsoft Excel spreadsheet. They did so by explaining that the fax contained a sign-in for a zipped file that must be opened with Microsoft Excel and required a password. People assume that if there's a security measure, like a password, the email must be legitimate. This Microsoft Excel spreadsheet contained a macro (a small program) that downloaded and installed a malicious program onto the computer. The program attached itself to the web browser and was used to hide or display information on webpages such as "verifying" a user accessing their bank account or just gathering information on webpages visited. Then, the bad actors sold that data on the Dark Web, the underground marketplace for cyber-criminals.

Here's another example. You get an email that has a compelling subject. These are often emails hoping for you to verify your information, check status, or sign in to a website to win a prize. The attacker often takes some current event to trick you into either being charitable, curious, or greedy.

As I write this, we are in the middle of the worldwide Coronavirus/ COVID-19 pandemic. This is a field day for cybercriminals. The emails might look like they come from your HR department or a government organization like the Center for Disease Control. They entice you to click on the link, and when you do, well, bad things happen. Be on the lookout for emails like that, and follow the advice that you will find later in this chapter before clicking on any links.

Here is an example of a forged CDC email.

"Distributed via the CDC Health Alert Network
January 31, 2020
CDCHAN-00426

Dear ███████████████

The Centers for Disease Control and Prevention (CDC) continues to closely monitor an outbreak of a 2019 novel coronavirus (2019-nCoV) in Wuhan City, Hubei Province, China that began in December 2019. CDC has established an Incident Management System to coordinate a domestic and international public health response.

Updated list of new cases around your city are available at (https://www.cdc.gov/coronavirus/2019-nCoV/newcases-cities.html)

You are immediately advised to go through the cases above for safety hazard

Sincerely,
CDC-INFO National Contact Center
National Center for Health Marketing
Division of eHealth Marketing
Centers for Disease control and Prevention"

Another example of phishing is when you get an email that looks like it came from your boss, a client, or a vendor. These are often extremely dangerous and seek to convince you to wire money or give up credit card information. They look legitimate and are usually researched by the criminal.

A nervous manufacturer called me one day and told me he just willingly wired $450,000 dollars to a hacker. I say "willingly" because he had instructed his accounting staff to send the money. What happened was the hacker had accomplished what is called a "man-in-the- middle" attack and posed as one of this manufacturer's biggest suppliers. The con was if they pre-paid their outstanding balance and pre-purchased $250,000 worth of material, they would get a 25% discount. The balance had to be paid before the end of the year. The hacker had broken into the manufacturer's email system and re-routed the email to the supplier to a fraudulent domain. Then, the hacker simply carried on a conversation about the discount with the unknowing manufacturer for over 40 days. The hacker, not being able to send email from the real supplier, used a remarkably similar domain name to fool the manufacturer.

Here are some example domain names to give you an idea of how this is done:

- Domains with an "m" in them look similar to an "rn" as with walmart.com versus the imposter domain walrnart.com

- Domains with a zero in them look the same in uppercase CORN. COM versus C0RN.COM
- Domains with the numeral '1' in them. They look like a lower-case L as with Paypa1.com
- Domains that are concatenated: www.amex.com vs. wwwamex.com
- Domains that are commonly spelled wrong: utube.com vs. youtube. com

There are numerous ways to protect your business from social engineering attacks.

A. The first way is to educate your users. Implement an on-going phishing-training and testing program. Phishing is the #1-way hackers will penetrate your business. We have found education to be highly beneficial.

Basically, we send compelling emails to your employees, and if they click on them, in a genuinely nice way, we educate them on what they did so they don't do it again. The fake phishing emails are always based on current events or from fake vendors similar to those with which the company does business. The idea is to reduce the likelihood the employees will click on bogus emails.

Companies really never want to spend money to educate their employees until after they have been hacked. Then, it's the first thing they want to do. Prevention, such as employee training, is a little like buying insurance. Nobody wants to buy it, but they need it.

B. The second way to protect your network from social engineering attacks is through a special protected DNS service that blocks your users from reaching known bad-guy sites that are used for phishing, malware, and ransomware. DNS or Domain Name System is the system on the Internet that turns names into addresses so that you can reach your destination. Think of this protected DNS as a safety harness so employees can't hurt themselves. In the years since, we have implemented a protected DNS service at our clients, we have noticed a reduction in malware, and a huge reduction in phishing with just that one tool. This protected DNS service sits in the middle and detects when there is a ransomware attack coming from a known dangerous site.

C. Third, make sure you have real-time active endpoint protection installed on all computers attached to your network. In the old days, we used to call this anti-virus, but today it is so much more. Hackers will look for the easiest way to penetrate your business. The easiest way is through your employees, but the second easiest way is from older unprotected or under-protected computers and network devices connecting into your business. Endpoint protection will mitigate some risk.

D. The fourth way to protect your business is to know your exposure. Just like you need to know what is going on with your credit, you also should be monitoring your company's exposure on the Dark Web. Sign up for an on-going Dark Web monitoring service that will alert you when your company's credentials are on the Dark Web. The service we offer our clients is very affordable, and I believe every company should be continually monitoring sources for intrusion. Sometimes the only way you will learn that your company has been the victim of a social engineering attack is when you find the evidence on the Dark Web.

E. Fifth, keep everything patched and up-to-date. Use a remote monitoring and management tool (RMM), or the services of a competent managed IT services provider, to keep everything up-to-date and monitored. A good RMM with a skilled staff behind it can not only make your life easier, but also it will protect you in a way that is much less expensive than having a team of IT personnel doing the grunt work of protecting your network. Often, when we begin working with a company, the ownership thinks everything is fine and dandy only to find machines not patched, old anti-virus with outdated definitions, and infected machines on their network. Without a managed service provider or a good RMM tool, these things are too often overlooked. An older automobile is a good analogy. You cannot skip changing your oil forever. You can run your car for a long time as long as you take care of it and maintain it up-to-date, but without that, it's going to fall apart and cause you problems.

No one likes spending money needlessly, but it is important to consider the age of computer equipment when addressing social engineering. Generally, PCs older than three years and servers older than five years can be a problem if they have been neglected. If they are up-to-date, managed, and running current software, then they are still safe. They're just slow, and employees are not as productive with them. Sometimes with these older machines—I'm sure you probably remember windows XP—the product and service patches have been discontinued, so they cannot be up-to-date. Once they have reached end-of-life from a patching point of view or a security update point of view, they are a danger to your office. Social engineering attacks may not seem to be linked directly to outdated equipment, but your employees might tell you otherwise. Employees whose computers are slow to begin with, may not be as willing to dedicate additional time to scrutinizing emails for bad domains, exacerbating an already big problem.

Finally, trust but verify. We often audit companies that either have in-house IT or are using another provider to manage their network. Having a regularly scheduled outside audit is the only way to really know what is or isn't happening in your IT environment. Some businesses require a strict compliance audit like PCI, ISO, or any of the regulatory bodies. Even if your industry doesn't require one, an outside audit is a good idea.

Ferris Bueller said, "Life moves pretty fast. If you don't stop and look around once in a while, you could miss it."

Despite the predictability of his antics, movie viewers are captivated by Bueller's stories and want to believe everything will somehow end well. Viewers want to believe in his good intentions. Social engineering capitalizes on our desire to hope in people's good intentions. The trouble is, life does move pretty fast. If you don't stop to look around your business and train your employees to look around, you could miss the warning signs that your business is ripe for a social engineering attack, or worse, has already succumbed to one.

About Terry

Terry Rossi is co-founder and CEO of PICS ITech, a leading Managed Service IT and Cloud Provider in the Philadelphia area. Over the last quarter-century, PICS ITech has worked with companies in 17 different countries, ranging from $10 billion-dollar multinationals to mom-and-pop operations in small towns. Their mission: *To help companies get the most value out of their investment in technology, while protecting them from cybercriminals, rogue employees, and state bad actors.*

Terry was drawn to technology as a young man, and his love for it has never waned. Working in the emerging "cellular phone" industry, Terry was introduced to computers. Starting on a DEC MicroVAX, he was instantly hooked on this new technology. Ever since, he has committed himself to find and share innovative solutions to help companies succeed in a competitive tech-driven environment.

Along with the engineers, consultants, and strategists on the PICS ITech team, Terry and his team have received numerous awards and recognition, establishing them as worldwide leaders in the managed IT space. Awards include the INC 5000, The Wharton School of Business Philadelphia Top 100, the *Philadelphia Business Journal* Soaring 76, the MSP 501, MSP 500, Pioneer 250, and many others. Terry is also a host of "The IT Provider Network" podcast and author of *Hiring in the Digital Age— How to Take the Pain out of Interviewing, Hiring and Onboarding New Employees for Your Small Business.*

In the cybersecurity world, Terry is proud to be a member of InfraGard, a partnership between the FBI and the private sector. The InfraGard program provides a vehicle for seamless public-private collaboration that protects critical infrastructure through timely communication and mutual learning opportunities.

And if your company is trying to get a step ahead of your competition in tech matters, look into PICS ITech. Terry and his team can help you with:
- Cybersecurity Protection and User Awareness Training
- Strategic and Tactical Technology Consulting
- IT Budgeting and Technology Lifecycle Management
- Hardware, Software and Technology Procurement
- Real-time US-based Helpdesk with 24/7 Emergency Service
- Centralized Services to Keep Your Company Safe

Contact Terry on the social networks at:
- @TerryRossi @PICSITech
- www.pics-itech.com

Or, phone at:
- +1-609-702-3920

CHAPTER 21

CMMC – ARE YOU PREPARED FOR THE NEW GOVERNMENT REQUIREMENTS?

BY AARON WYANT

Cybercriminals possess myriad ways to hack a network, which you may have learned anecdotally, or—although I hope not—through personal experience. The federal government knows this, too. The United States government has an inherent responsibility for record-keeping. Contractors that work with the government share many of those records, so it is only fair that some of the burden for safeguarding information and records falls to the contractors with access to sensitive information.

Before the government instituted these requirements, a company could hire whomever they chose to create their IT infrastructure without vetting that IT provider's cybersecurity credentials. Nearly anyone off the street that claimed to be a computer repair company could repair one computer problem then "fix" the company's network. This practice often created an easy way for hackers to access a network. The problem was, without compliance requirements, there was no incentive to increase security.

To that end, the government created a multi-level certification program called Cybersecurity Maturity Model Certification, or CMMC, comprised of a list of standards with which companies wishing to do business with the federal government must comply. CMMC brings a whole new level of security, or secure foundation, to government contractors and subcontractors. The requirements will help secure, protect, audit, and safeguard CUI (Controlled Unclassified Information).

The theory behind CMMC is that process maturity or process institutionalization, making an activity repetitive and standardized, will also make it rote. Employees, even in a crisis, will have followed the process so frequently that they no longer need to think about what to do. Under previous less stringent requirements, taxpayers faced a large potential burden should a data breach occur. With CMMC compliance, even the smallest company working with the government will have some security measures in place and some skin in the game.

If your company contracts with the government, or is considering it, are you prepared for CMMC? The compliance clock is ticking. Soon the government will have a list of those companies claiming to be compliant and know which companies have been audited already. In these initial days, the early bird that requests and completes its audit before its competitors do really will get the worm.

Are your subcontractors compliant? Do you know what will be required of them? By May 2020, the government wants companies to email them their security score so the government can perform an initial audit of the business before September 2020. After that, the government will periodically audit companies to see if they have maintained their score.

CMMC applies to every company with a government contract, from the landscaper that maintains a federal property to the highest-level defense contractor, and everyone in between. The government has already begun sending emails out, checking the security of the businesses with current contracts. For my company, that means we must become CMMC compliant while we assist over 70% of our clients to come up-to-speed too.

As with most government processes, CMMC paperwork is daunting. To work with the government, a company must be NIST SP 800-171A compliant. Now, they will also have a cybersecurity score and a maturity level rank. A company earns points for each element of NIST SP 800-171A achieved. The more points earned, the higher the company is in the pecking order and the more government contracts available to them.

So, let's go through the CMMC Model, the benchmark against which any organization can evaluate its current level of security methods, helping them set goals and priorities for improvement.

CMMC is a framework that consists of maturity processes and cybersecurity's best practices from multiple cybersecurity standards frameworks, and other references. There are five levels of CMMC processes and practices. Maturity Level (ML) 1, the lowest, to Maturity Level (ML) 5, the highest. CMMC measures process maturity and the implementation of 171 practices. At each level, a company must demonstrate the institutionalization of processes and implementation of practices for that level and preceding levels.

ML 1 is recommended for companies that don't work with CUI (Controlled Unclassified Information), but might work with or support a vendor that has CUI information. ML 1 is the *Performed* level. This is the basic cyberhygiene level focused on safeguarding federal contract information (FCI). ML 1 includes 17 practices. Are you keeping your passwords safe? Is two-step verification turned on? These are two examples of what a company should be doing to secure its data, regardless of if it's required to be CMMC or not.

ML 2 is *Documented*, giving your company intermediate cyber-hygiene. What good is it to say you should do something if it's not documented. You should change your password every 90 days. You should not use the same password in more than one location. If it is written down as a policy, then it's more likely it will be done and not forgotten. Documentation tells everyone this is the way we do things. For example, the HR Department does not have access to the Contract Department's files. This is written in company policy, reviewed regularly, and signed by each employee. ML 2 builds on ML 1 with 55 additional practices to master.

ML 3 is a *Managed* level. The company practices good cyberhygiene and covers access control, awareness and training, audit and accountability, configuration management, identification and authentication, incident response, maintenance, media protection, personal security, physical protection, risk assessment, security assessment, system and communications protection, and system and information integrity. The company continues to practice good cyberhygiene and focuses on the protection of CUI and all security measures as outlined in NIST SP 800-171A.

ML 4 is a *Reviewed* level. At this level, a company reviews and measures their activities for effectiveness. Additional practices are added in such as access control, audit and accountability, incident response and system and communications protection. ML 4 creates a security strategy and roadmap to its completion.

At ML 5, a business is **Optimizing**. They have standardized and optimized a documented security approach across the entire organization. The receptionist, as well as the CEO, will understand the rules. The company performs these actions with a seamlessness not found in the previous levels. The business ensures that all information processing facilities meet defined requirements for information security, continuity, redundancy, and availability, and they review the effectiveness of all security solutions at least once a year.

CMMC boils down to how the company is executing security measures. Configuring management: how are you doing that? Identification and authentication: how are they handling incident response? What do you do when something happens? How is your company maintaining the network and protections? If data is stored on CD ROMs, or wherever it is stored, is it being encrypted? Is it secure?

People often wrongly assume that the only threats to a network and the data on it come through the computer, but other real-world scenarios can be just as dangerous. Anytime there's an opportunity of access to that system from someone else, it could be an issue. An open door, for example, could be an invitation to steal classified information. Part of compliance includes having visitors sign in and out of areas, so you know who has had access to an area where data is housed. Anyone could walk right in, grab a computer or better yet plug in a USB Device or network device, and connect it directly to your PC, server, and/or network port in the wall and have full access to your system – if it is not protected correctly. They don't even need access to the building. They could just leave a USB stick with the receptionist or any employee that is not trained correctly, and they would inadvertently connect it to the PC. This could cost you thousands, even millions of dollars or more, depending on what data they are trying to get and why.

Computer screens facing public areas or security cameras facing computers that are used to access CUI information could potentially lead to the wrong individual learning a password or seeing a document that should not be public knowledge.

When we started in this business in 2008, cybersecurity was a sort of afterthought to most businesses. By 2018, cybersecurity had become a mainstream term, and companies understood at least the basics of passwords and backup data. Heading into 2020 and beyond, however, the best practices reflected in CMMC are applicable across all industries, not only those who are contracting with the federal government. Any company should be able to achieve the ML 3 guidelines and should make that their goal. Most of the benchmarks for an ML 3 rating are recommended best practices such as controlling connection of mobile devices to the network, restricting remote access, providing security awareness training to staff, and employing multifactor authentication.

To attain ML 4 or ML 5, an organization might need to allocate a little more capital for hardware to facilitate the right backups, because the more secure, higher-quality hardware comes at a higher price point. Overall, though, CMMC involves more layers of protection, greater accountability, and additional documentation.

While this level of security may not fit the budget or even make sense for every small company, every day, we find new ways to help our clients attain their compliance goals. Simple solutions like software that charges per user, instead of thousands of dollars upfront for licensing, translate to affordability for all our clients.

If your business has already been awarded a government contract, more than likely, you have at least heard of CMMC. Have you discussed your strategy with a cybersecurity specialist? Do you have the minimum two-step authentication turned on? Is anybody auditing your cybersecurity processes? When was the last time you spoke to someone about your system? Have you ever logged into your backups to see if they are successfully recording backup data because you cannot recover files that aren't there? CMMC's strength lies in documentation. A business won't be able to lie about the steps they have taken or their score and get away with it for long.

Attaining ML 4 or ML 5 will require a greater financial investment, but on the other hand, a company with those statuses is eligible for higher-level, more lucrative contracts as well. The financial commitment is one of the main reasons a business should begin the process immediately. The most pressing reason to begin today to become CMMC certified is that the lengthy and arduous process to become certified takes time because the associated documentation takes time. Companies should strive to have completed the steps for compliance early enough to be audited before the end of the year.

If you aren't certain with whom to address the daunting task of attaining CMMC, here are some recommendations based on how we approach CMMC with our clients. First, find an IT provider that is willing to make an appointment with you to come onsite, if possible, to perform an assessment. They should be looking at the simple things to begin with, like, is the place locked down? And do you need an access card to enter the building? What type of sign-in protocol is in place, if any? The IT company should want to cover all the bases. Then, they should investigate which monitors are in view in each area and whether the contents of the screen are easily seen? If the IT specialist can easily view those screens, so can everyone else.

Next, they should be estimating the age of computers. Are they outdated? Then, a good IT professional will want to evaluate the server room, making notes of any onsite servers, the brands of routers, and what firewalls, if any, are in use. They will question you to see how far along in the NIST process you are. They might ask how you are training your employees and what employee documents you maintain? Finally, they should ask to run a scan on the network to better understand any vulnerabilities of the network. Only then can an IT provider calculate a score and advise on what is needed to get your company secure and compliant with the government.

About Aaron

Aaron Wyant was brought up with a mom who had polio and kidney problems. Growing up and traveling to hospitals waiting for his mom on a weekly basis, he realized at a young age how much he wanted to help people. Aaron had to figure out how to earn money at a young age, and he would sell beach mats at age six. Then he would wash cars and sell Holiday/Birthday cards from 7-14 years old.

The year 1987 was the first time he started working on PCs. He got a computer and took the course that came with it. His friends would be playing outside while he was learning how to fix and build them. At age 14, he worked with the school district in the summers to pay for new clothes for the Fall semester. Then he worked for Red Robin from ages 16-23 and was Team Member of the Year in 1994. Then from age 18 to 23, he worked two more jobs with the restaurant job to pay for housing and his ITT College Degree. Both jobs had to do with Technology and PCs, so he learned a lot from them. After college, he worked for Banctec, fixing Dell computers and networking for the travel agencies.

Right before he started his own company, he worked with other companies in sales and PC Support and networking. With a passion for computers, and wanting to help people, he decided to work for himself starting Dispatch Tech in 2008, helping people in San Diego with their computer issues and networking problems. His favorite parts were learning how to fix things and making them work more efficiently. Installing solid-state hard drives with no moving parts for example, and teaching end-users how to protect themselves from cybercriminals. In 2018, he purchased a cybersecurity business to implement the best security for his business and his customers.

You can connect with Aaron at:
- https://dispatchtech.com/contact
- info@dispatchtech.com
- Tel: 858-344-3988

CHAPTER 22

INDUSTRY FOCUS: RESTAURANTS

BY ALEX HARB

Technology has become a critical aspect for all organizations large and small, including those centered in and around the restaurant and hospitality industry. Innovations in technology have fueled the ability for these businesses and brands to improve operations, reduce their costs, and apply technology in innovative ways to change how they connect with their patrons. And with technology advancements, there comes a significant increase in the amounts of data – payment and transaction data, customer information, and financial records, just to name a few examples. While it is no secret this data is extremely valuable to the business, it is also no secret that this same data is just as valuable to criminal hackers and bad actors who profit from abusing it if given the opportunity.

There is an onslaught of daily headlines proclaiming the latest data breaches resulting from attacks targeting both local and national brands in the sector. It's critical that we recognize and understand that no organization or business is immune to the threats they are facing today. Whether a smaller, locally-owned business or a larger multi-location franchise, the potential impact of a cyberattack or data breach is significant and relevant. From financial penalties to potential class action lawsuits or fines, there is inescapable damage for victims who suffer from such incidents. Furthermore, consider the impact on brand reputation, potential loss of customer loyalty, and other collateral consequences that cause the most damage to your bottom line following a cyberattack or data breach.

FINDING A START POINT

In the restaurant industry, the starting point for most businesses is centered around compliance with PCI (Payment Card Industry) standards. All merchants that process, store, or transmit cardholder data must comply with these standards. But it is important to note that compliance requirements may not encompass the necessary security measures to protect other aspects of your business. And compliance does not always equal security.

So, how can businesses protect themselves? Given the current and ever-evolving threat landscape, the question alone might seem like an impossible one for a business to even grasp. As cybersecurity might seem a vast or nebulous term, it is more or less the process of applying risk management principles – a fundamental most business owners understand. It is critical to understand that when it comes to risk management, it is centered around the process of mitigating a risk as opposed to eliminating a risk. See, you are never able to remove risk entirely, but you can still take steps to lessen its impact. As we cover this concept in the upcoming chapter, it's important to keep this in mind as we review ways to better secure your business.

Keep in mind the process of securing your organization, it's data and operational technology systems will be an ongoing and ever-evolving process. There is not a silver bullet or absolute answer to cybersecurity. Consider this, the process improvement programs within your organization are constantly changing and evolving as new standards are developed for improving cleanliness, or processes are instituted to enhance guest satisfaction. These programs must be adapted and reiterated to ensure a high-functioning outcome. And this is no different than your cybersecurity program. The threat landscape is an always-changing and moving target, which requires analyzing, reviewing and adjusting your various defensive security measures.

Addressing these threats can only be successful if there is a process to follow that is manageable and repeatable. To help provide such a process, industry organizations have worked to develop various standards or methodologies for businesses to follow – a framework of sorts. A framework is not a to-do list or checklist of things that must be done, but rather a guide to help how to attack the larger goal. It is designed to provide guidance that can be followed but is not necessarily a prescriptive step-by-step approach to reaching your desired goal or outcome. And a framework can be adapted and applied as appropriate to fit any size or type of business, including restaurant establishments, to help them manage and reduce cybersecurity risks. In this chapter, we'll cover the following five core functions of the popular NIST (National Institute for Standards and Technology) Cybersecurity Framework: Identify, Protect, Detect, Respond, and Recover. We'll dive deeper into each of these to help lay a path or create a cybersecurity blueprint that can be followed to protect your restaurant.

CREATING A BLUEPRINT

I. Identify

Risk management requires understanding what you are trying to protect, the risks posed in various scenarios, and then applying appropriate measures to mitigate those risks. In order to understand what requires protecting, it is important to go through the process of inventorying your information assets. Over time, most restaurant establishments will collect enormous amounts of data from various systems – POS software, online ordering platforms, mobile apps, marketing and loyalty programs, etc. Beyond operational platforms, your business may also be collecting back-office information such a financials and employee data. Identifying where data lives, the sensitivity of the data being collected, and how to securely store the data are all important questions to consider. Spending time in the identification phase is key. Without gathering actionable information, the following efforts and measures put into place may or not be effective to protect your business. You need to know what you have before you can protect it.

II. Protect

If it can be protected, then it should be. We've all heard the saying, *"An ounce of prevention is worth a pound of cure."* And while protection doesn't necessarily translate to prevention, by applying protective controls you can hopefully limit the potential for harm. Using the information gathered in the identification process, you can then begin to decide how and where to apply protective measures.

These measures should include technical controls such as: endpoint-monitoring tools to protect against malicious software, multi-factor authentication software to enforce stronger validation before accessing information resources, encryption technologies to secure the transmission of sensitive information, and the cloud-based data backups to protect against the risk of data loss. Also consider policy-based controls, which should include limiting the level(s) of system access to employees or establishing repeatable processes for applying updates/patches to information systems. Lastly, methods should be implemented for training employees in an attempt to build "human firewalls." Educating system users on how to identify or recognize attempted attacks, such as phishing, will go a long way in thwarting the success of these potential threats.

Since the majority of headlines we read regarding attacks in the restaurant industry involve breaches of payment card information, you might narrowly focus your protective measures on this area only. Unfortunately, these headlines often garner the spotlight from media outlets due to the widespread consumer and/or financial impact. However, they don't often shed insight on the destructive impact left on the business. Keep this in mind as you consider the various protective measures to deploy.

III. Detect

There is a saying in the cybersecurity community, "it's not a matter of if you will experience a cybersecurity incident, but rather when." Unfortunately, there are far too many restaurant owners and operators that feel their business is not a target. In an effort to refute this shortsighted way of thinking, security experts have hailed that there are two types of businesses today – those that have been hacked, and those that will be hacked.

Early alerting or recognition of an attack is critical, as it may give you the leg up in preventing the broader impact of an attack or cyberincident. But this requires you fully understand what you are trying to detect and, more importantly, what steps to put into action to respond. We'll address that next, but for now let's focus on detection. For most of us, we are already familiar with some of the modern-day detection techniques. Think about the physical aspects of your establishment and the systems you have in place – security alarms, smoke detectors, and food temperature sensors are just a few that may come to mind. Each of these is designed to provide an early warning indicator to allow you, the responder, to address the situation or event before it escalates further.

However, detecting something abnormal can be very hard if you don't know what is normal. To better understand this in the world of information systems, it is important to establish a "baseline" of normal activity. Once established, there are a number of different detection systems that can be put into place. Consider implementing systems and processes that allow you to establish a baseline of what normal systems look like. Then, by checking your systems at regular intervals or using automated alerting can lead to the detection of abnormal activity.

While this may seem like a lot of work, it's less costly to take steps now than to wait until an attack occurs. It has been widely reported that businesses are often notified by a third-party (their processor, for example) about a potential incident before they themselves are even aware of it. This is not a position you want to find yourself in. By using detection techniques ahead of time, you will put your business in a far better position to act when an attack does occur.

IV. Respond

As we have already covered, it is not a matter of "if", but "when" your business will face a cyberattack. While you may have been diligent in protecting your business by aligning your resources with your risks, you need to be ready to respond in a worst-case scenario.

Being prepared for a cybersecurity incident requires having a plan to follow. Furthermore, this involves having a combination of both technology tools and skilled experts to take swift action. Larger corporate establishments might have the ability to leverage shared IT/cybersecurity resources from a parent organization, but for most single-owner restaurants and franchisees, they may not have those luxuries. More likely than not, your business does not have dedicated technical staff or a team of cybersecurity experts it employs. As a result, you may want to consider partnering with a reputable, managed IT services provider with an advanced focus on cybersecurity skills with capabilities to assist your business.

Aligning these resources requires advance preparation and a detailed plan that outlines how you will respond when an incident occurs. This response plan should not be viewed as a one-time effort, and then placed on a shelf to collect dust. Instead, it is critical that your response plan is reviewed and reassessed regularly to ensure it is up-to-date – based on changes to your operating environment, technology, and evolving threat landscape.

V. Recover

Recovery focuses on planning for the inevitable. This is often referred to as business continuity and disaster planning. If (or, *when*) your restaurant suffers an attack, how will you restore systems and get them back to a normal operating state? And what will you do in the interim to continue operations while those systems are unavailable and being recovered? This requires creating contingency plans and processes. And not just creating these plans and processes, but actually testing them periodically to ensure they will function as expected.

One of the current cyberthreats posing the greatest risk to businesses over the past several years is ransomware. Ransomware attacks are particularly threatening as they attempt to maliciously encrypt your data in an attempt to then extort the business by essentially holding it hostage. Data backups have been hailed as the most effective remediation for these attacks. It is surprising, however, the number of victim organizations that either do not have good data backups or weren't prepared to actually recover from those data backups. As part of being prepared, it is critical that your recovery processes are frequently tested to ensure the plans and processes will be effective when they are needed.

Once systems are recovered, there are other important considerations to plan for. Did the cyberincident or breach result in a loss of data that triggers breach notification requirements? Are there other legal obligations, such as notifying law enforcement or other industry agencies? It is important to include this information in your plan so it is readily available for reference following a cybersecurity incident.

AN ONGOING, ITERATIVE PROCESS

As you examine these various components, keep in mind that it's a process. Think about your approach to food safety and how that has changed over the last few years. Undoubtedly, these processes have been modified and adapted as new research is released or new health standards are unveiled. We can agree it is an ongoing process. The same is probably true for food safety or cleanliness. These are never left alone, but instead are revisited as new impacts on our society are identified. Consider the global pandemic experienced this year and the changes every business made to so many of their processes. Cybersecurity is not about checking boxes and cannot be a "set-it-and-forget-it" process. Rather, cybersecurity is a continual process that you need to build into your daily operations. The threats facing your business may change, but if you remain vigilant in your approach to cybersecurity, you'll be prepared to respond accordingly.

Remember, there are no shortcuts. You may be tempted to focus more time and energy on the first two steps—Identify and Protect. While these may seem the most important, you need to be equally concerned about detecting, responding, and recovering from a cyberattack or incident. It's not a matter of if, but when.

About Alex

Alex Harb is the President and CEO of RBS IT Solutions. Headquartered in Wichita, Kansas, RBS IT Solutions provides world-class IT services and cybersecurity consulting to small and medium-sized businesses and organizations. Alex is highly-respected in the local business community, and his entrepreneurial spirit and hard work earned him the Kansas Small Business Person of the Year award in 2014.

Having years of experience in customer service and a deep-seated passion for technology, Alex has started multiple successful businesses with these core pillars as the foundation. In addition to founding RBS IT Solutions, Alex is also the creator of the fast-casual restaurant brand, Meddys, with multiple locations operating in the southeastern region of Kansas.

Alex is passionate about leveraging technology as a significant business enabler and delivering solutions that will have a profound impact on organizations. Through the years, he has learned when technology is teamed with great leadership, that which seemed impossible quickly becomes possible. Given his extensive and diverse background in information technology, cybersecurity, and the hospitality industry, Alex is well-positioned as an expert in offering critical recommendations, guidance, and best practices for this business in this sector on how to secure technology infrastructure.

Alex holds a Bachelor of Science degree in Computer Science from Wichita State University. During his free time, he enjoys reading and spending time with his family. Alex currently resides in Wichita, Kansas with his wife and their three children.

CHAPTER 23

ENGINEERING SAFER IT SOLUTIONS

BY CHARLES SWIHART

Would you prefer to be a member of the elite 20% or the 80% majority?

Your answer depends on who the members of the elite group are, right? Being part of the select group of Oscar winners might be exciting. How about being a member of a small group of lottery winners? Sure, that might positively change one's life. What about becoming a member of the elite 20% of small businesses that will suffer a cybersecurity breach this year? Hard pass. No one wants to become a member of that group.

Any business can be vulnerable to cybersecurity threats. The risks are greater for small to medium-sized businesses, as they experience 81% of network breaches. Worse still, 97% of those network breaches could have been prevented with technology that is already available.

Small to medium-sized businesses in specific industries have increased vulnerability due to the way they do business. For example, remote workers with engineering and construction firms make them an easy target. In manufacturing, the large numbers of people and equipment accessing the network offer an array of potentially open doors for cyberthieves.

Engineering and construction companies tend to employ workers at remote job sites who sometimes work there for months at a time. While they may excel in calculating loads, the strength of a foundation, and the best way to erect a multi-story building, they may be less savvy when it comes to preventing a network breach, and therefore, more vulnerable to cyberattacks. Engineers typically spend most of their time in the home office, but in the construction industry, nearly 70 percent of the workforce is in the field. In manufacturing companies, there is also the risk of attacks on remote workers, even when the CEO logs in to check email while grabbing his morning coffee on the way to the office. Of course, remote workers need to interact with office staff, sharing emails and documents.

When an employee is working in the company office on the local network, they are protected by the security infrastructure that their IT department has in place – from DNS filtering to antivirus and firewalls – but when an employee is working in a remote location, they can lose some of those protections, and their data and activity is often less protected. The engineering firm does not necessarily have a role in protecting the network at the job site. This makes it critical that any remote access into the company network from outside is carefully designed by, or at least reviewed by, a cybersecurity professional.

Even with the latest in cybersecurity protections in place on your office network, the weakest link in the company armor is the user. No amount of antivirus software and firewalls can stop a user from downloading and running malicious files or clicking on links in a phishing email.

The typical phishing email you might see today presents a scenario where you need to log-in to your email account to see a quarantined email or to respond to an administrator's alert that your email account will soon be deleted. You are instructed to click the link to log-in, and when you do, you see a website that looks legitimate but is not. When you enter your email address and password, the culprit now has that information. So, when someone tells you that their email was hacked, they are really saying that they unwittingly gave up their password and personal information directly to the "hacker" when they clicked the link in a phishing email.

Once the hacker is in your email account, he can see who you email, your calendar, and other personal information to use against you and your company. It all starts with that simple phishing email, "There's something wrong with your Microsoft account. You need to log in and change your password." Without thinking, any employee, or even the CEO, might have just clicked that link. It is not actually Microsoft, it is someone looking to profit off your company, and now he is in that email account with access to the names and titles of everyone in the company.

The case of one recent client perfectly demonstrates what can happen when someone inadvertently shares too much personal information through a phishing scheme. In this case, the company's owner clicked the link in a phishing email and unknowingly provided the hacker access. The hackers watched the company owner's calendar, and they could see that he was going to be at the dentist on a particular day and time. So, while he was in the dentist's chair, they sent an email from his email account to his comptroller that said, "Hey, I forgot to pay this vendor, here's the name and address. Send them a check." Fortunately, in this case, the controller was smart enough to know that her boss would not have sent a request like this.

However, another client wasn't so lucky. This manufacturer routinely ordered parts from China. They would receive an email when the parts had been shipped, and then they would wire the money to pay for the shipment. They received an email that said, "Your parts have been shipped, but we've changed banks, and we need you to wire the money over to our new account instead." They wired $28,000 to the wrong account, the hackers' account. By the time they discovered it, the money was gone.

How will you protect your company? A security assessment is an excellent place to start to establish a baseline for your risk and close any existing vulnerabilities. After an initial evaluation, most companies will create policies and procedures to protect the company. However, those policies are only effective if employees adhere to them.

Security awareness and employee education come next. An employer might think their engineers are too smart to click a bad link in a phishing email, but what about when a pop-up says that software needs to be updated? Will that engineer call IT and wait for them to do the update and verify its authenticity, or will he do it himself and potentially welcome ransomware into the network? Most employees in engineering, construction, and manufacturing are not cybersecurity experts. They understand the risks at a job site – they wear steel toe boots and hard hats to safeguard themselves – but they need specific instruction to protect their laptops from the enemy.

As mentioned before, remote workers represent one of the biggest vulnerabilities. Educating employees about email risks, regularly changing their passwords, and allowing only designated employees to update their software, all help in keeping a company secure. Other activities put company networks and data at risk, and they are rarely given a second thought.

An employee who is home sick with the flu might want to remote in to check emails or send that proposal they were working on the day before, right? Bosses love that. Look at that dedicated employee! The employee logs on from their PC at home on which their teenager plays video games. Now you've got a big hole into the network. When you VPN into that network, you've just brought that computer in with anything that might be on it. As IT specialists, we go to great lengths to ensure the antivirus is up-to-date on all the office computers, and now the sick employee just brought an unprotected computer onto the network. It's just dangerous. Who's knows what kind of viruses and keyboard loggers are on the home computer? A keyboard logger could be recording every keystroke, including company passwords. That home computer with no firewall protection just opened a back door for a dangerous virus or ransomware to infect the office network.

The need for protection extends beyond computers on which the employees work. We once were called in to clean up the aftermath when a company was infected with ransomware through their security camera system. The owner of the company wanted to be able to log in and monitor their security cameras. They thought, "well, it's just a security camera computer, so it won't be a big deal." However, that computer was on the network. Hackers got into it and then infected the entire network. They had to pay a sizeable ransom to regain access to their own network. People seem to be less diligent about security with their cameras because they assume no one wants or cares about the video feed, but every device connected to the network is a potential entry point for bad actors.

The two biggest cyberthreats to a company are theft of information and ransomware. Clients often think that losing proprietary or sensitive information is the worst result of a cyber-attack; however, ransomware can be an even larger threat. Ransomware locks a company out of its own network and data, forcing the company to pay for a "key" to unlock it.

How can an engineering or construction company protect its network from cyberthreats? Here are a few protections to consider:

1. Multi-factor authentication

Multi-factor authentication verifies your identity through two separate devices. For example, if an employee wanted to add their email account to their new cell phone or a new laptop, they would first enter their email address and password. The computer would then prompt for a code. That code would be texted to their cell phone or emailed to another device.

You never know what cybercriminals are after. You can't predict every possible way they might use some data. Some things that you might think are not that important might provide some valuable piece of information to a scammer. Seemingly innocuous information like an address or a middle name could be used to figure out a password and put the company computer system at risk. Companies using multi-factor authentication for log-in thwart the hackers that manage to figure out a password or two. If you're offered multi-factor authentication, use it.

2. Email encryption

Email encryption is the system your doctor might use when they send you a lab report via email. The sensitive document is not merely attached to the email. Instead, you are sent a link to log-in to a secure site where you can download the document. It is important to use a system like this to send any sensitive financial, banking, or personal information via email.

3. Next-Generation Antivirus

Not all antivirus software is created equal. The newer generation of antivirus software can prevent and reverse ransomware. Only about three of the approximately 200 antivirus companies out there do this. These new antiviruses quickly recognize ransomware, stop it, and restore the files.

4. User Training

Bring in a cybersecurity professional to conduct lunch-and-learns with your staff. They can discuss email safety and common mistakes employees make. This will promote conversation, questions and overall cybersecurity awareness in your company

5. Phish Testing

Have your IT department or MSP send phishing tests to your employees via email and review the results. You can see a detailed report showing you which users clicked the link and which provided their password. Those users can then receive more in-depth training.

There are many ways to protect a network. No tool can protect you 100% of the time, but with many tools covering different vulnerabilities, you get close. This doesn't mean you should just run out and buy the latest antivirus. To secure your company's network, you should start by understanding what it looks like today. This requires a cybersecurity assessment. Only then can you see what your weaknesses are and begin to strengthen them.

About Charles

Charles Swihart fell in love with technology as a teenager when he began writing software on a Texas Instruments TI-99A computer. He studied Engineering and Computer Science and started his Information Technology career at Bechtel in 1990, where he led AutoCAD training for Engineers and Designers both in the United States and in the Middle East.

Charles also developed applications to help AutoCAD users work more efficiently. Eventually, the focus of Charles' work moved from training and development around AUTODESK products to building software in the Oil and Gas industries to manage pipeline transactions, analyze laboratory samples, and manage well inventories.

In 2003, Charles left software development to start the Cyber Security Centric Managed IT Services firm, Preactive IT Solutions. The firm was named one of the top 501 Managed IT Service firms in the world by Channel Futures and was on the *Houston Business Journal*'s 2019 list of the 100 Fastest Growing Companies in Houston, Texas. Charles serves as a coach to other IT entrepreneurs, and was recognized as an industry leader by his peers when he was selected twice to be a finalist in the Technology Marketing Toolkit's annual "Better Your Best" competition. He won that competition in 2020 as the most profitable company in the competition.

Charles has led several Ransomware Remediation projects, and his company specializes in bringing IT Services and Cyber Security Protection to Engineering, Construction, and Manufacturing firms. With his background in Engineering, he understands the challenges these firms have and how to use technology to help.

Preactive IT Solutions manages IT systems for companies both with and without internal IT teams providing help desk, server management, cybersecurity, cloud, and backup services.

You can reach Charles Swihart at:
- http://preactiveit.com
- swihart@preactiveit.com
- (832) 944-6250

CHAPTER 24

BRING YOUR OWN DEVICE (BYOD): DEVISING A POLICY THAT WORKS

BY DEAN LAUSE

March 2020 – The world appears to be standing still…

Streets are blanketed in an eerie calm, virtually empty aside from the stray car or biker. Schools are closed and offices abandoned. Before COVID-19, only a portion of employees worked remotely. Now, 42 million Americans, about 29% of the U.S. workforce (Bloomberg), have been mandated to work from home. This is the beginning of a new "normal" as the pandemic spreads fear, uncertainty. In the blink of an eye, businesses must adapt and adjust. Bring Your Own Device (AKA, BYOD) is the practice of allowing individuals to use personal devices to perform company work. While some companies had already successfully adopted remote policies and technologies, others found themselves racing to conjure up BYOD plans overnight.

Preparations for a remote workforce can take months, if not longer, to implement. It is a challenge that becomes even more magnified when employees are abruptly expected to use personal devices for work. A lack of guidelines, education, and security measures is definitely a recipe for disaster. While the long-term effects of the current pandemic on business are unknown, it is clear organizations need to be prepared to embrace BYOD technology.

Even before the COVID-19 crisis, the BYOD market was on course to hit almost $367 billion by 2022, up from just $30 billion in 2014 (Intrado). I personally adopted the capability 25 years ago because it was clearly one of the easiest ways to finish my own work quickly and efficiently. Then, it was a convenience; today, it is a necessity. There are numerous advantages: reduced expenses, improved productivity, and greater employee satisfaction. Businesses that take advantage of BYOD practices can save at a minimum $350 a year per employee. Using portable devices for work purposes saves employees about an hour per workday, as well as improves productivity by up to 33 percent (Frost and Sullivan).

In order to implement BYOD properly, executives and IT teams need to structure a plan. That starts with understanding the proper precautions required to protect organizations from sensitive data leakage, potential lawsuits and even sabotage. BYOD definitely poses a risk to a company's network, files, phone systems, emails, and contacts. It also can threaten a host of sensitive information including human resources reports, health information, legal documents, trade secrets and even marketing lists.

Although the number of remote workers increased significantly during the pandemic and heightened the risks of fraud, threats and phishing attacks, the dangers have always been there. The formula for getting BYOD off the ground successfully is still the same – *cutting corners does no one any favors when it comes to security.*

Earlier this year, I received a frantic call from the head of a prominent law office. His firm had become accustomed to working remotely, and business was booming. He was enjoying the advantages – productivity was up, costs were down, and employees were feeling a greater sense of work-life balance. It only took a few seconds for that to change. Across town, one of its attorneys was running to an appointment while quickly sending a few emails. Suddenly, he froze and had an uneasy feeling. Did that last email go to its intended recipient? He checked his sent items and felt his knees buckle. Sure enough, that message, which contained its firm's entire customer list, had just been delivered to its biggest competitor. The fallout was tremendous. Not only did the head of IT find himself looking for a new position, but the law firm also found itself in a precarious position to re-establish trust with its clients after proprietary information had been disclosed so carelessly.

IMPLEMENTING A BYOD PLAN

As the Chief Technical Officer for Argentum IT LLC, it is my job to help companies implement BYOD strategies that work. There are four key brain-storming steps I always lead with when beginning the process of implementation.

Determine Your Needs. This is the most important item to adjudicate upfront. It is vital for companies to consider why they want BYOD in place and to examine their needs and concerns. Is it to improve workplace productivity, or is it to make a network more mobile? Whatever the reason, a BYOD policy should be designed to optimize goals and be based on a strategy.

Define What You Are Trying to Protect. There are numerous regulations (HIPAA, Dodd-Frank, Sarbanes-Oxley) that stipulate how data is stored and who has access to it. For example, for a medical or law office to be compliant, it needs to have a record of the information it has obtained, know who has access to it, and where that information is stored in the event a device is lost or stolen. The organization must also have a policy in place for wiping the device clean if the device is lost or stolen, so the PCI, HIPAA, or other compliant information stored is inaccessible to a third party.

As an IT provider, I am obligated by law to inform my clients of what the compliancy laws require and to provide the measures for protecting the data in an appropriate manner. I once onboarded an organization which stored unencrypted social security numbers in an open PDF format in its database system. I worked with the leaders to find a solution to ensure that the SSNs were masked/encrypted to be in compliance with HIPAA requirements.

Define Your Framework for Security and Assigning Protocol. Every business requires differing levels of security. Top-level security is defined as "least privileged access": the concept and practice of restricting access rights for users, accounts, and computing processes to only those resources absolutely required to perform routine, legitimate activities. In this type of restricted environment, many employees may simply have "read-only" capabilities.

You also want to create stipulations on passwords to ensure secure access to data. Most compliance requirements also require that files are encrypted at rest and in transit. Too many companies ignore or do not understand these encryption mandates. Encryption conceals files on a drive so that the data cannot be read without proper authorization.

Once these areas have been navigated, IT professionals within the organization can assist in mapping out a detailed plan.

FOUR ESSENTIAL ELEMENTS TO CONSIDER

1. SECURITY

Your mobile device policy is a place to outline the safeguards you have in place and what you reserve the right to do with them to protect the good of the company. For instance:

- **Make sure that all mobile devices are protected by a password** that meets the standards set by company's guidelines. Want to increase the chances that individuals accessing your company platform are authorized to do so? Require employees to log in with a multi-factor authentication process. This technology goes beyond the password method by asking users to enter a randomly generated code delivered via email, text, or key fob when signing in.
- **Require applications to be approved** by the company before they can be installed and used for work purposes.
- **Set limits** ensuring that only devices included in the BYOD policy, or are supported by IT, may be able to connect to the business' network.
- **Establish policies for lost devices and employee exits.** If a device is misplaced, IT detects a threat on it, or if the employee leaves the company, have a rule in place that the company can wipe that device remotely to protect company data. In most cases, prior to this happening, an employee will receive a 'click-through agreement' from a network administrator, along with a prompt, requiring them to hit "ok" before the action can take place. Make sure to include that all devices that are lost or stolen need to be reported to IT within 24 hours and the mobile carrier should be notified immediately.

- **Institute clear guidelines** dictating the terms by which employees are allowed to use their personal devices. What is acceptable on company time versus what is never acceptable, e.g., storing illegal materials, accessing certain websites, or conducting harassment? Which employees require remote access and what are the ways in which that access can be granted, i.e., is there specific data that should only be accessible from the office?

2. PRIVACY

When it comes to instituting these guidelines, the issue of privacy inevitably comes up. For the most part, when a personal device is placed on a company network, employees are handing employers control. Do not assume that personal emails, photos, and various applications will remain private. It comes down to this, "How concerned are you with your personal privacy?" If the answer is "very," consider having two devices, with one solely dedicated for business use. Some companies will even issue a floater that the employee will be responsible for answering and maintaining during the week. I will say, most BYOD policies are considerate of the employee, and the people that run mobile device platforms do not have the time nor the desire to go through personal information. It's basically a decision of how much trust the employee is willing to give the employer and vice versa.

3. UPDATES

Another area where employers walk a fine line is telling employees what they can and cannot do with their own personal devices, such as mandating system updates. Employees should always supply the latest security updates to make their devices less vulnerable to attack but authorizing them to do so can feel like an infringement. If employers don't want to include this point in the BYOD policy, at least make it a provision that the employee will be liable if data is stolen as a result of their device not being kept current.

4. EDUCATION

One final, but vital point I want to stress when setting up a BYOD policy, is to make sure everyone in the office is educated on the policies and restrictions. **If employees don't understand, have the ability to ask questions, or know which questions to ask, the**

policies put in place are going to fail. Make certain employees are comfortable having an open dialogue and are kept up-to-date properly. This rule not only applies to BYOD, but to the entire IT world as a whole. For example, one of the accountants at a firm we work with was told "never question the boss." He ended up transferring $50,000 to an individual who turned out to be phishing. Needless to say, that money was gone. There were numerous instances, prior to this happening, where I warned such an incident could happen, and had even laid out an email/phishing education plan for a nominal fee totaling around $1,200. Obviously, the business owner decided not to spend the money on the $1200 education phishing-awareness program, believing it unnecessary. Do the math and it's easy to see that decision cost his organization greatly.

Threats change on a daily basis. Assuming that your employees are smart and that they know what they're doing on all levels is risky. The world is always changing and, as they say, knowledge is power. In that vein, it is also important to keep BYOD policies fluid.

The needs included in a BYOD policy today may be different than those required in six months to a year, so arrange to have policies reviewed annually. Evaluate the items that are still applicable, find any holes in the network that may not have been addressed, and determine any elements needing to be loosened or strengthened. The policies put in place should protect both the employer and the employee, be addressed upfront, and be incorporated into employee manuals, contracts, and/or orientation pamphlets. Wording such as, "any employee who uses their mobile device does so, knowing that it signifies their consent to the Acceptable Use Policy, and their intention to abide by it," is also helpful to include.

VDI ACCESSIBILITY

Technology giants like Citrix and its cloud computing service, are looking into making VDI (Virtual Desktop Infrastructure) more accessible to businesses and consumers while Microsoft and VMware are following closely behind. There are individual providers that are providing virtual desktops or hosted virtual infrastructures and are a great option for companies hoping to achieve the ability to run anywhere-anytime securely. It offers almost exclusive control over data, because, if set up properly, all that occurs is the transfer of screen data back and forth – making it impossible for employees to walk out the door and take company data with them. Additionally, there's no chance of employee devices infecting an office network. Of course, without the appropriate policies in place, virtual desktops are just as vulnerable to data loss as any other system.

THE FUTURE OF MDM

As cloud and BYOD become more utilized, the lines between business and personal use are going to become increasingly blurred and laws are going to be tested. Currently, the reality is that you can access company data from virtually anywhere in the world using an application like Office 365, Cloud-based ERP (Enterprise Resource Planning) solutions and other web-based applications such as SalesForce or ConnectWise. There are some tools that are coming down the pipeline to help segregate data on mobile devices.

Apple has been on the front line with their MDM (Mobile Device Management) program, which they rolled out in the summer of 2019. This option is meant to protect sensitive corporate data and manage the software and settings available to users, while allowing users' private personal data to remain separate from IT oversight.

Android is also compartmentalizing with Mobile Device Management capable only of accessing data that was pushed out by the corporate environment. The tools are becoming more mature as major companies see the need, but we're not fully functioning to the point where users can completely separate corporate and personal data. For example, I can encrypt data on my iPhone, but there's no way to segregate that data to where an individual can use an encryption key on one part of a phone and not another.

CONCLUSION

In the end, the most successful BYOD policies are adaptable and fluctuate with our times and technological capabilities. It is never a bad idea to consult a managed service provider with professional IT technicians on staff, but regardless, always exercise due diligence and use common sense. There's really no such thing as a completely "secured connection" anymore. The most secure computer is the one that's locked away in a closet without network access. If you are working on something that you don't want the world to see, don't do it on an open Wi-Fi connection. If you've taken reasonable care to ensure that your device has current firewall and malware software, the chances of getting hacked are there but greatly minimized. If you receive a warning that your machine is being scanned, disconnect it from the network/WiFi. I've seen people ignore the warnings and continue to click. Technology cannot protect you from that kind of behavior. Read, be vigilant, install updates and educate your employees. Those will serve as your greatest tools.

About Dean

Dean Lause is a technologist to the highest degree. When he was in middle school, he learned and developed small programs using BASIC programming code on his Commodore 64. He was one of the first to post to bulletin boards on the newly-emerging "Internet" and built a mini-network in his home. He competed in his senior year of high school in computer specialist competitions, placing 1st regionally, 2nd in state and 17th nationally. Today, he enjoys technology as much as he did then. In fact, he has a "Smart Home," with connected devices controlled by AI, mobile apps, and voice commands. When he is ready to go to sleep, all he needs to say is "Good night," and Voila! all of the lights in the entire house turn off, the doors lock, the TV/DVR turn off, the house alarm is set and the alarm clock for the morning is ready to go!

After a 4-year stint in the Army as a computer specialist, Dean spent the next 20 years in Fortune 500 Enterprise IT environments. He quickly built his IT skill set, becoming an expert in VMWare, Citrix, and other various technologies. Dean served as the Director of Network Infrastructure & Security of North American Operations in his last role, before joining Argentum IT and completing his MBA with a specialty in Accounting in 2011. Dean understands not only the technical side of how devices work together and integrate within an environment, but also understands and designs the environment from a business point of view for productivity. He strives to provide cost-savings, efficiency, and practicality to solve the real issues that are present for each individual client he works with.

Leveraging his 20+ years' of enterprise-level experience, for the past ten years, Dean has consulted with numerous Fortune 500 companies across the country on issues relating to network infrastructure and security, Citrix XenDesktop, VMWare implementation and capacity planning, Office 365/Exchange Email Migrations as well as Mobile Device Management and Disaster Recovery Planning. He has also been engaged to develop and improve technology processes as well as accomplish technology projects on time and budget.

Today, Dean uses all of these skills and more to aid small to medium-sized businesses to utilize technology to run their companies more profitably and efficiently. As Chief Technical Officer of Argentum IT, LLC for the past ten years, Dean has supervised a proactive service desk which educates clients on technology best practices, designed multiple infrastructure environments for clients (both big and small), to fit their needs and built a sizeable hosted infrastructure environment – utilizing VMWare and Citrix products.

Dean's breadth of experience affords him a unique view of IT and business challenges, which allows him to help customize and develop unique solutions to solving IT and Cybersecurity challenges.

When he is not tinkering with IT, Dean enjoys dancing West Coast Swing and traveling.

You can connect with Dean at:
- https://www.linkedin.com/in/deanlause/
- dean@lause.net
- https://lause.net/

CHAPTER 25

PCI COMPLIANCE

BY JAMES EVANS

In 2006, the PCI Security Standards Council was founded by American Express, Discover, JCB International, MasterCard and Visa Inc. "PCI" stands for Payment Card Industry. The Council has developed the PCI DSS (Data Security Standard) which defines technologies, policies, and processes that protect payment systems. PCI DSS applies to **ALL** entities that store, process, and/or transmit cardholder data.

So, this is security? Not exactly. Compliance and security aren't quite the same thing. You can be compliant with the PCI DSS today, and out of compliance tomorrow. A good information security program will incorporate the requirements of PCI DSS into the organization's day-to-day operations, thereby keeping it compliant. PCI DSS is only concerned with payment card data, while your organization likely has other data that needs to be protected as well. Thus, compliance with PCI DSS is only one component of a complete information security program.

Why should you care? Generally, each card brand has its own PCI compliance program, many of which leave basic enforcement in the hands of the acquirer (merchant bank). When a business opens a merchant account with a bank/acquirer, it will inevitably be asked about its PCI compliance status. Failure to comply can lead to fines and eventually, the inability to process further credit card transactions. While specific fines are not published, it has been widely reported that normal fines range from $5,000 to $100,000 per month. PCI DSS provides a baseline security standard to protect the credit card information a company collects, processes, and/or transmits. As these credit cards belong to your customers, protecting customer data is just an all-around good thing to do. You should also care about liability. Becoming PCI compliant limits your liability in case of a breach.

"We're just a small company. Nobody is going to bother hacking us." Being a smaller organization makes you a bigger target. Hackers expect small organizations to have more resource constraints, and therefore, weaker security programs. This makes small companies a softer target, easier to compromise, and thus, less effort for the hackers to get their payday. That said, PCI DSS is not one-size-fits-all. The Council recognizes that some parts of the DSS just don't fit some organizations.

Small businesses with simple dial-out credit card terminals, like the standard ones that connected to a phone line and dialed a specific number to process, are becoming increasingly rare. Modern credit card machines are connected to the network and are using the Internet for processing. Even restaurants that traditionally had the simplest of transactions increasingly have converted to more advanced point of sale systems, with multiple terminals where servers can input orders. The orders automatically show up on a terminal in the kitchen. Later, when the customer pays for their meal, the server takes the credit card to one of those terminals, swipes it, and all that information is now on the network. Somewhere in the back, a manager pulls a report on what's going on that night. You might also have the head chef looking at what his food costs are for the night. All that activity happens in real-time while cardholder data resides in that system. We need to protect it, that is why PCI is a serious consideration.

1. Determine

Once you have decided to become PCI compliant, you first must determine what "level" merchant you are. Merchants are categorized into four levels based on their transaction volume and breach history:

- *Level One* merchants have over 6 million transactions annually or any merchant that has had a data breach. That's right, if you've had a breach, you go straight to the top.
- *Level Two* merchants process between 1 million and 6 million transactions annually.
- *Level Three* merchants conduct between 20 thousand and 1 million **online** transactions annually.

■ *Level Four* consists of merchants with less than 20 thousand online, or 1 million total transactions annually.

2. Select

Second, you must select the correct form for compliance reporting for your organization. Levels Two, Three and Four may complete a self-assessment questionnaire (SAQ) as part of their attestation of compliance. Level One merchants must submit an annual Report on Compliance (ROC) prepared by a Qualified Security Assessor (QSA). Obtaining an ROC (as required after a breach) could easily cost a company $50,000. All levels must also receive quarterly network scans performed by an Approved Scanning Vendor (ASV). QSA and ASV are certifications issued by the Council. Due to the cost of these certifications and their highly specialized use in the industry, a typical IT shop will not have QSAs on their staff.

Assuming your company is Level Two through Four, there are eight self-assessment questionnaires. The correct questionnaire will be determined by how your organization stores, processes, and/or transmits cardholder data. For example, Form B is for merchants that use only imprint machines and/or standalone dial-out terminals with no electronic data storage. Of the eight questionnaires, six refer to specific cases in which there is no electronic data storage on-site and no e-commerce business. Form A is for e-commerce in which all functions are outsourced with no data storage on-site. Everything else falls under Form D.

3. Complete

The third step is to complete the form. This is where I recommend you seek assistance. While PCI DSS has twelve formal requirements, Form D (as of this writing) is an 86-page document. Each requirement has a lengthy set of questions. If you answer "No" to any question, you are not compliant. Therefore, it is imperative to have a thorough understanding of each question, including the intent and method(s) of testing, to determine the correct answer. Fortunately, each question requires a yes-or-no response. It is also important to capture evidence supporting each answer and keep this in a file for future reference. Your IT staff, IT service provider, or Managed Service Provider (MSP) will have to answer many of the questions;

however, not all IT professionals have the expertise and experience to understand the meaning and intent of these questions fully. It is vital to choose an IT provider, MSP, or consultant with significant PCI DSS specific experience. Unfortunately, many people claim to be experts, but most have only a rudimentary understanding or worse.

The twelve PCI DSS requirements include:

1. Install and maintain a firewall configuration to protect cardholder data.
2. Do not use vendor-supplied defaults for system passwords and other security parameters.
3. Protect stored cardholder data.
4. Encrypt transmission of cardholder data across open, public networks.
5. Protect all systems against malware and regularly update anti-virus software or programs.
6. Develop and maintain secure systems and applications.
7. Restrict access to cardholder data by business need-to-know.
8. Identify and authenticate access to system components.
9. Restrict physical access to cardholder data.
10. Track and monitor all access to network resources and cardholder data.
11. Regularly test security systems and processes.
12. Maintain a policy that addresses information security for all personnel.

For example, requirement one currently contains 27 sub-questions concerning processes for making firewall changes, existence of network diagrams and other documentation, firewall security policy, firewall configuration and deployment specifics, and requirements for periodic review of all the above. It is not possible to look at the text of requirement 1: "Install and maintain a firewall configuration to protect cardholder data." and say, "Oh yeah, we have a firewall." and move on. A "No" to any of the 27 questions means you are not compliant.

Sample question 1.3.3: Are anti-spoofing measures implemented to detect and block forged sourced IP addresses from entering the network?

Most people don't know what this question means or how to test for it. Get help, and not from just anyone. If you have an IT provider or if you are hiring someone to assist you, ask about their prior experience. Ask them, "Have you worked with a Level Three merchant?" Question their credentials in the same manner you would if you were hiring a general contractor to make renovations to your home. If you were hiring a contractor, you would ask for recommendations, you would take a look at before and after photos of their work, you would request their license number and you might even contact the Better Business Bureau to see if any complaints have been lodged against them. Due diligence will pay off if you do the same with your PCI compliance.

4. Remediate

The fourth step is remediation. For any "No" response on your compliance form, you must come up with a plan to resolve that problem to become compliant. In some cases, there are easy fixes. For example, many organizations lack proper documentation of existing policies. Simply creating the documentation may be all that's required to remediate this type of problem. In other cases, complying with PCI DSS can require substantial remediation, which can literally change the way your company does business. If you're in this boat, don't be alarmed. Your business will be in a better position when you're done.

Get help. Just as it's important to have the right expertise to understand the questions, it's even more important to have the right skill set when it comes to planning and implementing solutions, especially the technical ones. While often helpful, it is not necessary to use the same people to remediate that helped fill out the questionnaire. In some cases, it may be advantageous to separate these teams as it provides some measure of checks and balances. While the bulk of PCI DSS is technical in nature, some accounting firms have taken on the assessment phase (filling out the questionnaire). Even if they do a great job in this regard, you probably don't want the accountants doing surgery on your network, configuring firewalls, and setting up backups.

Again, it may be helpful to think in terms of the general contractor remodeling your home. He can take down the wall, move the plumbing and remodel the kitchen. However, if when he takes down the wall he locates an old pipe that had been leaking that has caused mold to form, he might step aside and let the mold remediation team clean up the damage before the walls get closed up again. When dealing with fixes in the PCI remediation stage, success depends on using the right tools for the job.

5. Maintain

The final step in PCI Compliance is maintenance. You're at the end of the road. You've fixed all the "No" responses and now every question is answered with a "Yes." You're compliant at last! So, you're done, right? Not so fast.

As previously stated, "You can be compliant with the PCI DSS today, and out of compliance tomorrow." A good information security program will incorporate PCI DSS into day-to-day operations, keeping you compliant. Compliance is a state that is measured at a single point in time; you must maintain that state. Internally, when you make changes to the network, when you install a new server for example, you must scan the network to ensure you are still compliant.

If you didn't have a formal Information Security policy before starting the PCI DSS compliance process, you have one now. After all, that is the twelfth requirement. Now your job is to adhere to it. Review and update all policies, procedures, and documentation as needed. Perform regular, annual self-assessment for risk. Have your ASV perform quarterly network scans. Test your Wi-Fi annually. Periodically review the questionnaire and re-evaluate your answers depending on how your business changes over time. Stay on top of things. It is far simpler to maintain compliance once attained than to let things slide and be forced to start over.

About James

James Evans protects his clients from disasters and cyberthreats while keeping their business operations running smoothly and efficiently.

James started down the road towards an IT career in 1983 with a Radio Shack Color Computer, transitioning into the IBM PC world in 1988. Later, he would share his knowledge by helping people who were new to computers with basic PC setup and operation, often providing this assistance at no cost to help those who needed to learn basic computer skills. An avid user of local Bulletin Board Systems (BBSs), he predicted the future importance of online services and began writing new BBS software. The goal of this new software was to expand these online "islands" into a much larger community, a precursor to the modern Internet. In 1993, James began incorporating fledgling internet technology into the project, but by late 1995 phased-out the BBS entirely in favor of becoming a dedicated Internet Service Provider (ISP.)

He transitioned out of the ISP business in early 1998. Subsequent roles at new companies, including at two private R&D labs, a dot-com, and an e-healthcare SaaS provider, presented him with exciting new challenges. These paths took him through the worlds of intellectual property, software and hardware engineering, and compliance. During this period, he was charged with the protection of millions of patient records and millions of dollars in credit card transactions.

Always creating with a passion and with an eye towards future advancement of technologies, James has had 37 patents issued by the United States Patent and Trademark Office. In his work, James created early Wi-Fi products, multi-tenant high-density routers, and specialty server hardware designs, while pioneering today's modern e-commerce and e-healthcare applications.

After more than a decade of building companies for others, in January 2011, James decided to return focus to his own company, American Frontier. True to his history and experience, the mission was simple: bring IT functionality typically reserved for "big companies" to small and medium-sized businesses. From assisting people with basic PC setup and operation in the late 1980s to managing corporate networks and protecting businesses from cyberthreats today, the theme of helping others navigate sophisticated technologies and murky tech-speak to find real solutions has been clear and consistent for decades.

James and his team at American Frontier are located in Apex, NC, and primarily serve the Raleigh/Durham, Research Triangle, and surrounding areas of North Carolina. American Frontier is a Managed Services Provider which also operates a Disaster

Recovery and Business Continuity facility to help business owners get operational again after the worst disasters. Assisting others and being a community partner, the company routinely gives back to that community by making meeting space available to local organizations for various events. This includes public events, such as business networking, educational, and health and wellness gatherings, as well as private events, such as meetings and training classes.

You can contact James at:
- www.amfrontier.net
- 919-741-5468
- https://www.linkedin.com/in/evansjames/

CHAPTER 26

DO YOU KNOW WHAT YOU HAVE, AND WILL YOU KNOW IF IT CHANGES?

BY JAY FERRON

If you don't know what's on your network today, how will you know what has changed if you get hacked? You won't. If you don't know the configurations of your machines and which machines are working, how will you know what's changed? Do you know what's in your server room? Do you have a diagram of how everything connects? If today, you don't know precisely what hardware and apps your business utilizes, which versions of those apps are running, and how and why the network is configured the way it is, your business could be in trouble. In the event of a disaster, you will need to rebuild. No baseline means no blueprint to reconstruct what you had. How will you get to know what you've got?

If you don't know the details of your server configuration or if your version of QuickBooks is up to date, you are not alone. Many small to medium companies don't know their configurations because nobody bothers to document it. They have no idea what the server configuration is supposed to be; therefore, they won't know if they've been hacked. Two hundred days later—when the breach is discovered—the risk to the business will have compounded.

It's easy to see how this can happen. A small to medium-sized business probably doesn't care about what their computers do or how they are configured. They just need their applications. Most of the time, they hire somebody to set up their system and expect that person to know what they installed. Maybe they hire a managed service provider that is also a security specialist to document those settings. They might just pick up the phone when something breaks.

You might think that large companies always know what's going on with their networks because they have IT departments handling those issues. Realistically, however, the larger the company, the more users and workstations they have, and the harder it is for anyone to keep track of what they've got. Who should be tracking it? Generally, it's either the IT department, if they have one, or the security vendor if the company has hired somebody to manage that. With any size company, the same foundational security rules apply:

1. **Understand, prioritize, and manage what you have.**
2. **Patch and update when necessary.**
3. **Get rid of anything you no longer need.**

Locking valuables in a safe isn't of any value if you cannot prove what was in the safe if someone breaks in. No cybersecurity efforts will be worthwhile without an inventory. If you don't do this, I don't care what you do in security, you're still going to be vulnerable. Even if you do all your patching and everything else, you won't know what's there. Here's a technical example: DNS works on port 53. If I installed a piece of malware software on your computer that gave me remote access and I connect it to port 53, would you say, "Oh, that's just DNS" and forget it, or would you say, ""Wait a minute, DNS wasn't running here. What's running here? That's a hole that somebody got access to."" That's the mindset that I'm trying to drive. Knowledge is power.

When hackers gain access or when computers are compromised, typically, there are two types of compromises. One is ransomware, in which they encrypt all of a company's files. In the other, a hacker breaks in—potentially even a nation such as China, Iraq, North Korea, or Russia—trying to harvest information. However, once somebody breaks in, they become what's called an advanced persistent threat. What that means is they give themselves ways to come back and forth. So, if you plug the first hole, there are other holes where they can get in. They can go back and forth in that network as much as they want, whenever they want. If I'm a hacker, I am going to make a hole in the network, and it's going to be a service, a port, or something that's open, which is going to allow me to connect to it. If a business doesn't know what it has and how its network is configured, how will it know what I've added there?

It isn't unheard of for hackers to be in a network for nearly a year before somebody figures out what's going on. That's a long time for somebody to have access to your company's data. Businesses must start thinking about what they have, what they need, how it's configured, and what to do if that changes. You can't have proper security without answering those questions.

Your primary business might not focus on the network or the server. If you own a catering company, your primary focus is probably on food, clients, and the equipment in your commercial kitchen; however, if you own a server, you have it for a reason. The server houses the information for the thousands of clients whose events you host annually. What value do you place on those records? Without your client records, all the accouterments of food preparation will be completely unnecessary.

Building on the catering company example, if someone recalibrated the oven you use to prepare catered meals so it was 50 degrees hotter than normal, you would want to know that information because that's your business line. If you didn't know and suddenly somebody changed it, that would be a big issue, right? You could burn thousands of meals, losing revenue and, potentially, the clients who trusted you to do the job correctly.

Every business needs a baseline for the system so that they know 'what' and 'where' everything is. Take an inventory of the hardware, the software, and the configurations, so you can say, ""Okay, wait a minute, something is not right.""

A cybersecurity professional needs to know what you have before they can protect what you have. So, the first thing they should do when a business calls with a problem is to take an inventory of their network to find out what is there: what services they have, what they are doing, and why they are doing it. Do they have an application they haven't used in ten years that is still talking to the internet? Maybe that needs to be eliminated. Only after an inventory can you make intelligent choices. When your car breaks down, the mechanic runs a diagnostic test on the vehicle to see what it says and proceeds from there. That's the recommended approach for cybersecurity as well.

If you don't know what you have, you're not thinking about it, patching it, updating it, or managing it. This increases the risk to the business because the more issues that it has that are not managed or understood, the more vulnerabilities it has, and the easier it is for somebody to attack it. Potential security issues begin the minute the system is installed. The operating system and driver updates are regularly released, and a missed update equals a hacker opportunity. Update notifications are like car recall notifications. If you received a recall notice from your auto manufacturer that said there's a problem with your car's steering wheel assembly and it could randomly fall off, would you drive your car? Probably not. However, if you never paid attention to the recall notice to know that you have a problem with your car, you're an accident waiting to happen.

Simple inconsistencies can result in significant cybersecurity issues. I recently serviced a customer whose small business had several seemingly trivial issues. The software was stored on computers, not a server. Everyone had administrative privileges. One employee had Adobe Photoshop Version 1, and somebody else had Adobe Photoshop Version 3. No one considered the possible vulnerabilities in Photoshop Version 1. Understandably, people are busy working the business that they run, and they're not thinking about if Windows is regularly updating on every machine, if the antivirus is updating, or if the backup is working.

A business might add an external hard drive to the laptop, and make it backup files to that hard drive. That sounds reasonable, except if you get ransomware, it's also going to take down the hard drive to which you backup files, right? From the hacker's perspective, if he can find a hole that's well known that the business hasn't patched, why should he work harder to break in when he could work smarter and easier? If he can exploit the vulnerabilities of the old version of Photoshop, he can waltz right into all the files backed up on the external hard drive too.

So, exploited holes in any system can lead to disaster. A recent example in the news involved Android cell phones. Android phones that are two years old, or older, have a security hole in them. They are unpatched—most carriers don't patch the phones—so there are over a million Android phones with this glitch—any hacker can direct the user to a webpage and take over the phone. Now, you're probably saying, ""So what? It's just my phone?"" Oh, but the phone is also your contact list. It's your email. It's probably the same password you use to log in to social media and half of your credit cards. How about if the hacker just downloads your phonebook and then sends an email to your boss telling him that you quit?

To be fair, the same can be said of a PC, a Mac, and a Linux machine. It doesn't make a difference which tools you're using. If you have an inventory of what you have and how it should function, then you can prioritize based on the risks of the organization and take care of those things that are critical and not worry about those things that are minor. Once you know what you have, then you can say, "Okay, what's the most critical thing to my business? What are the risks of that thing? How do I protect that thing?" Sadly, too often, people go the other way around and try to fix all the little patches first, when some of those might be minor, instead of addressing the critical issues first. It makes sense to methodically prioritize and address the concerns after a risk assessment with a security professional.

Even devices like printers have vulnerabilities. Older network protocols that once facilitated communication between devices require upgrading to current protocols. Older ones still in use could allow a bad actor to access the buffer overflow attached to a printer and use that to gain access to the data on the printer. If that printer has a hard drive storing frequently used documents, etc., as many of the larger models do, essential data could be stored on it. Do you know what's stored on the printer in your office? If the service technician must replace the old hard drive, would you know what information he could be carrying out of the building if he takes the old hard drive with him?

Knowing what you have is critical, so you can say with certainty, "Wait a minute, you can work on my printer, but I won't allow you to leave the building with a storage device. You can replace it, but you can't take the old one away with you because I'm worried about my confidential data." A doctor's office, a law firm, and a small financial organization all have regulations with which to comply, but they don't think about the risk of a printer on their network.

Know your risk. *Risk equals asset-with-value x(times) threats x(times) vulnerabilities.* Once you find a risk, there are only four things you can do.

- One, deny the risk. If you're not jumping out of an airplane, it doesn't matter whether the parachute works.
- Two, share transfer the risk. Auto insurance is an example of share transfer. You have auto insurance so that if you get in an accident, the insurance company will pay for a percentage of my damage.
- The third option is to reduce the risk to an acceptable level. You will never eliminate all risks, but you can minimize the risk to an acceptable level.
- What's leftover, the fourth option, is residual risk? How can you make those decisions, those risk decisions, around your computer, network, and phone infrastructure unless you know what you've got? You can't.

Sometimes the simplest services can create serious risk. Take the office phone, for instance. Do you have a traditional landline or VoIP? If you cannot answer that question, that could become a problem. If it is VoIP, it is connected through the network to the internet. What are the holes? Is the VoIP secure or not? Do we need a patch? I've had clients say to me, "What do you mean you need to patch our telephones?" Well, they are network devices now, so they need security patches. What is the risk to your business if somebody can get in and take call manager down, preventing employees from conducting business?

When providing cybersecurity, I begin with a simple investigation into the network for IP addresses or services that are running. That tells me how many computers a business has. Sometimes, they may not even know where their computers are. When I scan the network for hardware, then I locate the servers.

It is certainly possible, especially in larger organizations, that hardware goes missing. While inventorying at a client's office, I asked, "Where's the Novell file server?" The owner looked at me, puzzled, and said they no longer had a Novell server. However, there was a Novell server currently online. I asked to speak to the employee who had been there the longest and asked him, "Did you have a server called Nile, because it's still running?" He denied that was possible but eventually directed me to where there used to be a room that housed that server. We walked around the walls, but we couldn't see anything. We finally poked our heads up in the drop ceiling and looked down, and in the middle of what used to be a closet was a server sitting on the floor. It was still running. Talk about skeletons in the closet.

Do you know what's still running on your network? Learn what you have. Identify the risks to the business. Rank those items from most critical to least critical and address them in that order. Address them in that order because most companies don't have an unlimited budget for their cybersecurity. You prioritize because you might have the budget to fix thirty little things or one critical thing in your business. The most critical thing to the business is what you should address first.

About Jay

Jay Ferron is the founder of Interactive Security Training, LLC. Interactive Security Training has been in business for over 30 years, with the goal of helping customers to secure business and company data. Interactive Security Training listens to customer's needs, helps them develop solutions, implements those solutions, and then trains staff to maintain those solutions. Interactive Security Training customers include Cigna Insurance, Travelers Insurance, Microsoft, Rogers Communications, AT&T, US Marine Corps, US Air Force, US Army, and Defense Information Systems Agency. Other customers include banks, government agencies, health agencies, and service providers.

Jay Ferron is a multi-certified Information Security Subject-Matter-Expert (SME) with more than 40 years of professional experience, including Security & Compliance, Integration and Transformation Initiatives, IS Management Process and Operational Metrics Definition and Documentation. Jay's extensive certifications include: CDPSE, CEHI, CISSP, CHFli, COBIT, C)PTEi, CISM, CRISC, CVEi, MCITP, MCSE, MCT, MVP, & NSA-IAM.

Jay has written over 19 technical courses for Microsoft, Global Knowledge, and others. Jay is quoted in *Channel Pro*, a reseller publication, and his blog is at: https://www.channelpronetwork.com/blog/231/Jay-Ferron. Jay is a Microsoft MVP and President of the Connecticut chapter of ISACA. Jay is also Co-Director of the NY Metro Joint Cyber Security Conference (NYMJCSC.org). NYMJCSC is now in its seventh year—featuring keynote speakers, educational panels, and sessions aimed at various aspects of information security and technology.

Jay's blog is: http://Blog.mir.net, and you can find information about the conference at: http:// nymjcsc.org.

You can connect with Jay and his team at:
- 203-675-8900
- Info@interactivesecuritytraining.com
- www.interactivesecuritytraining.com

CHAPTER 27

IS MY PASSWORD GOOD ENOUGH?

EIGHT PASSWORD TIPS TO KEEP YOUR DATA SAFE

BY JEFF JOLL

ABOUT PASSWORDS

Though their demise has been predicted for years, passwords are here to stay, at least for the immediate future. Somewhere in the early-2000s, Bill Gates predicted the demise of the traditional password, because he knew of the security flaws. Passwords weren't up to the challenge of keeping important information genuinely secure. And yet even today, our digital lives are heavily reliant on the passwords and codes we choose to keep our data safe.

With all of the services and sites we access online today, we mostly operate from a state of being logged in. Whether that's to access our account information, files stored in the cloud, or even preferences, our internet life is highly personalized. We are all inundated with a need for passwords. I, personally, have hundreds across just as many sites and services.

How can we best deal with the fact that we need secure logins for so many different uses? As we continue to create and maintain accounts, how do we best keep our lives and businesses secure?

IS MY PASSWORD GOOD ENOUGH?

Chances are it's been a while since you gave the passwords you use much thought. For most people, it's easy enough to meet the minimum requirements, opting for passwords with words or numbers that we can easily remember. When forced to change them, most people are guilty of changing only a character or two. And when we do have to create a new account and password on a site, a majority of us are probably guilty of using the same or a similar one that has been used elsewhere, perhaps even on a banking site.

The way we use passwords (and password requirements) today isn't the most elegant solution, but given technological factors and user challenges, using them is ubiquitous with going online today. When we are asked to create a password, we are forced to comply (or not use the given website or service). Most of us pick an old standby favorite, with a subtle variation that will meet the requirements of the site. We have it memorized, write it down, or save it to the site or browser and move on with our day. But by doing so, we're incredibly vulnerable to fraud, hacking, and phishing.

I know, passwords are a pain. But, think about it this way, what is really at stake here? Have you ever spent the afternoon locked out of your bank account? What would the ramifications be if your passwords were breached?

What if someone suddenly had access to your business bank accounts, and all your funds were transferred to an offshore account? Would your business survive? Imagine having to notify your employees, your customers, your vendors, and your family that you were out of business because your bank accounts were hacked. All because you used a wimpy password that was easy for you to remember.

So, how can you ensure that your passwords are the safest and most secure? My recommendation is to use a combination of the following methods:

1. **Use a password manager**
2. **Use long passwords**
3. **Never save passwords in your browser**
4. **Don't reuse passwords**

5. Never send passwords in plain text
6. Change your passwords
7. Make your secret questions "secret"
8. Enable multi-factor authentication wherever possible

Let's dive into each of these recommendations, how they work, and why I encourage you to employ them.

PASSWORD MANAGERS

There are countless benefits of using a password manager. Probably the most obvious advantage of a password manager is that you don't have to remember the long, complex passwords you are going to use. You can also use a password manager to generate complex and unique passwords for you. Most password managers work by using a combination of strong encryption algorithms, multi-factor authentication, and a local-only encryption (which means your data is kept secret at the device level). There are various password managers out there, including LastPass, 1Password, Dashlane, and BitWarden. The trick for most of these password managers is that you'll need to be able to come up with—and remember—one strong password. This single password to a password manager is how all other accounts stay secure and safe, so choose wisely.

I believe in the importance of password managers so much that I started including one in the basic security offering we provide to our clients. There are plenty to choose from that range from free to a nominal fee for more advanced features or multiple users.

I use LastPass personally, and I use it to store a lot more than just passwords. You can use it to store crucial encrypted information, such as building codes, passport numbers, and other valuable content you want to keep safeguarded.

One final note on password managers: be sure to implement all of the security features that you can, in order to keep your password manager secure. While a password manager keeps you and your passwords secure from various threats, you still must ensure no one can get into your computer and gain access to your password manager. Precautions include having a strong and secure password, utilizing biometric features (such as using your fingerprint), and routine or automatic logging out of the site after a certain amount of time.

LONG PASSWORDS

We've all experienced a site that refuses to accept a weak or short password. These are usually "guessable" names or words, and easy number combinations. Wherever possible, passwords should be long and complex.

If you aren't using a password manager to generate long random passwords, or you want one that you have a decent chance of remembering, my approach is to think of memorable phrases and word combinations. From there, I suggest that you vary the password using special characters, numbers, capitals, and lowercase characters.

Here's one example: Say I needed a password for a bank account where I had a loan payment, I might start with the thought, "This is my worst nightmare." From there, I might come up with the following: *$Th1z!sMyWURSTN1ghtmar3*.

Using just brute force, it would likely take years to crack this password. The longer and more varied the contents of your password are (such as special characters, numbers, lowercase, and uppercase), the more secure it is.

CHANGING PASSWORDS

One of the "best" practices that had been around for years likely contributed to the use of weak passwords, and those were the policies that required people to change their password every 30, 60, or 90 days. By requiring the password to change so often, people would pick any easy password and just add or change a single character, which really isn't much of a change at all. I recommend making updates or changes to your password in the following cases:

- You've had the same password(s) for more than one year.
- You suspect there was malware on your device.
- An online service where you have an account reveals they had a security incident.

- You shared your password with an individual, and you no longer want that person to access your accounts or services.
- You suspect that there was unauthorized access to your account.
- You logged into an account on a public computer.

Even if the password you've been using is long, or you're using a complex passphrase, there are good reasons why you should be updating your password. These examples mostly involve security issues or incidents, but also can be about interpersonal issues. In any of the above cases, always be sure to update your password to keep your accounts secure.

DON'T REUSE PASSWORDS

While reusing passwords can undoubtedly make it easy to recall and reuse them on various sites, simply doing so makes it very easy for a hacker to have free reign over your accounts. It also provides a great starting point for guessing your passwords on other sites. Should one of your passwords get compromised (for example, guessed correctly by a hacker), a natural next step would be to test that password on your account across other sites and services. Now you have to be concerned about all of those sites where you use that password.

When creating unique passwords, follow the advice given in previous sections above. I do not recommend reusing a password – even a strong one. When it comes time to create new or alter these passwords, I strongly urge you not to reuse even parts or aspects of a password you feel confident about. For example, I would classify using "rover123" and "rover456" as being an example of "reuse" as the root word is the same, and the numeric variation is not particularly different. Make sure your passwords are different on each site and service you use for your own safety.

DON'T SAVE PASSWORDS IN YOUR BROWSER

This tip is certainly one that applies to almost everyone. Many people rely on their web browsers to save and manage their passwords and account information. While this is convenient and super-easy, it likewise makes it super-easy for a hacker should they gain access to your computer. If your device is lost or stolen, whoever ends up with it can have easy access to your accounts if the passwords are stored in your browser.

Aside from the very real danger of hackers or losing your device itself, there are other things to consider about using a browser to keep your accounts secure. For example, you may not want family members, visitors, friends, or roommates to have the opportunity to access your accounts when you aren't around. At a minimum, this may be embarrassing, but it can also be something more nefarious or dangerous. My strong recommendation is to prevent this risk entirely by not storing any logins and passwords in your browser.

Many password managers can integrate with your web browsers, giving the same kind of convenience in a more secure fashion. I highly suggest you go this route for the safety of all your accounts and data.

UNENCRYPTED EMAILS

With so many web services these days, it's understandable that we sometimes may need to share a password with a coworker, family member, or friend. However, sending over the password in plain text is a risky proposition. Should your email (or theirs, for that matter) be hacked, you are a sitting duck.

There are a couple of ways to share passwords without sending them in plain text. Many businesses have a way to send secure email, but it typically needs to be "triggered" on a case-by-case basis. If you don't know if you can send a secure email, ask your IT or Ops team, or someone in leadership, about your office best practices for sending important data.

This is another endorsement for using a password manager. I frequently share passwords through my password manager when the need arises. This allows me to track who I have shared the password with, when, and even prevent the recipient from being able to see the password.

There's an analog option for those of you who just need to share information once, and perhaps do not have a business team to consult or haven't yet set up your password manager. If the sharing of critical information is necessary, the safest way to do so is an old-school phone call to share the password.

SECRET QUESTIONS

Many sites ask that you supply answers to various secret questions for secondary authentication. In some cases, this method is still used for resetting passwords. Just remember, "secret" information is much harder to keep secret these days. With social media and the vast amounts of information available about all of us on the internet, something that you think is secret might not be all that difficult to uncover. Names of pets, parents, and even former street addresses are easy enough to uncover.

Here are a few guidelines to make yourself think deeper and make your secret questions truly unguessable. Give it a try yourself.

- Use questions that are not easy to discover the answers.
- When given the choice of picking the secret questions, mix them up. Don't always choose, "What was your mother's maiden name?"
- Look for the most obscure question in the list, one that you alone have to think of the answer. Ask yourself if this question could be guessed by a close friend or partner.
- In fact, to get extra secure, you can always use trickery and deceit when coming up with answers to the secret questions. This probably requires a good memory or a password manager where you store the answer.

MULTI-FACTOR AUTHENTICATION

For any site that allows it, I highly encourage you to turn on multi-factor authentication (MFA). While this chapter is about passwords, using MFA introduces another layer of security that is a powerful tool in keeping your data and accounts secure.

The most common implementation of MFA is a subset called two-factor authentication (2FA). You are probably familiar with it: this happens more and more with mobile and desktop devices being used for the first time, on new networks, or when traveling. One common way 2FA works is by sending a one-time passcode via text message or email. This ensures that the person trying to gain access to the account also has the secondary authentication method (i.e., is able to receive a code via text message on the device associated with the account). Another method is to use an authenticator app that generates a 6-digit number, such as Microsoft Authenticator, Google Authenticator, or Duo.

All of the critical applications we use in our business are protected using 2FA and an Authenticator app. At first, I thought this would be a significant inconvenience, but it really hasn't been. That is, as long as I have my cell phone handy. 2FA can be validated in just a few seconds, and I really appreciate this extra layer of security.

IN CONCLUSION

The reason password security is important is based on the real and valid threat of fraud, phishing, and data breaches. While most everything has risk these days, simply taking a few easy steps can significantly minimize your risk and vulnerability. These eight password tips can help ensure your profiles and data remain safe and secure. By following the guidelines I have provided here, you can be empowered to drastically reduce the chances of a breach or hack that leaves your accounts vulnerable.

Businesses will continue to raise security awareness with campaigns and training. Whether it's the banking websites or e-commerce stores we use, it's essential to own your data and passwords, as they are truly the keys to our virtual (and often, very real) kingdoms. Just remember, the reason for having a secure password is not to satisfy your IT Department, the bank, or any of the sites you use, it is about keeping what is YOURS—yours, safely, and securely.

About Jeff

Jeff Joll has worked in a wide range of industries with organizations both in the United States and internationally throughout his career. The common thread has been helping these organizations improve their use of technology, which has been Jeff's lifelong passion. Jeff started working in the "computer" field as a fulltime professional before he graduated from high school and has never looked back.

Jeff has been helping Pittsburgh area businesses leverage technology for over 25 years. He has worked with businesses both large and small, but his passion is assisting small organizations to succeed. Jeff began his career developing software, and when he started his own company, he decided to focus on developing software for small businesses. However, he soon found his software clients looked to him to be the one-stop-shop for all things technology related. Jeff's broad experience in the tech field allowed him and his staff to bring a consultative approach to helping clients maximize their technology investment in order to achieve their goals.

Jeff's approach to technology is somewhat unique for a person who has spent his whole career as a technologist. He is not "enamored" with technology for technology's sake. Rather, he seeks to provide his clients with common-sense, cost-effective solutions – the same kind of solutions he would deploy in his own small business.

In 2010, Jeff purchased a Computer Troubleshooters franchise to improve his ability to deliver technology services to Pittsburgh area businesses. As a locally-owned small business, he found there were benefits to being part of a global organization, including having access to highly skilled technical resources without the need to have them on his payroll. Since then, Jeff and his local team have helped keep small organizations safe and secure through their "Trouble-Free" managed service and security plans.

Jeff likes to say, "We are the IT Department for small business." Most of his clients don't have their own IT staff and depend entirely on Computer Troubleshooters-Pittsburgh for the planning, implementation, and support of their technology infrastructure.

As cybercrime has continued to increase, Jeff has increased the focus on keeping his clients safe from criminals who could ruin a business or non-profit overnight. By making sure data is backed up, networks are secured, and client staff members are trained to be "security aware," his clients continually improve their defenses. At the same time, Jeff and his staff are continually evaluating how to better protect their clients against a constantly changing threat landscape.

Jeff and his wife, Eileen, are lifelong residents of the Pittsburgh area. They have four adult children, enjoying traveling and being outdoors. Jeff has a BS degree from Robert Morris University with a major in Accounting, and passed the CPA exam in a single sitting once upon a time.

You can connect with Jeff at:
- www.ct-pgh.com
- https://www.linkedin.com/in/jeffjoll/
- 412.462.3400
- jeff@ct-pgh.com

CHAPTER 28

SOLVING THE MYSTERY OF SOC COMPLIANCE FOR APPLICATION HOSTING

BY MARK RICHTER

Large, small, or somewhere in between, every business would like to keep costs low, keep the business secure, and manage risk. SOC (Service and Organization Control) compliance helps businesses achieve those goals. SOC is the auditing of a company's data security practices against a framework of standards in multiple categories designed to protect mission-critical data and mitigate cybersecurity threats. Although SOC specifically addresses the regulations and needs of government, banking, and medical industries, SOC compliance is more recently sought after by businesses in other industries hoping to increase their business opportunities. Meeting SOC compliance shows Insurance underwriters that your business manages risk in an acceptable way.

The SOC criteria, developed by the American Institute of Certified Public Accountants, creates a security framework for third-party software companies to give confidence to organizations when they engage with those third-party vendors. Every SOC-certified company has been audited by an independent CPA who certified that firm has the appropriate SOC defenses and procedures established. SOC includes 450 standards with which to comply in areas including business continuity management, configuration management, data backup, human resources, information security policy, logical access, network monitoring, organization overview, physical security, risk assessment, and vulnerability management.

There are two phases of SOC compliance: SOC 1 and SOC 2. In SOC 1, a company has completed all the requisite paperwork, and an auditor has signed off that the business, as of a specific date, has addressed everything in that paperwork, and everything is in order. Companies are required to follow documented standards or regulations that work with SOC 2-compliant organizations. For SOC 2, the auditor will test during either a one-month or a three-month period that the company is doing the things that they said that they were doing. SOC 2 audits different subject areas.

SOC 2 assesses all the key elements with which a company must comply and have policies, processes, and procedures in place. Then, they must be implemented from the human employee standpoint, and from a technological standpoint. Everywhere that company data flows must be protected under SOC, and that extends to applications local or off-site. Those are the subject areas that are part of the SOC audit that need to be addressed by the compliant company in full, without exception, so that they can achieve their certification.

There are two ways to obtain SOC certification. The first, and more expensive way to get certified, is to hire an organization that conducts audits. Generally, these organizations bill hourly for their auditing time. If the average audit takes one to three months to complete, the cost can be exponential. The second way of doing it is to be self-compliant. It depends on the industry as to which SOC compliance is required.

What does SOC compliance look like? Business continuity management, for example, includes having several sets of backups. It's generally advisable to have three sets of data: one copy that's running on the machine that you use every day, a second local backup in case the equipment used daily fails, and a third copy in another location, normally in the cloud. The concept of least privilege means people only get access to the parts of an application related to their job. Least privilege, under information security, protects everybody else's jobs from somebody who does not know what they are doing; think of it as <u>access on a need-to-know basis</u>. Vulnerability management, another SOC compliance category, closes the gaps that might lead to compromised data. Application hosting is one area where a company's data is particularly vulnerable. Application hosting is the process where any business-critical application from any vendor is hosted on a local or cloud server. For the safety and integrity of their clients' data, vendors may require their hosting partners to be SOC compliant.

Most people are probably familiar with application hosting, even if they do not realize it. Businesses utilize application hosts daily without giving it a second thought. As an example, the recording software that an attorney uses in client interviews is "in the cloud" and, therefore, is hosted on a specific server. Business accounting software often is hosted in the cloud, as well. The rub is that they are not hosting those applications just for your business. Your business is just consuming it. Even though you bought the access to that application, you do not fully control it as you once might have. That said, who is controlling that server? A business' mission-critical software should have as much security, reliability, and user-access capabilities available, whether it is an application for one person, 1,000 people or 10,000 people.

Let us use a large soda manufacturing company mythically called Cola Company, as an example. Cola Company needs to run its massive supply chain to get its supplies, which include things like sugar, water, other sweetening, or flavoring syrups. They also track bottling supplies like aluminum cans, glass or plastic bottles, and which facilities need those items. On top of that, they track the packaging supplies, such as cardboard or plastic loops, pallets, and crates. They manage shipping in trucks, and they manage the distribution of those products to sales outlets. Cola Company products are ubiquitous. Their critical software application runs via a hosting software from a company called SAP. There are a handful of large companies that offer this software: SAP, Oracle, and Microsoft are a few of the biggest. The process of hosting that application and the massive amounts of information requires servers, data centers, and networking and storage for the thousands of people using it, often simultaneously.

All that information bouncing around and stored within that application framework is mission-critical; one lost data set triggers the proverbial domino effect. Therefore, the continuity management required for SOC certification is also critical. Stakeholders, or family shareholders in smaller companies, demand security, availability, and processing integrity—assurances that the information required to keep Cola Company productive is secure, and that multiple copies of that data are stored in case one fails.

Cola Company wants its communications with its customers and suppliers to be secure, confidential, and protected from cybersecurity threats like ransomware and hackers. Hackers would love to get into their network and mess with them. SOC policies, processes, and procedures also address protections for communications and correspondences.

Forward-thinking CEOs and boards of directors should take a "zero trust" position on how data should be managed securely in their application hosting infrastructure. In the case of client interview recordings, as a law firm might use, the firm does not want anyone listening to confidential client recordings. So, the recording application has SOC procedures in place to safeguard those files. Security measures are amped up even more for industries like healthcare with HIPAA compliance.

Cola Company may be more amenable to doing business with companies that have SOC certification in place. It keeps the bad actors from using third-party software as a back door to perpetrate malicious attacks into a company's active directory or to worm their way into all the different systems. Bad actors and cyberthieves from foreign countries make their living hacking United States companies so that they can get in, use what they call ransomware, and compel any size business to pay a ransom in Bitcoin to get their data back. With SOC compliance standards in place, a business is more trusted. Without them, just one cyberattack can put a business underwater. SOC also ensures that applications are firewalled with hardening techniques to prevent these attacks from happening.

Unless a company is required by its industry to be SOC certified, the decision comes down to business risk. One of the jobs of the CEO, the board, and the executive team, is to mitigate business risk. For a smaller or medium-sized business, complying with 450 items to be SOC certified is very daunting. I recommend those businesses begin by addressing about 65 different areas such as business continuity, logical security, change management, configuration management, and human resource policies to increase threat awareness and protection.

Compliance is clear-cut in banking or medical industries with regulations and HIPAA because not adhering to those measures have legal ramifications. Becoming SOC compliant enables a business to expand its client base to customers that they could not have before. If a company wants to do business with that bank or that medical office, they must also be SOC or HIPAA compliant. The ultimate objective is expanding the pool of potential customers. One of my clients, a manufacturer of high-volume printed material like newsletters, postcards, and billing, wishes to expand their client base into the medical arena. They have chosen to become SOC and HIPAA certified so that they can work with medical clients for their printed materials and mailings.

SOC compliance does not need to be a mysterious process, unattainable to the average business, but it does require the assistance of trained professionals to help businesses prepare by formulating plans and checking off items well ahead of auditing. The decision comes down to risk and reward. Is your company willing to assume the risks associated with remaining non-SOC compliant? Even for a family business, the risk might be substantial. Conversely, what greater rewards might your company receive in the form of new business by implementing the SOC policies and attaining SOC certification?

SOC best practices have been consistent in the modern computing era. The highlights revolve around the key policies of configuration management, change management, patch management, vulnerability management, server, router, and firewall hardening and hardening policies.

It all starts with configuration and change. An information system is composed of many components that can be interconnected in a multitude of arrangements to meet a variety of business, mission, and information security needs. How these information system components are networked, configured, and managed is critical in providing adequate information security and supporting an organization's risk management process.

Implementing new information systems and changing existing systems result in some adjustment to the system configuration. To ensure that the required adjustments to system configurations do not adversely affect the security of the information system or the users from operation of the information system, a well-defined configuration management process that integrates information security is required.

Policy objectives call for:

    (a) establishing and maintaining baseline configurations and accurate and up-to-date inventories of organizational information systems (including hardware, software, firmware, and documentation) throughout the respective system development life cycles.

(b) to establish and enforce security configuration settings for information technology products employed in enterprise and organizational information systems.

A well-implemented configuration management policy of a SOC compliant organization consists of a 3-tier computing environment to include development, QA/test, and production tiers. Developers must have the freedom to create an SW code that solves business problems. Hardening the server environment to reduce vulnerabilities and threats should be part of the configuration plan. The Center for Internet Security (CIS) has hardening plans for all the common operating systems. While this development is happening, production systems – already delivering business value – must remain locked down and unchanged. Surprise changes may cause a company to be unable to process its business, resulting in critical downtime and revenue loss. The right way is to extensively test new code in a QA/Test tier with a subset of users, and only until the code has proven to be production-ready does it get moved to production. Application code changes are NEVER made to a production tier. It is a common error for SMB executives not to be aware of the ramifications of not following this policy.

Change policy considers that Information Systems components are continually facing the need to change to meet the variety of business, mission, financial, technical, and information security needs. How this is done will ensure all needs are considered, communicated to the key people, and performed in a consistent way. Whether it is a new information system or a change to an existing configuration, a process of change that involves the key people, the process and the technology involves a documentation format standard. The standard enables all personnel to be notified and made aware of who, what, when, where, and how the change is to occur and be concluded.

The policy must establish when any production data or subset of production data is moved or copied to a development or test server or environment, and the environment at that point will be considered a production system and requires compliance of the Change Management policy, procedures, and processes.

Configuration and change highlight just two of the major categories of SOC and HIPAA compliance requirements. At the beginning of this story, I pointed out there are 450 standard components. These two were chosen to provide an executive-level example of why SOC and HIPAA are best not viewed as a chore, but as tools to make the business more secure and to lessen risk. Your employees, customers, and your insurance agent will all benefit from your compliance.

About Mark

Quality and integrity are the principles Mark Richter had top of mind when he founded his business, iStreet Solutions, in 2004. He felt that small and mid-sized companies would benefit from having an enterprise mindset of peace-of-mind and always-available IT solutions.

Mark holds Electronic Engineering and MBA degrees and is a proud founding member of the Vistage Small Business (SB) 2476 executive coaching group formed in 2015. His training came from 20 years at the Hewlett-Packard Company, where principles of quality, integrity, and the *HP Way* were instilled in him as he worked with enterprise customers.

It was also at HP that he gained in-depth knowledge of the telecommunications and electronic manufacturing industries and why businesses rely on always-available technology systems. During this time, he provided customers with HP's data acquisition and control solutions to help them achieve 100% available systems. He complemented this by working with enterprise companies to outsource their SAP solutions.

The change management expertise that he perfected at HP has kept him evolving iStreet Solutions and his role. Shortly after opening he implemented his business plan. He acquired a data center and focused on hosting Enterprise Resource Planning (ERP) solutions from SAP. During this time iStreet Solutions achieved numerous hosting certifications from SAP. The industry demands high levels of quality and assurance, and Mark answered by achieving SAS70, SSAE16/18, and SOC 2 certifications as well as compliance with HIPAA standards.

Mark clearly recognizes that his customers have a business strategy to execute. In this light he works with them to provide IT solutions that facilitate positive business impact. By ensuring business and technology alignment, and complying with best practices and regulatory standards, he ensures his customers manage risk and costs, by providing always-on information systems.

During the years, the principles of peace-of-mind through always-available technology have not changed, but the technologies and methods have. To accommodate these changes, Mark's technical staff includes senior security and networking experts who focus on information systems and hardening the edge of networks to resist threats.

iStreet Solutions' Microsoft skills include broad and deep expertise in Windows Server, including Active Directory for zero trust/least privilege solutions, MS-SQL, and

Microsoft 365 offerings. Featuring hybrid clouds iStreet Solutions, helps customer merge the best of cloud and on-premise solutions.

Today Mark leads iStreet Solutions to help customers enhance their business outcomes with IT Support, apps in the cloud, cybersecurity, and compliance solutions. He directs the implementation of IT Solutions that are compliant with the latest standards that serve to protect his customers from cyberthreats and disasters.

The Industries they focus on are in the manufacturing supply chain and, in general, businesses with 10 to 150 employees.

Based in Sacramento, the company works with customers there and in the San Francisco Bay area and has customers throughout the USA.

You can connect with Mark at:
- www.istreetsolutions.com
- 916-269-1916
- markr@istreetsolutions.com

CHAPTER 29

KEEPING YOUR BUSINESS SAFE FROM MOBILE DEVICE ATTACKS

BY OSCAR DIAZ

Cybersecurity is a critical component in your organization. However, many businesses overlook a crucial component used to conduct business: mobile devices. Today, mobile devices account for approximately 60% of all internet usage and are used by employees and workers of all kinds of workplaces, including hospitals, non-profits, yoga studios, tech startups, retailers, even small independent businesses. However, for most businesses, mobile devices are a cause for concern for security and IT teams.

It's essential to understand that mobile devices are a critical issue for security and need to be protected to mitigate risks. For example, you probably have already spent thousands of dollars implementing a security system that can be compromised by a $500 smartphone, because you didn't think it could be a way to access your network.

In this chapter, we will explain mobile device vulnerabilities and what you can do to improve your organization's security. First, we recommend a few immediate and simple precautions to take when it comes to using mobile devices. Second, we suggest you share information and use a strategic approach to plan and implement security improvements.

Think of it this way. You are already spending time, money, and effort protecting the hardware and systems (whether desktop or laptop computers, your wireless network, etc.). However, if you still allow employees or people to use their personal mobile devices to connect to your wireless network, your policies and encryption leave a vulnerable gap in your business. This chapter will help you fully protect your business assets, as well as keep your business safe from mobile attacks.

In the simplest terms, a mobile device is any "mobile" or portable piece of hardware that can access the internet. Most mobile devices are smaller—there are hand-held devices such as tablets, as well as the smartphones most of us have had for years. These mobile devices access the internet either via a SIM card using LTE, the cellular network, or through a wireless connection.

What makes mobile devices vulnerable to attacks, and how does it happen? One obvious way is the device itself getting lost or stolen, then accessed by someone who intends to do harm. However, some more egregious ways a mobile device can be compromised include accessing a compromised wireless network, using open public networks, falling for spam or phishing, etc. Always be aware that the mobile devices your employees use are an easy way for attackers to get into your network.

There are three immediate and simple precautions your business should take when it comes to mobile devices:

1. **Avoid Free Wi-Fi**
2. **Use a VPN**
3. **Be Skeptical of Links Via SMS**

AVOID FREE WI-FI & USE A VPN

An incredibly common situation we all face is checking our mobile devices in between home and the office. Perhaps you are traveling and away from your hotel, or maybe you are just out getting a coffee at a local cafe. You may even be out of data on your wireless plan and decide to access an open free internet connection. There are usually many free and open wireless connections that do not require a password or a purchase to access them. When you look for open Wi-Fi networks available on your mobile device, you'll notice businesses with wireless access using their names (e.g., Starbucks, Apple, Tim Hortons, etc.). However, it is possible for anyone to create a network and name it after a reputable company without verifying whether it is legitimate or not.

Sure, free Wi-Fi is tempting. The problem here is that you don't know who is on the other end of this supposedly free internet access. And since it's open to anyone, you don't know what that person/entity is going to do with your data. With a free connection, whoever is providing internet access has the ability to see your activity: that means the sites you are browsing, where you're shopping, and most nefariously, they may have tools with the potential to access your passwords and data.

Let's say, for example, you're using mobile banking while on a free network to check if a transaction or paycheck has come through. The suppliers of this free Wi-Fi might be able to capture the password you used to log into your bank. They may then try to use that password across other services and sites to gain access. Worst-case scenario, hackers would be able to exploit a security issue on your phone and install malware.

Why is that a problem? Well, there are many concerns here. In the instance of malware, it grants access to your phone without your knowledge—which puts everything at risk, including your business network, your data, and potentially your customers. In a short amount of time, the free access you gained for the time it took to have a coffee has given an intruder or hacker access to your entire business network. In doing so, you have bypassed all the security measures that you have in place for a regular work laptop or company computer (firewall, security rules, company policies, etc.). All this was done by using a mobile device on a non-verified network.

What happens next? Usually, when a company is compromised, the intruder or hacker that breaks into the system will not act immediately. They will start doing something called enumeration, which is trying to figure out what type of access they can get from the device they compromised. (In this example, they could be exploring the employee's mobile phone, which was briefly on an unverified free network.) The next steps may include accessing your business network and compromising other systems and computers, including installing additional malware. From there, hackers will continue to gain information and intelligence about your network and data. For example, they might learn about your network devices, the variety of your printers, and continue to spread malware on the various pieces of the network.

Though this moves slowly and behind the scenes, the entire business is compromised. When the time comes, they will unleash the attack on your business' systems: whether that's stealing information or a ransomware attack. However it plays out, your organization will be taken hostage for a ransom in order to get your information back. So not only is there the risk of losing information and the cost of getting the data back, but additionally, there is no guarantee when dealing with hackers (not to mention damage to the reputation of the company and potential legal consequences). All of this fallout was caused by a quick connection to a free network. How can your company avoid this from happening? Simply put, don't trust free Wi-Fi, and don't allow your coworkers to do so using their mobile devices. If you absolutely need to use Wi-Fi, use a VPN to protect the connection.

BE SKEPTICAL OF LINKS VIA SMS

Not everyone knows that phishing can occur via SMS just as it does via email. Today, there are SMS-based messaging for all kinds of services and products: political campaign marketing, location of shipments and deliveries, updates to important documents, status for loan materials, etc. These come through your preferred SMS application: iMessage, WhatsApp, or whatever you use for texting. And SMS phishing attempts may be more difficult to spot than in email since text messaging already uses abbreviations, shortened URLs, and other truncations.

Here's one predatory example of a phishing attempt via SMS. You receive a text message inviting you to click a link to access an update about government assistance you've heard about on the news (e.g., small business loans, stimulus packages for Covid-19, the Canadian Government [CRA], and the US Census). Sounds legitimate, right? How can you know for sure? Something security and IT professionals know is that programs are often announced but not available immediately. Hackers, on the other hand, capitalize on current events to send fraudulent phishing messages, inviting recipients to "click on this link to apply."

And what is happening is that you are receiving malicious notification, not by email, but via your SMS. Assuming you click on it and it is indeed fraudulent or a phishing attempt, you may be allowing a third party to install malware on your phone. So the reality is that your mobile device is a computer connected to the internet that can be compromised as easily as your computer, should you not take adequate measures.

SMS is just another way for someone to take control or compromise your mobile device. SMS links from unknown numbers are a perfect ground for criminals, attackers, and hackers to take advantage of unsuspecting users.

Now that you've learned a few of the risks attached to mobile devices and how to avoid them, the next big step your organization should take is working towards a security plan for your business.

Why is it essential to incorporate mobile devices into a security policy? One way to think of this is by using a simple metaphor of cars parked on the street. Let's say there are two cars, both on the same street, and there's a criminal looking to break into one of those cars. We know that chances are, with enough time, that a criminal is going to be able to break into both cars. However, the reality is that most criminals want to act quickly to make sure they can be successful and not get caught. So, what might they do when faced with this "two-car" scenario? A criminal will break into the car that has the least security and the fewest barriers to entry. Metaphorically speaking, the same thing is true for technology and cybersecurity. Think about it this way – more security doesn't guarantee you will never have a breach or attack, but it will make it more difficult for hackers to break into your network or compromise your data.

What else can be done to keep your business safe from mobile device attacks? There are two potential strategies for protecting your company from mobile device attacks:

- **A technical approach**
- **A company cybersecurity policy**

1. **A technical approach** will limit what technology can do with company-provided devices. For example, implementing tools like

MDMs (mobile device management) as well as tools that align with your business's software programs and tools. This approach gives your IT team control of mobile devices when needed, for example, to only allow the device to connect to a specific network, or even wipe a lost or stolen device remotely. There are many pieces of technology that control the mobile device: for example, the ability to lock down the device remotely in order to minimize the risks when an unauthorized user is accessing the network.

2. **A company cybersecurity policy** would utilize your company's Human Resources. These policies determine how your employees are going to use their personal devices within their business network. There will need to be training, documentation, and awareness among staff members, perhaps in Ops and HR. A company's policies are where you define policies around "acceptable usage of company resources," as this applies to mobile devices. For example, your policy might say that personal devices can only use the company's network as long as they abide by these policies (e.g., IT must install certain tools). These policies could even be a combination of technical and HR requirements. For example, you can implement policies around it so that if a device is reported as lost, company policy requires that you wipe the device.

If an employee does not consent, or in the case, say, of an intern or contractor, one approach might be to have them use a guest network (i.e., a combination between technology and human resources). Of course, IT needs to make sure that the guest network doesn't have access to the company's resources, and it's completely isolated from the system or the company's network.

In the end, you have to measure which parts of these approaches work best for your business. Some companies only allow employees to access the company's network with vetted devices, whereas others may be more lenient, but regulate usage with an HR policy. No one solution works; the best approach is a balance of both. A working combination is essential to have both the business and human resources involved when creating these policies. With a strategy that uses both technical and policy approaches, the final piece of the puzzle is documentation and training.

So the final question on how to keep your business safe from mobile device attacks is how to proceed. Some good questions to ask your leadership, HR, your technical team, and even legal advisors, are the following:

- What are you trying to accomplish?
- What are you trying to protect?
- What are the company goals?
- What are some of the key security concerns?
- What outdated practices need to be eliminated?
- What is the budget and/or timeline?

From there on, your business can begin collaborating on a plan. When you're preparing to work around a security policy that allows you to protect your most valuable assets as well as your network, you have to also take mobile devices into consideration as a piece of the puzzle. Otherwise, all efforts are ineffective. Ultimately, it doesn't matter how much money or time you put into safeguarding your system if you're leaving the weakest link unprotected.

The best champions and allies often are those who work closely with IT—Office Managers in charge of running or overseeing operations. In an increasingly complex world, technology risks are all around us. Having an improved understanding of what we can do to keep employees supported and our company data and information safe can start with a few key pieces of understanding.

In conclusion, you can keep your business safe from mobile device attacks with this five-step process:

1. **Determine what your business goals are.**
2. **Put together a plan.**
3. **Look to implement policies from both a technology and HR perspective.**
4. **Create documentation.**
5. **Communicate, inform, and train.**

Mobile devices are a critical piece of security and must be protected to mitigate risks and keep the business safe and secure. As I always say, you might have a quarter-of-a-million-dollar security technology implemented, but it's worthless if you fail to account for all potential weaknesses in your network. Mobile devices are most vulnerable to hacks, phishing, and fraud— in a matter of a few clicks from a mobile device, your entire network may be at risk. However, with a strategic set of policies, training, and education, you can ensure the safety and security of your business across all devices and locations. The safety of your business depends on it.

About Oscar

Oscar Diaz has 20 years of experience in the IT industry. Oscar studied Information Technology Engineering at UNITEC (http://www.unitec.edu.ve/). During his five-year program, he worked as a Coding Instructor and participated in several university programs to attract new students to the faculty.

After graduating, Oscar started working in the Telecommunication Industry at Digitel Corp (www.digitel.com.ve). His first position at Digitel was as a System Administrator, where he had several servers under his responsibility, including the email system that supported 3000 users. In the next five years, Oscar demonstrated he was willing to take on new challenges and responsibilities; this allowed him to climb the organizational ladder and earn a management position where he was in charge of the server infrastructure running on Microsoft products (200+ servers and 10+ engineers on his team under his direction). After that, Oscar moved to the position of Application Manager, where he was in charge of (a) Business Intelligence, (b) Web Application Development, and (c) Customer Liaison Units (where he had 20+ engineers, business analysts and team leads working under his supervision).

After ten years working in the Enterprise world and seeing the opportunity of bringing Enterprise IT practices to small and medium-sized businesses, Oscar founded Tecbound Technology in 2011. The goal of the company was to bring quality IT service to business owners and help them navigate the challenges of using IT in their business. Tecbound has grown ever since and now has a presence in Calgary, Vancouver, and Latin America.

Oscar sponsors several children through not-for-profit organizations like World Vision and Christians Children's Fund, and has a passion for helping kids to get involved in sports activities to promote family values, respect for others and encourage them to become the best they can be.

You can connect with Oscar at:
- Email: oscar@tecbound.com
- Phone: 403-926-1754
- LinkedIn: linkedin.com/in/oscarddiazb/

CHAPTER 30

LAW FIRM SECURITY: PROTECTING LAWYERS AND CLIENTS

BY MICHAEL GLASSER

An infamous cybergang infiltrates a prestigious law firm's computer system, quickly deploying malware that enables them to surreptitiously access the firm's proprietary information. In most cases, such a security breach might be of little interest to those outside of the legal community and IT security professionals. In this case, however, the cybergang commands international attention because they carried out this attack against New York City's premier celebrity client law firm: Grubman Shire Meiselas & Sacks.

The firm's A-list clients include Lady Gaga, Madonna, Elton John, and LeBron James. These clients, among others, risk having confidential information released to the public, information that likely ranges from the mundane to the embarrassing, and even to potentially professionally/ personally damaging. The cybergang also claims to have stolen files from the firm that relate to President Trump (the firm denies that he is or was a client), and are threatening to release incrementally all this firm's information they currently hold unless Grubman Shire pays more than $40 million in ransom. If the firm refuses to pay, the cybergang threatens to seek bidders on the dark web for the data.

Whereas most ransomware attacks are settled quietly between the victims and increasingly ambitious and sophisticated perpetrators, a high-profile security breach such as this is impossible to hush up. Grubman Shire has already suffered a significant hit to their reputation (with a commensurate hit to their bottom line as well), and their degraded professional status will sustain well beyond the resolution of this attack.

That Grubman Shire attracted the attention of cyber thieves is unsurprising, but the legal industry needs to be aware that cybercriminals consider all law firms rich pickings because they hold valuable and exploitable personally identifiable information (PII) about firm members and about clients, including birth dates, social security numbers, email addresses, and bank account numbers (including accounts that hold client escrow funds). Chinese, Russian, and Ukrainian crime rings are currently hacking into law firm computer systems with ever-more sophisticated ploys to steal that information, presenting an ongoing and potentially expensive risk. For instance, an IBM Security-sponsored 2019 data breach study found that the average cost of a cyberattack on organizations across 17 different industries, including the law industry, was $3.92 million. Therefore, a single cyberattack may not only negatively impact a firm's productivity, but it will also degrade the firm's reputation and may potentially devastate the firm financially.

Do not assume that your firm's computer system is unlikely to suffer a cyberattack or that if you are targeted, you can do little to stop the breach. Cyber thieves thrive on these "it-can't-happen-to-me" misconceptions, and so you want to consistently maintain vigilance.

The monitoring, alerting, and response posture of my organization was tested one Sunday night in January 2019. That night, a tech alerted me about a possible attack on a law firm client's computer system. My team took a closer look and determined that we were witnessing, in real time, a ransomware infiltration. Our protocols and mitigation systems allowed us to detect the breach almost immediately and respond. In contrast, a typical data breach takes, on average, more than six months to discover and an additional 69 days to contain. Because the law firm had advanced protections in place, Glasser Tech immediately thwarted the ransomware and made all requisite repairs. By 6:30 the next morning, it was business as usual. Had that law firm not taken the precautionary steps to install heightened safeguards and a reliable backup system, the loss of the law firm's data, time, and money could have been catastrophic, potentially totaling up to $100,000 a day. Instead, our client lost nothing.

Sadly, the preceding scenario is not unique. Glasser Tech has shepherded hundreds of law firms through similar situations. Proactive firms that allowed us to enact all necessary measures to enable us to readily detect and handle attacks suffered little or no damage when the inevitable attacks occurred.

Not all firms are so lucky, though. Business owners often call desperately for help after a ransomware attack or devastating virus. Firms that approach us during or after a breach pay a heavier price, both because "fixing the problem" is not as easy, and because victims of cyberattacks are often blamed for their lax security. Because lawyers have a fiduciary duty to protect client data, a law firm's victimhood often elicits less sympathy and understanding than victims of other crimes such as burglary or carjacking. You will be investigated and questioned about your preventive measures, and if your answers are not adequate, you may face onerous fines and lawsuits.

As every lawyer knows, ignorance of the law is no defense. Neither is ignorance of information technology (IT) security threats and a firm's legal and ethical requirements to address them. Cybersecurity is no longer a want, it is a must. Each of the 50 U.S. states has enacted computer crime laws, which they periodically revise as cybercriminals become savvier. Two recent examples are the Stop Hacks and Improve Electronic Data Security (SHIELD) Act and the California Consumer Privacy Act (CCPA).

The New York SHIELD Act requires businesses, including law firms, that employ a New York resident or hold any New York resident's PII to comply with a stringent cybersecurity plan. Violations of the act may incur fines of up to $250,000. On the other side of the country, significant policy changes to the CCPA took effect in January 2020. The CCPA places consumers in control of their personal data, allowing consumers to request information that companies have saved, and a list of third parties with whom their data has been shared.

Aside from state laws, attorneys have an ethical duty to implement reasonable safeguards to protect against and to respond to data breaches. Failure to do so has resulted in professional malpractice lawsuits. In 2016, for instance, a class-action lawsuit was filed against the Chicago-based firm Johnson & Bell for allegedly having inadequate data security measures that put client information at risk.

The risks enumerated in this section extend beyond law firms themselves. A recent attack on TrialWorks, a cloud software vendor for the legal world, illustrates how these breaches affect not only your company but also all those connected to it. In October 2019, lawyers throughout the United States were locked out of their accounts and could not access critical data, including business files and legal documents. The TrialWorks platform, which services 2,500 firms, had been infiltrated by malware. Can you imagine a law firm surviving without its data? Many lawyers were forced to request extensions—attorney tweets from the time record the anxiety and terror for posterity.

For obvious reasons, TrialWorks did not want this attack publicized, perhaps especially because of speculation that the company paid a ransom to remove the malware. Although we might look askance at payments to cyberattackers, TrialWorks's supposed payment is not an absolute right or wrong. Without proper backup systems in place, a business might have no choice but to pay. Even then, however, you're dealing with criminals, which means no guarantees. The attackers might decide not to release your data or give it back intact. They may even ask for more money. All our clients are protected as outlined in the following section, and so theoretically, they should be able to recover all their data if something of this nature were to occur.

DATA PROTECTION:
HOW TO DEFEND YOUR BUSINESS

To protect yourself against hackers, you must first understand how they gain network access. One common method of attack is phishing, which is when an unknowing victim opens a seemingly legitimate email that lures the victim into clicking a website link embedded in the email. The link leads to a fake website that provides hackers an open door to infiltrate the victim's computer. Once in, criminals can freely deploy ransomware, which is what can essentially take down a business. Thus, an unwitting employee is the biggest risk to your company's infrastructure. Simply put, a person behind a keyboard who unknowingly clicks a link or responds in error to the wrong email can compromise an entire system.

To counter cybersecurity threats, Glasser Tech executes a multistep security-enhancement process that includes phishing awareness and advanced endpoint protection. The more security layers in place, the harder it is for attackers to access and compromise your valuable information. For law firms, we recommend eight proactive security layers, as follows:

1. Advanced Endpoint Protection

Traditional reactive endpoint security tools generally depend on the information of known threats to detect attacks. Advanced technologies go further and utilize live agents who are available to review and report threats as they arise, which helps to minimize and mitigate attacks.

2. Firewalls with Security Suites

Firewalls are filters that control access between networks by screening and blocking traffic. A business-class firewall, with enhanced persistent threat protection, halts incoming threats to your network, such as malware, spyware, and viruses.

3. Dark Web Monitoring

Also known as cyber monitoring, Dark Web monitoring scours the Internet for any sign or trace of your personal data. Personal data found online may include social security numbers, credit card information, bank accounts, and anything else that could be used for identity theft.

4. Phishing Awareness Training for Employees

Because phishing is the most common security breach, phishing-awareness training is key. We offer employee training by purposely and routinely deploying tests that replicate the signs of malicious email. The biggest part of prevention is education.

5. Patch Management

Patches are software/firmware updates designed to fix potential security gaps or vulnerabilities. Testing patches is an important step in minimizing data breach probability.

6. Advanced Spam/Threat Protection

Threat protection technologies defend against spam, malware, and known threats while maintaining access to email during and after emergencies. Our email protection enables companies to access email even while their server is down.

7. Image-Based Backup

Compromised or corrupted systems can be restored through an image-based backup, which allows systems to be recovered and restored to an earlier moment prior to an attack.

8. Compliance-Management Service

Glasser Tech's compliance-management service ensures that law firms comply fully with cybersecurity laws, ethical mandates, and insurance requirements. Critical aspects of such compliance management include risk assessments and monitoring, critical security policy implementation, an incident response plan, and compliance reporting.

For Glasser Tech, staying one step ahead in the IT world means continuously reviewing and expanding each of these security layers. (For example, consider advanced endpoint protection—a few years ago, it didn't exist.) Therefore, we constantly assess new processes and procedures so as to provide clients the best technology available to ensure their systems' efficiency and security.

A CYBERSECURITY TEMPLATE

The National Institute of Standards and Technology (NIST) offers a template that allows firms to implement a baseline security culture. These standards outline how a firm's data risks compromise, and describe distinct actions to mitigate those risks. The template consists of five essential functions, as follows:

Identify

The Identify function helps companies pinpoint system threats to cultivate understanding and awareness of the most critical system vulnerabilities. This principal understanding identifies where your company should direct its time and effort to develop software solutions and systems.

Protect

The Protect function entails several procedures to increase your data security functionality and to reduce the number of cybersecurity attacks and limit their impact.

Detect
The Detect function outlines monitoring and detection practices to increase a firm's reaction time. This function is essential to a vigorous security posture. After all, according to Quartz.com, in 2016, more than 25% of data breaches went undetected for more than a month, and 10% of breaches went undetected for more than a year.

Respond
Whereas the first three functions (Identify, Protect, Detect) focus on mitigating the risk of a cybersecurity event, the Respond function proposes guidelines to develop and implement a response plan tailored to your company in case a breach occurs.

Recover
The Recover function presents steps your firm can take toward a successful recovery following a security breach. The ultimate goal prioritizes a timely return to normal operations.

PROACTIVELY PLANNING YOUR PREVENTIVE MEASURES

According to the American Bar Association Legal Technology Resource Center's 2019 Legal Technology Survey Report, 26% of respondents reported that their firm experienced a security breach, and only 31% of respondents had an incident response plan. These numbers do not surprise me. I am well aware that business leaders can become overwhelmed with cybersecurity lingo and become numb to it. However, simply assuming that you are protected, or choosing to ignore potential security threats altogether is not the answer. Businesses can and do become educated about the protections they have and the ones they need by using a full-service IT company such as Glasser Tech. We can assess needs, implement software and hardware solutions, make network design recommendations, and help companies become safer and more productive through support and training. Our job is to stay on top of the cyber evolution so that you can concentrate on your company and maintain peace of mind. The truth is, even if you take every preventive measure, an attack may still occur. By creating the proper environment, though, the surface risk and the potential loss of data and time to your company will be negligible.

Security is not a *should*, it is a *must*, and it starts with you. To adequately protect your law firm, you need certainty that your security defenses are optimal. You know how much you have invested to reach the point where you are, and you know the value of your reputation. Do not let a cyber thief take that away from you. Get the facts and ensure your protection. I am always happy to help a fellow business owner. Visit our website, www.GlasserTech.com, and request a consultation to review your firm's current cybersecurity posture.

About Michael

Michael Glasser is President of Glasser Tech, the legal industry's most in-demand IT Consulting Firm. Glasser Tech is the only IT company that exclusively specializes in providing highly effective solutions for law firms in New York.

Glasser Tech is Michael's direct response to law firms' need for high-value IT consulting that understands the legal field's unique technology needs and security demands. Michael and his team work closely with each client to ensure improved security and maximized productivity within their law firm.

Michael has over 25 years of experience in legal technology consulting and has worked with hundreds of law firms across the State of New York. A majority of those firms are still active clients to this day.

Michael's tenacious leadership and technical experience have propelled Glasser Tech past the boundaries of a traditional IT service provider. His proven reputation, access to superior technology tools, and a hand-picked team of experienced IT technicians make him uniquely positioned to empower law firms to achieve success through premier legal technology consulting.

A well-known and respected speaker, Michael regularly presents at events such as local chambers, legal associations, educational institutions, and law firms on various subjects including Cybersecurity, and Disaster Recovery and Backup solutions.

Connect with Michael today:
- www.LawTechnologySolutions.com
- 516-762-0155
- Michael@GlasserTech.com
- www.LinkedIn.com/in/GlasserTech

CHAPTER 31

WHAT IS A SECURITY FRAMEWORK?

BY RAFFI JAMGOTCHIAN

A security framework is a guideline on how to develop an organization's security program using a consensus of best practices by the team that put together that framework. Think of it as the constitution that sets the rules on how laws are created and how departments function. There are around 250 different security frameworks around the world; some are specific for a country or business industry.

A security framework can save your business time by giving you a structure from which to work. Most frameworks can provide your company a guide of where they are in terms of security maturity, identify gaps, and give you a roadmap for the future. Most frameworks are universally applicable, even those that are industry-specific. More than likely, that industry framework was based on a universally-accepted one. Frameworks will also allow you to explain your security program in common language to both tech and non-tech alike, and it aligns business goals with technology.

SECURITY FRAMEWORK -> POLICIES -> PROCEDURES

The prescriptiveness of frameworks varies from framework to framework. It may not necessarily tell you what to do or how to do it, just that something needs to get done. The map can be either sparse and vague, or it can be very detailed.

Without a security framework, however, it becomes difficult, especially for a small and medium business owner, to know what to invest in when it comes to security. The key is to pick one that you are comfortable with, maybe with a trusted advisor and your industry's regulations in mind.

If you are already working with an IT company, ask them what security framework they have adopted. It makes sense to also keep you in alignment with what they are already doing if you have not found one that works better for you. However, it is key that your business management has bought into which security framework you will be using for adoption.

Small and medium businesses, unless they have a specialty that requires something different, would benefit from one of these frameworks:

1. **NIST Cybersecurity Framework** (NIST-CSF). Also known as the NIST Cybersecurity Framework for Improving Critical Infrastructure Cybersecurity is a more recent development from the National Institute of Standards & Technology (NIST) department of the US government. It focuses on risk analysis and risk management through five major phases: identify, protect, detect, respond, and recover. NIST-CSF can be used across multiple industries and is very flexible, but not very prescriptive.

2. **CIS Controls** (formally called the SANS Top 20) focuses more on technical controls and best practice configurations. It tends to be the first choice for IT and Security teams because it initially came out of the SANS Institute, one of the most influential training organizations for security professionals. CIS does not focus on risk analysis or management directly, as NIST does, but does so indirectly because of the hardening process that it defines. CIS Controls work well in collaboration with another governing framework like NIST-CSF. There are several spreadsheets and tools available that have done this work for you.

   HIPAA/HITRUST compliance requirements added additional language specific to health care. It also includes a few other compliances.

3. **COBIT** stands for *Control Objectives for Information and Related Technology* is an older framework developed by IT governance professionals. Businesses that adopted frameworks long ago may have started with COBIT. It originated as a method of reducing technical risks but has expanded to include alignment of IT and business strategy. COBIT is typically used by companies that need to comply with Sarbanes-Oxley.

4. **ISO 27000** is an international framework that is extremely broad, encompassing, and can be applied to companies of all sizes and shapes. ISO 27000 is like the ISO 9000 that was developed for manufacturing quality and has similar certification processes. It consists of many sub-standards, including sub-standards in healthcare and specifics on cloud computing. ISO 27000 is commonly used by larger or international organizations, as well as cloud providers.

5. **SCF**, S*ecurity Controls Framework*, focuses on internal controls for both cybersecurity and privacy. The SCF is considered a meta-framework or a framework of frameworks. One could also think of it as a blending of both the NIST-CSF and the CIS 20 with additional enhancements. The SCF is designed to provide strategic, operational, and tactical guidance through the adoption of the principle that if you build for security, you will automatically meet your compliance obligations. SCF consists of 32 domains and 750 controls. Each domain has a defined set of principles and a specific intention.

   Examples of SCF include Asset Management, Business Continuity, Change Management, Monitoring, and Endpoint security. According to securitycontrolsframework.com, "The SCF's mission is to provide a powerful catalyst that will advance how cybersecurity and privacy controls are utilized at the strategic, operational, and tactical layers of an organization, regardless of its size or industry."

What frequently happens is that a business needs to look at several frameworks because of the nature of their business. A small business that works in the financial services sector with clients in California, for instance, may want to integrate several such as CIS, NIST CSF, and blend those with FINRA and CCPA regulations.

Once you have identified which security framework to adopt, evaluate where your company stands. It can be as simple as taking a spreadsheet and listing all the controls and requirements of the framework and identifying if you have something in place that covers it. Use a simple scale such as no coverage, partial coverage, and near full coverage.

Once you score your organization, take a step back, and see where your gaps are. Where do you think your business is at most risk? Set those for your next major milestones to tackle. Identify how or who will address those (and it may not be technology). Then, repeat this annually as part of your annual review.

Scoring and tracking will help you clearly define where you are today and where you should go. It will help identify the resources you may already have or that you need to acquire, and ultimately help you to budget.

Frameworks help you do several things. Most importantly, they give you guidance on how to build a security program that works for your business. But there are some other benefits. More than likely, you are on the earlier side of the journey, most businesses are. That means that if (God forbid) an incident occurs while you are still filling in the gaps, you may not have all the defenses you need to protect yourself. However, if the regulators come in and you can demonstrate that you have been effectively implementing security controls through a framework, it could go a long way to mitigate any potential regulatory damage.

THE PYRAMID OF SECURITY

The frameworks identify what may be tactically needed, but in a generic sense, and typically there are solutions that help check off a lot of the boxes if done correctly; therefore, we developed the Pyramid of Security to help guide conversations with our clients about the minimal requirements of a security program.

Please note, putting these in place does not mean you have a security program, it just means you have done some things to secure yourself. Having a securing program that these items "talk to" is equally, if not more important. However, these will raise the bar of where you are from a security and resiliency standpoint.

Updates

Your computer operating system has updates available each month, and many of these are security-related. Your software applications, including web browsers, Adobe acrobat reader, and others, are frequently updated. Some update themselves and just require a restart. Others will prompt you to download an update.

Your hardware manufacturer will update its firmware and drivers. These are the specific programs that interface between your software and the hardware it runs on. Many of these are performance and security related.

Passwords

Passwords are still the primary way we access systems. Password re-use and poorly selected passwords are the primary reasons accounts get breached. Use a password manager to remove the burden of remembering a unique password for each account. Use multi-factor authentication wherever possible such as a hardware token (IE. yUBIkey), a software authenticator (Authy, google, duo), or an SMS or email code, which is not recommended but is better than nothing.

Backups

Keep multiple backups of your data, including at least one copy offsite. Cloud storage is a decent offsite option. Keep multiple versions, not just the latest, and keep your backups for at least 30 days, although 90 days is better. Test your backups frequently to make sure you can restore your data if needed.

Endpoint protection

In a cloud-first world, our endpoints—computers and mobile devices—are our first line of defense after the human. Traditional anti-virus programs are no longer enough. You must detect and prevent known and unknown problems, provide digital forensics to understand what happened and identify issues, enforce policies on the endpoints, and identify and remediate against footholds. Additionally, you should consider application whitelisting, which means identifying the applications that should be allowed to run.

Email Security

All emails should be filtered both inbound and outbound for viruses, spam, and potential phishing. Sensitive information sent via email should be encrypted, and all message traffic logged to ensure that data can be reviewed later.

Next-Gen Firewall

The router provided by your internet provider is not enough. You should employ a next-generation firewall or a unified threat management system that provides advanced filtering. Basic routers lack the ability to log activities for future review and correlation. Alternatively, there are ways to get that functionality in a distributed environment, including your remote workers, even if they are working from untrusted locations (homes, coffee shops, shared space). Along those lines, consideration should be taken to segment networks. In other words, keeping certain devices from being able to talk to other devices: phones, Internet of Things, cameras, servers, guest computers, etc.

Mobile Security

Our mobile devices have access to more information than ever before. As a best practice, use a mobile device management system to keep mobile devices in compliance and secure. If your employees are unwilling to have a corporate application to manage their personal device, consider deploying a company-owned device instead.

Cyber Insurance

Add cyber-insurance to your current policy or as a stand-alone to cover you in case there is an incident. Recovery can be expensive and potentially fraught with legal potholes. Be mindful that Cyber Insurance does not mean that you can skip other security measures.

Logging

Log everything you can! Preferably, centrally log all security events, and if you can afford a security operations center or an MSSP to monitor and correlate events, even better. Logs can be useful to figure out what happened to whom and when.

Threat Intelligence

Learn about the threats associated with your industry. We recommend a blend of public and paid resources/threat intelligence feeds, if needed. Ask your security vendors what threat intelligence sources they use.

Asset Management

You cannot protect what you do not know. To that end, catalog all your computer assets, whether they are at your office or in the cloud, including what data you have stored and where it is stored.

Minimize Administrative Rights

Do not extend administrative rights to users. It gives malicious software direct access to everything on the computer. If your employees can install their own software, provide them a separate login for that function.

Web Filtering

Use the next-gen firewall in your office to filter internet browsing. Remote users may require an additional application installed to provide filtering and protection whenever they are traveling or working remotely.

Continuous Scanning

Scan your networks for new assets and vulnerabilities. Vulnerabilities are constantly arising, so if you do not scan your devices and network frequently, you will not know when a new risk occurs.

User Awareness and Training

Above all, your employees and contractors are your first line of defense.

A predominance of breaches occurs due to phishing and human error. Keep employees trained on the latest cybersecurity threats and privacy issues, and test your employees against their training through physical penetration tests and simulated phishing attacks.

SUMMARY

Security frameworks are updated regularly as needs evolve; they are not written in stone. The beginning is always a good place to start, and a security framework is your operational outline. The procedures you choose to implement within that framework are the tactical things that you need to do on a regular basis. As the requirements in your industry or the daily battles against cyberthreats change, so will your strategy.

About Raffi

As the son of a mainframe programmer, Raffi Jamgotchian has been around computers since the age of seven. Raffi joined and then later ran a successful Bulletin Board Service (BBS) out of his bedroom while in High School prior to attending Rensselaer Polytechnic Institute and receiving a BS in Computer and Systems Engineering.

Raffi joined a control systems manufacturer and helped implement some of the largest distance learning and conference systems in the United States. In 1995, Raffi joined as a general IT technician and scriptwriter for a mid-tier investment firm but eventually was the Director of IT Infrastructure for the New York region. During his tenure at that investment firm, he served as an advisor for emerging technology investments and managed many of the large scale IT integration projects, including the first cybersecurity teams. During this time, Raffi obtained an MBA in Information Systems.

In 2006, he left that firm to assist in the startup over another smaller independent investment fund.

In the fall of 2008, in the middle of the financial crisis, Raffi saw an opportunity to service small investment firms that were now cropping up. They needed the same technical, compliance, and cybersecurity that larger investment firms did, but didn't have the resources.

Raffi's highlights:
  a) He earned the Certified Information Systems Security Professional (CISSP) in 2005.
  b) Past Councilman for the Borough of Northvale.
  c) Past Board of Education member for Northern Valley Regional High School, Technology Committee lead.
  d) Member of the Northern Valley Rotary Club.
  e) Member of the US Secret Service Joint Electronics Crimes Task Force NY/NJ Chapter.
  f) Member of the New York InfraGard Chapter.
  g) Past Advisor to the ASCII Group – the largest IT industry association.

To contact Raffi:
  • triadanet.com
  • 201-297-7778
  • rj@triadanet.com

CPSIA information can be obtained
at www.ICGtesting.com
Printed in the USA
BVHW040013221120
593844BV00015B/74/J